Paul Auster

D1563704

MANCHESTER
1824

Manchester University Press

Contemporary American and Canadian Writers

Series editors:
Nahem Yousaf and Sharon Monteith

Also available

Douglas Coupland   Andrew Tate
Philip Roth   David Brauner

Paul Auster

Mark Brown

Manchester University Press

Manchester and New York

distributed exclusively in the USA by Palgrave

Published by Manchester University Press
Oxford Road, Manchester M13 9NR, UK
and Room 400, 175 Fifth Avenue, New York, NY 10010, USA
www.manchesteruniversitypress.co.uk

Distributed exclusively in the USA by
Palgrave, 175 Fifth Avenue, New York,
NY 10010, USA

Distributed exclusively in Canada by
UBC Press, University of British Columbia, 2029 West Mall,
Vancouver, BC, Canada V6T 1Z2

British Library Cataloguing-in-Publication Data
A catalogue record for this book is available from the British Library

Library of Congress Cataloging-in-Publication Data applied for

ISBN 978 0 7190 7396 0 *hardback*
ISBN 978 0 7190 7397 7 *paperback*

First published 2007
16 15 14 13 12 11 10 09 08 07   10 9 8 7 6 5 4 3 2 1

Typeset
by Florence Production Ltd, Stoodleigh, Devon
Printed in Great Britain
by Biddles Ltd, King's Lynn

For Fay

Contents

Series editors' foreword

This innovative series reflects the breadth and diversity of writing over the last thirty years, and provides critical evaluations of established, emerging and critically neglected writers – mixing the canonical with the unexpected. It explores notions of the contemporary and analyses current and developing modes of representation with a focus on individual writers and their work. The series seeks to reflect both the growing body of academic research in the field, and the increasing prevalence of contemporary American and Canadian fiction on programmes of study in institutions of higher education around the world. Central to the series is a concern that each book should argue a stimulating thesis, rather than provide an introductory survey, and that each contemporary writer will be examined across the trajectory of their literary production. A variety of critical tools and literary and interdisciplinary approaches are encouraged to illuminate the ways in which a particular writer contributes to, and helps readers rethink, the North American literary and cultural landscape in a global context.

Central to debates about the field of contemporary fiction is its role in interrogating ideas of national exceptionalism and transnationalism. This series matches the multivocality of contemporary writing with wide-ranging and detailed analysis. Contributors examine the drama of the nation from the perspectives of writers who are members of established and new immigrant groups, writers who consider themselves on the nation's margins as well as those who chronicle middle America. National labels are the subject of vociferous debate and including American and Canadian writers in the same series is not to flatten the differences between them but to acknowledge that literary traditions and tensions are cross-cultural and that North American writers often explore and expose precisely these tensions. The series recognises that situating a writer in a cultural context involves a multiplicity of influences, social and geo-political, artistic and theoretical, and that contemporary fiction defies easy categorisation. For example, it examines writers who invigorate the genres in which they have made their mark alongside writers whose aesthetic goal is to subvert the idea of genre altogether. The challenge of defining the roles of writers and assessing their reception by reading communities is central to the aims of the series.

Overall, *Contemporary American and Canadian Writers* aims to begin to represent something of the diversity of contemporary writing and seeks to engage students and scholars in stimulating debates about the contemporary and about fiction.

Nahem Yousaf
Sharon Monteith

Acknowledgements

I would like to thank the following for their help, guidance and comments during the development of this book: Tim Woods, Laurence Marriott, Chris Ringrose, Nick Heffernan, Douglas Tallack, Oliver Harris, Sharon Monteith and Nahem Yousaf. I would like in particular to praise the unstinting support and friendship of Peter Brooker, for which I will always be grateful.

The University of Northampton provided the financial support which enabled me to visit the Auster Archive in the New York Public Library, and the Berg Collection staff helped to make my time in New York very productive. I would particularly like to thank Paul Auster for the evening he spent chatting with me while I was in New York.

Parts of Chapter 6 originally appeared in ' "We Don't Go By Numbers": Brooklyn and Baseball in the Films of Paul Auster', in John B. Manbeck and Robert Singer (eds). *The Brooklyn Film*. Jefferson, NC: McFarland, 2003.

I would like to thank all my family and friends who have assisted and supported me throughout the process of writing this book. In particular I want to thank Fay for her love and support.

1

Rooms

Paul Auster has consistently taken the city of New York as a central feature in his work. The city inhabits his essays, novels and films both as a backdrop against which the plots unfold, and as an active agent in their outcomes. In 1988, Auster told Allan Reich: 'New York is the most important place for me' (Reich, 1988: n.p.). Around the same time, in a comment subsequently edited from the published interview, he told Larry McCaffrey and Sinda Gregory that New York is the main character of *The New York Trilogy* (1988), and that he is both attached to and hates the city (Gregory and McCaffery, undated: 11).[1] In 1997 – in conversation with another confirmed New Yorker, Lou Reed – Auster avowed that New York is a special place, distinct from the rest of America. 'New York I don't even think of as part of America, it's not even a part of New York state', he says. 'It's a separate little city state that belongs to the world' (*South Bank Show*, 1997).

The compelling nature of New York City encapsulates two primary themes in Auster's work. Contemporary literature is often concerned with representations of the complexity and scale of living in this era of late capitalism and global culture, and so engages with the processes that allow New York to be at once isolated while belonging to the world. At the same time, Auster's literature is centrally concerned with how we, as individuals, live collectively. In his early poetry, this is as much a question about society in general as it is about metropolitan living in particular. As the work develops and Auster turns increasingly to prose, and then to fiction, the questions of living in the metropolis, of anonymity and alienation, come to the fore.

Jean Baudrillard, on visiting the city, recorded similar concerns in his study *America* (1988). 'Why do people live in New York?', he asked.

There is no relationship between them. Except for an inner electricity which results from the simple fact of being crowded together. A magical sensation of contiguity and attraction for an artificial centrality. This is what makes it a self-attracting universe, which there is no reason to leave. There is no reason to be here, except for the sheer ecstasy of being crowded together. (Baudrillard, 1988: 15)

Auster explores these same concerns. Like Baudrillard, he finds New York at once compelling and menacing. He tells Lou Reed that he is struck by the 'filth and the density of population', and 'the absolutely staggering range of humanity that walks by you at any given moment' (*South Bank Show*, 1997). This urban contradiction, of being at once attracted to and repelled by the metropolis, surfaces many times and provides a fascinating and productive tension in Auster's work.

Auster's concern with how we live collectively in large cities – 'the monstrous sum / of particulars' or 'the life that extends beyond me', he calls it in the poems 'Disappearances' and 'White Spaces' – is in part motivated by his interest in how the individual locates her or himself in the world (Auster, 1991: 61 and 83). His characters need first to locate themselves in the world through a matrix of situated and relational coordinates, before going on to establish stable relationships with others and a coherent sense of themselves. That is to say, in Auster's work, not until the metropolitan subject has established where they are through the landmarks and symbols of a knowable locale, and where that place is in relation to the rest of the physical and social world (and, in turn, how they are connected to it), can they begin the work of 'selfhood'. For Auster, this is the establishment of a stable and productive 'I'.

Auster explicitly acknowledges the importance of this theme. He told Joseph Malia that *The New York Trilogy* is about 'identity':

The question of who is who and whether or not we are who we think we are. The whole process . . . is one of stripping away to some barer condition in which we have to face up to who we are. Or who we aren't. It finally comes to the same thing. (Auster, 1997: 279)

Throughout the Auster canon, who his characters are (or aren't) is repeatedly forged from their connections to the social world, which they establish through friendship, love and the family.

Each of the following chapters traces the metropolitan conditions Auster presents as necessary for the founding and construction of an 'I' for his characters. These include satisfactory and supportive correspondences between characters' subjective 'inner terrain' and their physical, invariably metropolitan, outer one. As he shows, social connections and stable and coherent identity are only possible in the metropolis when there is a reasonable degree of coincidence between the self and the physical environment. Equally, where the 'outer terrain' of the physical metropolis is volatile and complex, the opportunity for harmony between individual and environment is drastically diminished. Consequently, any stability that Auster represents for his characters remains fragile and temporary, always contingent on the flexibility of the urban subject and her or his capacity to adapt to a complex and constantly shifting metropolis. As Peter Brooker points out in New York Fictions (1996), 'Auster's stories reflect on . . . interlaced concerns of language, literature and identity, seeking moments or types of stability between the extremes of fixity and randomness' (Brooker, 1996: 145). This study traces the stages in Auster's literary career which demonstrate three shifting understandings of identity in the metropolis, and explores fixity and randomness when experienced under these different perceptions. First, there are nihilistic representations of fragmentation and break-down. These are followed by a locally found familiarity and stability that remains fragile and contingent because of metropolitan volatility. Finally, Auster's characters develop an urban vision able to incorporate both local knowledge and a view of the wider social world, providing stability through flexibility.

Repeatedly Auster demonstrates that writing can be a way of mediating metropolitan experiences, and how storytelling and language are mythical dimensions of life which have the potential to overcome or alleviate urban predicaments. As this and subsequent chapters show, an essential element of Auster's varied and far-ranging artistic project is to recover New York (in particular) as a place to live. He shows how, when the metropolis is encountered as only a physical and social reality, it swiftly becomes an overwhelming and disorientating environment. However, when that physical reality is overlaid with a poetical dimension, the city is invested with symbolic and lyrical qualities able to 'disalienate' and 're-enchant' it.

For Auster, storytelling represents the illusory and mythical powers needed to 're-enchant' the metropolis, and characters who are able to deploy storytelling as an urban strategy come to find some sort of stability in their lives. As he told Mark Irwin, 'stories are the fundamental food for the soul. . . . It's through stories that we struggle to make sense of the world' (Auster, 1997: 336). He goes on:

I believe that the world is filled with stories, that our lives are filled with stories, but it's only at certain moments that we are able to see them or to understand them. You have to be ready to understand them. (Auster, 1997: 329)

Storytelling in Auster's work functions as a means by which the alienated individual can share with others, and reconnect to the social realm. The new poetical and social geography created by stories then overlays the city as an insubstantial and mythical dimension. Kevin Robins, discussing his sense of the postmodern city, sees a need to 'attempt to re-imagine urbanity [by] . . . . recovering a lost sense of territorial identity, urban community and public space. It is a kind of return to (mythical) origins' (Robins, 1993: 304). The re-enchantment of the life of cities, he writes, is able 'to revitalize tradition and community and to revalidate the kinds of particularity that have been lost' (Robins, 1993: 321). It is the assertion of community and the particularity of storytelling as a way of sharing that has the capacity to re-enchant the metropolis in Auster's work. Similarly, Donattella Mazzoleni, in her essay 'The City and the Imaginary', calls for a new relationship between the 'I' and the metropolitan environment 'by positing a possibility of a new imaginary' because the 'city is . . . a site of an *identification*' (Mazzoleni, 1993: 286 and 293, original emphasis).

Auster shows, through the movement in his texts from nihilism to a qualified optimism, that by reimagining the physical city the individual can achieve a relatively stable purchase on selfhood and social being in metropolitan life, suggesting that the process of reimagining is a dialectical one. James Donald, in *Imagining the Modern Metropolis*, also considers the relationship between the poetical imagination of urban stories and the material reality of the metropolis. He describes the exchange between the two in this way:

> It is not just that the boundaries between reality and imagination are fuzzy and porous. In the development of cities can be discerned a traffic between the two, an economy of symbolic constructs which have material consequences that are manifested in an enduring reality. (Donald, 1999: 27)

On an individual level, Auster presents characters who negotiate between the reality of their physical environment and the metropolis of their imagination (their 'inner terrain'). The greater the correspondences between place and self, the more secure a character's social connections, and the more coherent their sense of identity.

Auster's poetry, books and films have always focused on characters moving through space, and so the 'spatial turn' of the new cultural geography offers a particularly productive analytical approach to Auster's work. As Sara Blair comments, since the 1970s 'a constellation of texts and scholars drawing on cultural theory, anthropology, sociology, and philosophy has . . . declared . . . that temporality as the organizing form of experience has been superseded by spatiality' (Blair, 1998: 544). This new cultural geography includes the inaugurating figures of Henri Lefebvre, Edward Soja and David Harvey, and maps contemporary spatial practices alongside their cultural consequences. Cultural geography, then, examines the 'contested border between literature and culture, the aesthetic and the social', while at the same time admitting representations of spatial experience to the enquiry of geographers (Blair, 1998: 545–6).

This book sketches how the new thinking associated with cultural geography echoes many of Auster's own concerns. It also indicates how fiction is able to imagine beyond the limits of empirical social science to encounter spaces and places of the metropolis at its extremes, and how cultural geography too is beginning to use the imaginary as a way of interrogating its own practices.

I have organised my examination of Auster's central themes and their attendant concerns into a series of spaces and geographical scales and richly textured spatial experience. Consequently, my argument moves from the writer's room in this chapter onto the eerily uninhabited streets of New York City in Chapter 2, then to the social spaces (bars, restaurants, galleries, and so on) of 'downtown' Manhattan in Chapter 3. It then travels out of the metropolis and measures the way in which Auster represents cities and spaces beyond New York in relation to his home city in Chapter 4. Chapter 5 more fully enters the realm of the imagination and considers the spaces of dystopia and utopia, and the power of the symbolic in spatial constructions and the creation of place. Finally, the study returns to the metropolis to explore how Auster's geographical imagination is able to create a particular sense of place in Brooklyn, while at the same time exploring how it relates to the global processes of New York City as it becomes a global capital. Each chapter takes one or two texts (novels or films) and focuses in detail on how Auster's key themes of identity, loss and disconnection, language and storytelling, and illusion are affected by place. Auster moves from urban nihilism to qualified optimism in his work as he searches for forms of social life and community in the contemporary metropolis, and the chapters trace this shift from the early poetry, through the first fictions, to the films of the 1990s and the subsequent novels.

The chapters trace correspondences between the perspectives of cultural geography, the phases of identity in Auster's work, and his 'ways of telling' – from poetry, through fiction, to film. Auster comes to argue persuasively for the power of fable, magic, imagination and storytelling as one way of locating the self and creating a coherent and stable sense of identity in the complex contemporary metropolis. Thus he proposes a compelling corrective to the rational theories of space, that is a 'poetics of place', a poetics of New York.

Auster's early career was spent as a translator (he lived in Paris during his twenties), an essayist and a poet. He contemplates this period of his life in the memoir, *Hand to Mouth* (1998), subtitled 'A Chronicle of Early Failure', where he describes a life lived in penury. During this time he was married to the translator and novelist Lydia Davis and together they had a son, Daniel (who will be discussed, in fictionalised form, in Chapter 4). The rest of this chapter will deal with this predominantly neglected period of Auster's career (roughly 1970 to 1982), and will trace his route from poetry to prose. I will focus in particular on the writer's room as a site of literary production, and how this space shapes Auster's treatment of the key themes of language, memory and writing.

While, as Auster himself insists, he has always written prose in the form of literary essays and novels in progress (portions of which emerge in the published works later on), poetry was the dominant form in his early career (Auster, 1997: 298). By paying close attention to a number of key poems, I will demonstrate Auster's early concern with language and how it is affected by metropolitan living. The transition from verse to prose came with a 'prose poem', 'White Spaces', which explores the relationship between language, writing and space, both personal and metropolitan. Auster's first major prose publication came with the appearance of *The Invention of Solitude* (1982), an extended meditation on the life and death of his father, Sam Auster, and the capacity of language and writing to capture the qualities both of the man and of loss.

Taken together, Auster's urban experiences at home and in Europe, and his engagement with these experiences as a poet and as a writer, combine to foreground a concern with the capacity of language to capture and communicate metropolitan existence. In the earlier work,

Rooms
7

the problematic relationship between the word and the metropolitan
world is emphasised along with his concern with how the poet is to
locate himself in the myriad social interconnections of the metropolis.
Paradoxically, what emerges most strongly in response to this concern
is the image of the poet isolated in his lonely room. This image
resonates with that of the alienated poet in the crowd, and is part of a
long literary tradition which Auster invokes to represent the artist's
struggle. The poet struggles with language to describe his place within
the social world, and as he feels progressively disconnected from the
world the site of that struggle becomes his room.

If for the urban poet the city is the object of study, then for Auster
the room comes to represent a place to write it from. However, a
contrast emerges between the poetic method of earlier poets – such
as Edgar Allan Poe, Charles Baudelaire and Charles Reznikoff – and
that adopted by Auster. As will be discussed in Chapter 2, Auster's
wanderer-observers often fail to create a legible urban record. However,
Poe, Baudelaire and Reznikoff do employ the methods of the *flâneur*
– wandering the streets and recording the sights and sensations of the
metropolis. Auster, through his autobiographical character A. in
Solitude, employs the example of the influential German poet Friedrich
Hölderlin (1770–1843), who confined himself to his room after the
death of his lover, but continued to write feverishly (Auster, 1982:
98–100). By adopting Hölderlin's method, A. does not so much engage
with New York as a material and present fact, but chooses instead to
re-present the city from the raw material of memory. By calling upon
and adapting an earlier tradition Auster is expressing a contemporary
response to the complexities of the metropolitan environment. A. is
unable to experience and record *his* New York in the same way as
the *flâneur's* itinerant method because of the scale, complexity and
intensity of the contemporary metropolis. Instead the city must be
committed to memory and recorded through the mediating abstractions of language.

In Auster's poetry and early prose works there are distinct correspondences between the experience of language and the experience of
metropolitan living. Many times we see how the relationship the poet
or character forms with language is governed by the conditions under
which she or he experiences it. Under certain extreme conditions the
individual comes exclusively to view language as a large, complex and
remote system which manipulates them, and to which they cannot
effectively relate. As a result the individual suffers a breakdown of her

or his language function, experiencing, at its most critical stage, the condition known as 'aphasia'.[2] The concept of aphasia, as I am employing it here, will prove valuable in a number of contexts in the following chapters. It will be useful first, then, to sketch out what I mean by the term. Effectively, aphasia causes a disjunction in the mind of the sufferer between their experience of the world and their ability to deploy language to describe it. In short, words and things no longer correspond. In Paul Auster's work characters suffer from 'aphasic' episodes under conditions of severe isolation and loneliness, causing them to become disconnected from their physical and social worlds. As an 'aphasic' disjunction between the word and the world develops, so characters struggle with many aspects of their metropolitan condition. Consequently, a coherent relationship with language emerges as an essential component in stabilising the urban lives of Auster's central characters. To them, New York presents a large, complex and unpredictable environment, and the conditions under which they experience it make it difficult to compose the world and language into any sort of unity. The catastrophic consequences of such 'aphasic' episodes will be discussed in greater detail in Chapter 2.

To an urban poet such as Auster, then, language becomes a central theme. Again and again he confronts the task of representing the city through a medium which is often inadequate to its subject. To inaugurate a language sensitive to the complexities and contradictions of the metropolis has been a concern of poets since the emergence of the modern metropolis. Auster's urban representations have been richly influenced by the nineteenth-century Parisian poet Baudelaire, who was himself strongly influenced by Poe. The different ways in which Poe and Baudelaire respond, as poets, to their metropolitan moments are reflected in the ways in which Auster's characters respond to their experiences in late twentieth-century New York. Later chapters examine Auster's updating of the characters that people Baudelaire's Paris, and how he has contemplated appropriating titles from Baudelaire for his own work. As a nineteenth-century urban poet Baudelaire sought a poetics adequate to both the rational and the phantasmagorical elements of his experience of Paris, just as Auster and the Objectivists have done for their New York. In an echo of the two parts constituting his own definition of modernity, Baudelaire wrote of his poetry:

> Who among us has not dreamt, in moments of ambition, of the miracle of a poetic prose, musical without rhythm and without rhyme, supple

and staccato enough to adapt to the lyrical stirrings of the soul, the undulations of dreams, and the sudden leaps of consciousness. This obsessive idea is above all a child of the experience of giant cities, of the intersecting of their myriad relations. (Benjamin, 1997: 119)

In 'The Painter of Modern Life' Baudelaire attempts to describe the experience of modernity and the modern metropolis in relation to art. Modernity is, he suggests, 'the transitory, the fugitive, the contingent; it is one half of art, the other half being the eternal and the immutable' (Benjamin, 1999: 239). The complexity of an environment emerging from these conditions clearly requires a mode of expression equal to the volatility which results. Consequently, according to Benjamin, Baudelaire's poetic project was to create a prose adequate to the metropolis of his age. What Baudelaire seeks then is a mode of representation that engages with the eternal and (seemingly) immutable physical metropolis in terms which at the same time are able to capture the ephemeral and fugitive interrelations he finds so compelling. He identifies nineteenth-century European urban phenomena, the turmoil of the city and the human consciousness, which are simultaneously in conflict with each other and with the structures of language.

In the contemporary American metropolis, where these tensions are multiplied, the correspondence of language with the physical metropolitan environment is yet more problematic. Poets have continued to respond to the metropolis by seeking out new vocabularies and lexicons adequate to the deepening complexities and the consequent alienation of their contemporary metropolitan moment. The Objectivist poets, for example, sought a poetics of 'clarity', of 'seeing and of saying' that strongly influenced Auster (Auster, 1997: 36). That is to say, they attempted to apprehend the material world, and translate the image into words, and so give the world form through language where it can be re-represented. Amongst the Objectivists, Auster cites the New York poet Charles Reznikoff as a particular influence who explicitly pursues the object of a language appropriate to the 'strange and transitory beauty of the urban landscape' (Auster, 1997: 40).

The image of the poet in the metropolis, from Poe and Baudelaire onwards, has been that of the isolated and lonely figure moving along the streets, at once a part of the crowd and separate from it. Walter Benjamin, in 'Some Motifs in Baudelaire', describes how Baudelaire associates himself as a poet with marginalised urban subjects as an attempt to appoint himself a new urban hero.[3] Benjamin identifies a number of the individual 'urban types' who populate Baudelaire's *Les*

Fleurs du mal (1857). In this discussion, Benjamin traces Baudelaire's interest in figures who have been cast out and marginalised by modernity's advance, and whose appearance in the city he sees as fugitive and ephemeral. He isolates the ragpicker and the *flâneur* (along with the prostitute and the dandy) as types with whom Baudelaire associates himself as a poet. Auster borrows these figures from nineteenth-century Paris and translates them to the American metropolis of the late twentieth century, where they become the confused, alienated and disconnected walkers of his New York fiction.

One of the most famous urban pedestrians in American fiction, and one who influences the origins of Auster's wanderer-characters, is Poe's 'The Man of the Crowd'. Benjamin contrasts Poe's tale with Baudelaire's crowd scenes. He describes how Poe characterises the crowd as unknowable, which makes it compelling and menacing, investing it at once with a sense of alienation, anonymity and fascination (Benjamin, 1997: 126–8). In comparison, Baudelaire's poem 'To a Passer-by' invests the crowd with the potential to offer exciting but fleeting metropolitan encounters. The poet describes a brief and anonymous encounter with a beautiful widow who is borne first to him and then, tantalisingly, away from him by the crowd. Benjamin writes: 'far from experiencing the crowd as an opposed, antagonistic element, this very crowd brings to the city dweller the figure that fascinates. The delight of the urban poet is love – not at first sight, but at last sight' (Benjamin, 1997: 125). Thus, Benjamin is able to describe this mass as an 'agitated veil; through it Baudelaire saw Paris' (Benjamin, 1997: 123–4). The way in which the crowd conveys this mysterious beautiful woman to the gaze of the poet illustrates both the anonymity and the fascination of the crowd. However, Benjamin detects an ambivalence in Baudelaire's attitude to the crowd. If the masses are 'a part of Baudelaire', they are also the origin of a deep fear that refuses to allow him to submerge himself utterly in the crowd (Benjamin, 1997: 122, 128). It is Baudelaire's very status as a poet which prevents him becoming fully immersed in the city; both his class position and his professed role as dispassionate observer must separate him from the mass. The result is that 'the allegorist's gaze which falls upon the city is . . . the gaze of the alienated man' (Benjamin, 1997: 170). The urban poet, then, is an allegorist, who attempts to translate urban experience into language, and whose failures further alienate him from the environment he endeavours to capture.

Auster has inherited the concern of the poet in the city, and has contemplated it since his formative years as a poet in Jersey City and Newark, through his Columbia years in New York, to travels in Europe, and his writing career living in Manhattan and Brooklyn. In Newark, where his father was a ghetto landlord, Auster helped to collect rents and undertake house repairs. People he encountered during this time impressed themselves upon his imagination, and would later return as characters in his fiction (Auster, 1982: 56–9). Between high school and Columbia, Auster visited Europe. In Paris he enjoyed 'extraordinary encounters' and worked on a (now lost) novel, the story of which he lived in parallel with his 'real' adventures in the capitals of Europe (Auster, 1998a: 19). On this trip Auster visited Dublin to experience something of James Joyce's *Ulysses* (Auster, 1998a: 19–20). Here, after wandering 'like a ghost among strangers' in the city, 'the streets were transformed into something wholly personal' such that they began to correspond to his interior sense of self, and so became a map of his 'inner terrain' (Auster, 1998a: 22). Because he was geographically disconnected from his own social world across the Atlantic, Dublin became the analogue of his isolation and alienation. In 'the loneliness of those days', he says, 'I had looked into the darkness and seen myself for the first time' (Auster, 1998a: 23). For the eighteen-year-old poet the connection between metropolitan experience and the work of identity was clearly emerging. Auster finds a connection between his experience of Dublin (measured in the painful steps caused by an in-growing toenail), his interior self and the world of literature, in terms of both Joyce's legacy and his own emerging work and talent.

Paris too has had a profound effect on Auster. Paris plays a central role in *The New York Trilogy*, and exemplifies a city of the old, European order. As well as the trip before Columbia, Auster visited the city on a college exchange programme in 1967 and again from February 1971 until July 1974 when he translated Sartre, Foucault, and the constitution of the communist North Vietnamese government. On this third stay in Paris he edited and published a small journal of French poetry in translation called *Living Hand*.[4] This was sponsored by an unnamed wealthy benefactor, and ran for only a few issues. While Auster has a tendency to record his life in detail in autobiographical accounts and references in his fiction, this episode receives no coverage in the published works, suggesting either that he wishes to protect the name of his benefactor or that the failure of the magazine remains a painful event for him.

The relationship between metropolitan experience and the attempt to re-present it from memory though language can be seen in the poems 'Lapsarian', 'Scribe', 'Disappearances' and 'White Spaces'. In *The Invention of Solitude* the experiences of other isolated poets inform A.'s own solitude as he attempts to contain a deepening sense of panic when his metropolitan world is reduced to his bare and lonely room. The isolation from the world that is reflected in the young Auster's experience, is expressed later in the poetry as an equation between the singularity of an individual's life and the world of social pluralities in which that life takes place.

Poetry - 'an art of loneliness'

Auster's concern with language can be traced back to his earliest unpublished writings (deposited in the Berg Collection in the New York Public Library) and through the poetry he produced in the 1970s. His interests are twofold. First, he attempts to understand the 'distance' between the material world and the words that are meant to represent it. Secondly, he is concerned with the ability of the poet to position himself between the monolithic structures of the material world and language in such a way that the words he uses to represent his experience are adequate to that experience. While still an under-graduate at Columbia in April 1967, Auster recorded some thoughts on the relationship between language and art 'in haste' (Auster, 1967: n.p.). These thoughts have the quality of a 'manifesto' which Auster describes as 'the dis-jointed skeleton of something less than an argument' (Auster, 1967: n.p.). Amongst the statements that comprise the 'argument' are these:

Part IV
Item 15
. . . not only is man's perceptual capability limited – his language (the chief means of his expression) is also limited, that is, fails to represent the feelings, thoughts that wish to be expressed.
Item 16
Language is not experience. It is a means of organizing experience.
Part V
Item 17
The fall of man was not the result of moral turpitude; rather [of] epistemological blindness – the fall of the world into the word, the fall of vision from the eye to the mouth.
    About four inches.
                                                                (Auster, 1967: n.p.)

Time and again Auster's poetry and fiction refer back to these concerns: the capacity of language to represent; language as a way of being in the world; the failure of language symbolised as the fall of man. The concept of the image falling from the eye to the mouth as the word recurs explicitly in Auster's third novel, *Moon Palace* (1989).

Two issues are at stake for Auster in the relationship between the word and the world: first, how the user of language (the poet, in this case) sees the world; secondly, how closely language relates to the object being described. Auster has made three American poets who address these concerns, and have particularly influenced his work, the subject of critical essays: the Objectivists Charles Reznikoff, Carl Rakosi and George Oppen.[5] The Objectivist concerns revisited by Auster include the 'clarity of vision and utterance', and the objectification of the poem so that it is properly formed and most readily able to represent the world (Auster, undated a: 3).

In his notes for the Reznikoff section of 'The Poem as Object' Auster identifies four main themes running through Reznikoff's poetry: 'Seeing', 'The City', 'Language', and 'Stories' (Auster, undated a: n.p.). Seeing refers to the eye, the city is the object, language is the inadequate medium of translation between the two, and stories are how the poet attempts to make sense of his metropolitan world, forming the narratives that weave through both his experience and his imagination. Auster proposes the poet, and particularly Reznikoff, as Adam, the man charged by God with giving names to everything in the Garden of Eden. But the poet is at the same time 'the mute heir of the builders of Babel', which reduces him to a futile searcher for words appropriate to the world they are supposed to represent (Auster, 1997: 35). The act of writing, then, becomes 'a process by which one places oneself between things and the names of things, a way of standing watch in this interval of silence and allowing things to be seen – as if for the first time – and henceforth to be given their names' (Auster, 1997: 35).

Objectivist poetry attempts to occupy this very space and to locate the poet between the material world and the verbal world. The Objectivists did this by approaching the poem as a way of seeing the material world and a means to precise expression, which Auster describes as 'a poetics of approach rather than method – a way of placing oneself in the world' (Auster, undated a: 3). Repeatedly Auster returns to the idea of locating oneself so that the writer is able to see and write about the world simultaneously. Allied to the poet's desire to stand in the interval between language and the metropolis is the capacity of the artist to absent himself from the urban landscape while in the act of seeing and recording it. Of Reznikoff Auster writes, 'only in the modern city can the one who sees remain unseen, take his stand in space and yet remain transparent. . . . What counts is the thing itself, and the thing that is seen can only come to life when the one who sees it has disappeared' (Auster, 1997: 38). This key concern has important implications for the later fiction and, as discussed in the following chapters, manifests itself as hunger, starvation and a consequent reduction of the character's corporeal self in the cityscape.

Auster's concern with language's proximity to and distance from the world is foreshadowed by the Objectivists, but it is Rakosi who states his case most directly. In the essay 'Resurrection' Auster describes Rakosi's early poems as 'compact, incisive, vividly sensual in their grasp of physical things', and quotes this poem:

This is the raw data.
A mystery translates it
into feeling and perception;
then imagination;
finally the hard
inevitable quartz,
figure of will
                and language.

(Auster, 1997: 129)

For Rakosi, as for Auster, experience of the material world is the 'raw data' that language translates by a 'mystery'. Because it is the poet who needs to stand between the material world and words, he needs to be in possession of a vision of absolute clarity to convey the world's complexity. It is Reznikoff's ability to transcribe 'the visible into the brute, undeciphered code of being' that leads Auster to call him 'a poet of the eye' (Auster, 1997: 35). By seeing the object with optimum clarity, the poet is able to bring language much closer to it and, as Rakosi suggests, invest descriptions with feeling, perception and imagination. In turn, Auster describes the way that George Oppen sees the world as originating in the 'perception of objects, in the primal act of seeing' (Auster, 1997: 116). This mode of seeing, however, does not privilege the poet with any special knowledge of the world. Auster quotes from Oppen's poem, 'The Last Day', to demonstrate that Oppen, although closer to the material world, is conscious of its mysteries:

Impossible to doubt the world: it can be seen
And because it is irrevocable

It cannot be understood and I believe that fact is lethal
(Oppen quoted in Auster, 1997: 116)

Language, ultimately, for the Objectivists as well as for Auster, is a way of accessing an unformed world and an attempt to 'take possession of our surroundings' (Auster, 1997: 35–6). The poem then becomes 'an effort to perceive, . . . a moving *outward* . . . less a mode of expressing the world than it is a way of being in the world' (Auster, 1997: 37, original emphasis). For Auster, art – poetry, fiction, dance, music and painting – is a means by which the individual may place her- or himself in relation to the environment: 'a way of being in the world'. To this end, his poetry concerns itself with the relationship between the eye and the word, the connection between the word and the world, and the capacity of language as a system to represent the world. In his poetic output he has sought 'a uni-vocal expression . . . concerned with essences, with bedrock beliefs, and . . . a purity and consistency of language' (Auster, 1997: 304).

Auster's poetry encompasses, in equal measure, the concerns of this chapter (language, writing, a place to write from, the city as object), which his prose work then goes on to develop. Poems such as 'Lapsarian' chart the violence that language's failure to represent can inflict on the individual consciousness. 'Scribe' relates the poet's room to the rooms of the Tower of Babel and so connects to the theme of the lonely room as the site of the struggle with language, a theme returned to in the prose poem 'White Spaces'. 'Disappearances' takes Auster a step beyond the poet's room and considers, as Baudelaire had done, how the poet as an individual might respond to the multitudes in the metropolis.

'Lapsarian' grapples with the problematic idea that man both forms and is formed by language. Auster returns, like Reznikoff, to the natural world of Eden and Adam to trace man's relationship to the word. His conclusions are bleak:

I speak to you of speech
. . .
A man
walks out from the voice
that became me.
He has vanished.
He has eaten
the ripening word
that killed you and
killed you.

He has found himself,
standing in the place
where the eye most terribly holds
its ground.

(Auster, 1991: 53–4)

Auster's belief in the potentially 'lethal' violence of the word is apparent here, as it is for Oppen. The fall of Adam and his expulsion from the Garden of Eden are related to language through the eating of 'the ripening word'. Auster also suggests that the 'me' of the self derives from the collective 'voice' and words of others, and that when those words fail they have the power to obliterate the self constructed through language. The social nature of language, its reliance on shared conventions between speakers, and how this connection can be problematised by a breakdown of understanding is apparent in the poem 'Scribe':

The name
never left his lips: he talked himself
into another body: he found his room again
in Babel

It was written.
A flower
falls from his eye
and blooms in a stranger's mouth.

(Auster, 1991: 33)

In the first stanza of this poem Auster appeals to the biblical story of the Tower of Babel in Genesis to explore ideas of language. This story engages with themes of language, rooms and the city through man's attempt to build a tower to challenge God's power. God strikes down the tower and condemns the peoples of the world to speak in different tongues as a punishment. From the stones of the tower, man builds the first city: Babylon. The themes of the Tower, the fall of man and the failure of language introduced here recur, to one degree or another, in 'White Spaces', *The New York Trilogy*, *Moon Palace* and *Leviathan* (1992).

In the second stanza Auster again presents the potential slip between the eye and the word, between seeing and saying which, as he says in his early 'manifesto', is a distance of about four inches. However, for the poet to be able to present the material world to the reader – here symbolised by a flower – it must be 'speak-able' from the mouth of another. Auster extends the concept of translation between the eye and

the mouth to the way in which language is a collective habit of practice
and convention in which the word is a socially negotiable quantity.
Without the social habit of language, the object becomes unavailable
beyond the original material and tactile experience. That is to say, the
flower is available as a material experience to the poet, but can only be
available as an image to the reader through the shared experience of
language. When the object of the poetic representation moves into
the complex realms of the metropolis, the capacity of language to
adequately represent the 'objective' world becomes a deep anxiety.
'Disappearances' takes up the theme of the city as the object of the
poetic gaze. It considers how the solitary poet experiences the multitudinous city, how the eye attempts to decipher the city, and how
language attempts to engage with the complexities of this environment.
In the first part, Auster explores how the poet's eye relates to the city,
and how both language and the city are an accumulation of elements
– one of words, the other of people, both symbolised here as stones
in a wall:

> He is alive, and therefore he is nothing
> but what drowns in the fathomless hole
> of his eye,
>
> and what he sees
> is all that he is not: a city
>
> of the undeciphered
> event,
>
> and therefore a language of stones,
> since he knows that for the whole of life
> a stone
> will give way to another stone
>
> to make a wall
>
> and that all these stones
> will form the monstrous sum
>
> of particulars.
>
> (Auster, 1991: 61)

In the sixth part Auster deals with how 'the blinding / enumeration of
stones' (Auster, 1991: 66) and words obscures the city from the eye
of the viewer. The seventh and final part of the poem expresses the
solitude of existence in the crowded multiplicity of the metropolis as

'[p]lural death / born / in the jaws of the singular'. The city, like language, inflicts damage on the individual's sense of self: 'For the city is monstrous, / and its mouth suffers / no issue / that does not devour the word / of oneself'. These lines are vital to the understanding of Auster's attitude to the city in this poem and the others considered here (Auster, 1991: 67). The city and language are intrinsically linked here, and so is the sense of the self, given form through language. However, the city devours that self because it has a destructive effect on language. Also, the double sense of the word 'issue' prompts the reader to think of language both as a medium and as a way of problematising understanding. In the sense of topic or matter at hand, these lines suggest that the issue of forming a sense of identity through language is devoured by the mouth of the monstrous city. When 'issue' is considered in the sense of originating (as in the issue or broadcast of seed), these lines turn the reader once more towards the story of the Tower of Babel in Genesis, and the use of its stones to build the first city. 'Disappearances' consistently represents the city and language as indecipherable and overwhelming domains.

Charles Reznikoff's poetry has a similarly strong urban dimension. Like Auster, Reznikoff lived in New York and walked its streets every day. In his discussion of Reznikoff's work, Auster acknowledges that the problem for the urban poet has always been the need to simultaneously write the city and be a part of it. Crucially, Auster describes how Reznikoff enters the city 'precisely because he is apart from it'. He goes on:

> And therefore this paradox lodged in the heart of the poem: to posit the reality of this world, and then to cross into it, even as you find yourself barred at all its gates. The poet as solitary wanderer, as man in the crowd, as faceless scribe. Poetry as an art of loneliness. (Auster, 1997: 42)

Here then is the most precise expression of the legacy of Baudelaire and Poe, a man of the crowd but not in the crowd, a figure in the cityscape yet trying to diminish his presence in it: an alienated allegorist.

Finally, the poem 'In Memory of Myself' asks if 'the beating / drum of words' should really be able to represent the material world '[a]s if this were the world' (Auster, 1991: 97). If words had a harmonious relationship with the world, the poet's task of representing it would be less problematic. However, such a relationship becomes an increasingly distant proposition, and Auster's treatment in poetry of the themes of language, representation and the metropolis becomes predominantly nihilistic in tone. The poet is condemned to search for words that are inadequate, and the multitudinous metropolis condemns him to the 'monstrous sum / of particulars' where 'these many lives / shaped into the stones / of a wall' are piled on top of each other (Auster, 1991: 67). These precise concerns in Auster's poetry prompt Norman Finkelstein to describe how Auster 'seeks to renew the balance between the writing subject and the world outside' and to name him as heir to the Objectivists (Finkelstein, 1995: 47).

Prose – journeys across white spaces

At the time he was writing the later poems in the late 1970s, Auster was also experimenting with prose pieces. He describes the movement from short, austere and univocal poems 'that resembled a clenched fist' to an opening out of form and tone. He wrote four one-act plays, one of which was performed. But 'the bridge between writing poetry and writing prose' (Auster, 1997: 301, 302) was 'White Spaces'.[6] This prose piece was inspired by a dance rehearsal and reflects on poetic composition in terms of the relationships between movement and writing, thinking and language, and again on the nature of metropolitan life. Auster's stated original intention was 'to speak of arms and legs, of jumping up and down, of bodies tumbling and spinning' which would lead on to 'enormous journeys through space', 'cities', 'deserts' and 'mountain ranges' (Auster, 1991: 86). But instead of Auster imposing himself on the words, they impose themselves on him. At the same time he feels himself forced into a small and empty space – his room. He describes how the process of composition takes place in this way:

I remain in the room in which I am writing this. I put one foot in front of the other. I put one word in front of the other, and for each step I take I add another word, as if for each word to be spoken there were another space to be crossed, a distance to be filled by my body as it moves through space, even if I get nowhere, even if I end up in the same place I started. It is a journey through space, as if into many cities and out of them, as if across deserts, as if to the edge of some imaginary ocean, where each thought drowns in the relentless waves of the real. (Auster, 1991: 85)

Once again, the poet finds himself in his lonely room, and once again he places himself in the interval between the word and the world, a space that can only be filled by his own body. At the same time, although the poet remains in his room he can, in a sense, go anywhere he wants. This freedom prompts Auster to predict an insight resulting from his wandering reverie, but one that is just beyond his grasp. The 'light, streaming through the windows, never casts the same shadow twice', he records, 'and at any given moment I feel myself on the brink of discovering some terrible, unimagined truth' (Auster, 1991: 85). The fear Auster expresses here is that in understanding how he exists in the world, he may discover a whole world of terror connected to it. 'To begin with this landscape . . .', he writes, '[o]r even to note the things that are most near, as if in the tiny world before my eyes I might find an image of the life that exists beyond me, as if in a way I do not fully understand each thing in my life were connected to every other thing, which in turn connected me to the world at large, the endless world that looms up in the mind, as lethal and unknowable as desire itself' (Auster, 1991: 83).

The poet tries thus to find a way of placing himself in an unknowable world. Like Reznikoff and Oppen before him, Auster is searching for a location, and like Oppen, in particular, he fears that the mysteries of the world are impenetrable and potentially lethal. The poet's room, then, represents a place from which to view the metropolis while simultaneously sheltering from its overwhelming turmoil and confusion. For Auster, language is a medium fraught with problems, particularly when employed in representing the city, and his words are dedicated 'to the impossibility of finding a word equal to the silence inside me' (Auster, 1991: 86).

What emerges in 'White Spaces' is a representation, through an inadequate medium, of an environment unsympathetic to the scale of individual endeavour. It is exactly this complexity of urban living that Auster contemplates in 'the monstrous sum / of particulars'. Oppen confronted a similar 'shipwreck of the singular' and sought 'the meaning / of being numerous', which Auster feels emerges 'more from a feeling of isolation and loss than from a naïve hope in the future' (Auster, 1997: 117–18). For Auster, then, his solitude as a poet has been a paradoxical attempt to enter the world of men while also remaining in his room. In the subsequent prose fiction, Auster has remained committed to the Objectivist poetic principle of striving to present the world as it is apprehended. Language can merely attempt to represent the world, and the writer must be bound to the idea of the eye dominating the word, while also being wary of the four inches between the vision and the voice. However, to attempt to express something of the complexity of this world by overcoming this obstacle is the worthy pursuit of the writer. 'To invoke things that have never happened is noble', he says of the storyteller's art, 'but how much sweeter to remain in the realm of the naked eye' (Auster, 1991: 87).

The Invention of Solitude is Auster's first published prose book, and it takes up the themes of the solitude of living and the solitude of writing. *The Invention of Solitude* recounts the sudden and premature death of Auster's father, Sam, at the age of sixty-seven. But Auster goes beyond a description of bereavement to explore the difficulty of writing about the loss of his father. The sense of solitude is threefold as he struggles simultaneously to comprehend the isolation in which his father lived, his own loss and the solitude of the writer. As Auster told Larry McCaffrey and Sinda Gregory in a 1989 interview: '[o]ur sense of self is formed by . . . the endless monologue, the life-long conversation we have with ourselves. And this takes place in absolute solitude' (Auster, 1997: 314). In exploring the problematic duality of isolating oneself from the world, while at the same time trying to write about it, Auster again probes the relationship between the writer and writing.

The first part of the book, 'Portrait of an Invisible Man', explores Auster's difficulty of knowing the man who was his father. The second part, 'The Book of Memory', explores the nature of the writer's task in writing about a world that he does not always understand, and having to do so from a vantage point that seems external to the world that is being written. For Auster, this disconnection from the world is the paradox that alienates the writer from his environment and condemns him to remain in his room. Baudelaire and Reznikoff both experienced this 'poetic paradox' – Baudelaire standing outside the crowd to record it even as he attempted to participate and experience it, and Reznikoff endeavouring to absent himself from his poetic record of the New York cityscape. Auster takes up his own position in his room, and attempts to reconcile the contradictions of observation, experience and transcription from there. In doing so he connects memory, language and the solitude of the lonely room through an exploration of his father's relationship to the world, his own relationship with his father and the capacity of literature to represent these complex matters.

The problem of writing about his recently dead father is closely allied to the problems Auster grapples with in his poetry. The poetry was about locating the self in relation to the material world, and finding that place (the room) from which to write about it. 'Portrait of an

Invisible Man' attempts to locate the writer in relation to the subject of his father, and his father in relation to the world. However, Sam Auster's relationship with the world is problematised by his refusal to be known to others. Consequently, Auster has trouble locating his father:

> [w]hat people saw when he appeared before them . . . was not really him, but a person he invented, an artificial creature he could manipulate. . . . He himself remained invisible, a puppeteer working the strings of his alter-ego from a dark, solitary place behind the curtain. (Auster, 1982: 16)

Sam Auster was solitary 'in the sense of retreat. In the sense of not having to see himself being seen by anyone else' (Auster, 1982: 16–17). Because his father is all surface, Auster's subject matter becomes elusive, slipping from his grasp and defying description. However, Auster begins to piece together parts of his father's life from the fragments left behind. As William Dow notes, Auster's approach here emphasises unknowability, while at the same time he 'continually points to the importance of fragmented or partial knowledge'. The result, Dow insists, is that Auster 'places a new value on the elusive and discloses a longing for a stable self' (Dow, 1998: 276, 279).

The most compelling of these fragments is a family photograph taken when Sam Auster was a baby. Sam's father has been cut out and the picture clumsily recreated. The partial knowledge Auster divines from this picture distorts an important aspect of his family background and his own origins, and, subsequently, his sense of self. Auster's grandfather has been expunged from the family record physically and from the legacy of memory through silence. What this evasion hides is the murder of Auster's grandfather by his wife in Kenosha, Wisconsin in 1919. The result of the grandfather's erasure from the record and from memory is that he has been 'exiled to another dimension' (Auster, 1982: 34).

Sam Auster was a man with many hidden places, who hid behind a 'curtain' of solitude created by layers of artifice and mystery. Auster describes the process of writing about such a complex subject:

> Again and again I have watched my thoughts trail off from the thing in front of me. No sooner have I thought one thing than it evokes another thing, and then another thing, until there is an accumulation of details so dense that I feel I am going to suffocate. Never before have I been so aware of the rift between thinking and writing. . . . I have begun to feel

that the story I am trying to tell is somehow incompatible with language, that the degree to which it resists language is an exact measure of how closely I have come to saying something important, and when the moment arrives for me to say the one truly important thing (assuming it exists), I will not be able to say it. (Auster, 1982: 32)

The capacity of the writer to represent other people, thoughts, feelings and emotions through language is problematised for Auster by the scale of the task he has set himself. As in 'White Spaces', some terrible, unimagined truth that is 'incompatible with language' is lurking beyond understanding, and so beyond the grasp of the writer. 'The Book of Memory' is predominantly concerned with how to write and the conditions for writing. Auster's writing begins with memory and it is a consistently solitary pursuit. In this section of *The Invention of Solitude* he explores his own solitude, the reasons for it and how this affects his writing. In contrast to 'Portrait of an Invisible Man', 'The Book of Memory' is narrated in the third person, and Auster refers to himself only as A. This is because, as he explained to Joseph Mallia in 1987, *The Invention of Solitude* is not only autobiographical, but also 'a meditation about certain questions' in which he uses himself as the central character, and to write about himself he had to treat himself as someone else (Auster, 1997: 276–7). It was also a necessary strategy for Auster to observe a painful episode in his life. As he told novelist Jonathan Lethem in a more recent interview, 'I managed to get a certain distance from myself, and that made it possible for me to see myself, which in turn made it possible to write the book' (Vida, 2005: 40).

A.'s solitary condition is brought about by the breakup of his marriage and estrangement from his wife and young son. The result is disconnection from familiar relationships. On leaving the family home in Duchess County he moves into a room in an old office building on Varrick Street in Manhattan. Here he contemplates other writerly exiles in other lonely rooms. A. thinks about Hölderlin and his isolated madness, and Van Gogh, whose painting of his room is described as 'the substance of solitude' (Auster, 1982: 143). But most profoundly he describes visiting the room in Amsterdam in which Anne Frank wrote her diary. This is the place that Auster feels he first conceived of the 'Book of Memory', because here it is possible to 'imagine a solitude so crushing, so inconsolable, that one stops breathing for hundreds of years' (Auster, 1982: 82–3).

Auster describes A.'s room in Varrick Street on Christmas Eve, 1979. It is a room formerly occupied by an electrician whose name is still stencilled on the frosted glass of the door, and the room still carries the depressing remnants of its former purpose. Auster describes the bleakness of A.'s room:

> He cannot call it home, but for the past nine months it is all he has had. . . . By staying in this room for long stretches at a time, he can usually manage to fill it with his thoughts. . . . Each time he goes out, he takes his thoughts with him, and during his absence the room gradually empties of his efforts to inhabit it. When he returns, he has to begin the process all over again, and that takes work, real spiritual work. . . . In the interim, in the void between the moment he opens the door and the moment he begins to reconquer the emptiness, his mind flails in a wordless panic. It is as if he were being forced to watch his own disappearance, as if, by crossing the threshold of this room, he were entering another dimension. (Auster, 1982: 76–7)

The degree of A.'s social alienation is summed up by his exile, not just to the top of a disused office building, but like his grandfather's memory, to another dimension. The consequence of A.'s isolation is the need to constantly reconquer the space he inhabits and overcome the 'wordless panic' of this emptiness.

Hölderlin, Van Gogh, Anne Frank and A. all struggle with the dangers that lurk inside their rooms. Dominant amongst these dangers is the recall of past events and a descent into despair. A. remembers his family and his life before he lived on Varrick Street. Auster describes how thinkers such as Cicero have related memory to a room, and how memory can be explored as if it were a space. 'Memory as a place, as a building, as a sequence of columns, cornices, porticoes', Auster writes. 'The body inside the mind, as if we were moving around in there, going from one place to the next, and the sound of our footsteps as we walk, moving from one place to the next' (Auster, 1982: 82).[7] Memory is 'the place in which things happen for the second time' (Auster, 1982: 83), and when those memories are written down, becoming a record through language, they can be repeated infinitely. If they are painful memories, they can inflict violence upon the consciousness of the recorder and the reader. This is the kind of violence A. experiences when he studies the photograph that omits his grandfather from the family history. For Hölderlin, meanwhile, the result of constant recall through memory is delusion, mental breakdown and a thirty-six-year exile in his own room.

The relationship between writing and memory is crucial in 'The Book of Memory', as is the relationship of the writer to language. In this respect 'The Book of Memory' emerges directly from Auster's poetic concerns and, in part, from Reznikoff's influence. Of Reznikoff's view of the world, and the poetry that results from it, Auster says, '[as] soon as there is more than one thing, there is memory, and because of memory there is language' (Auster, 1997: 39). For A. 'the act of writing' poetry is 'an act of memory' (Auster, 1997: 142) making the recall of that which is memorialised possible – in this case the paintings of Van Gogh in Amsterdam (and so the chain of associations grows from Van Gogh's room, to Anne Frank, to the Van Gogh museum in Amsterdam). As memory is an important way of relating to the world, language becomes central to its expression, and so the writer seeks a stable relationship with the word. To explain the importance of language in relating to the world, Auster describes the different ways in which adults (possessors of the word) and children (preliterate possessors of the image) access memory. For adults '[w]ritten language absolves one of the need to remember much of the world, for the memories are stored in the words', while for the child it is the image that is associated with the place (Auster, 1982: 165).

It is clear though that the capacity of the adult individual to remember will influence their capacity to use language to represent their experiences. Throughout Auster's work, and in 'The Book of Memory' for A., language is always a random collection of symbols with an arbitrary relationship to the world it is meant to represent. For language to carry meaning a degree of stability must be achieved in the relationship between the individual, his environment and language. Quite simply, socially shared meanings will only become possible if individuals relate to their environment in similar ways, and mediate it with the same words.

Two aspects of this philosophy of language illuminate the way that language works for Auster at this early stage of his career. First, he identifies the relational nature of language, with each word deriving meaning more from its relationship to other words than to the object to which it corresponds, such that 'to enter any part of language is to enter the whole of it' (Auster, 1982: 160). Secondly, and at the very centre of Auster's understanding of language and art, '[l]anguage is not truth. It is the way we exist in the world' (Auster, 1982: 161). Where the individual suffers a problematic relationship to the world, as in the case of A., they have a problematic relationship with language. Of course, the reverse holds true as well. A. rapidly becomes alienated from society by both his isolation and his problems with language. He is unbalanced in his room by the lack of comfort, the loneliness and the disconnection from the things that give his life meaning – such as his family. The room holds 'only the signs of his own disquiet, and in order to find some measure of peace in these surroundings he must dig more and more deeply into himself' until he runs the risk of using himself up (Auster, 1982: 78–9). During these moments of disquiet, the dangers of the room emerge in the contemplation of the 'space between utterance and act' until 'a chasm begins to open and for one to contemplate such emptiness for any length of time is to grow dizzy, to feel oneself falling into the abyss' (Auster, 1982: 127). The implications for the writer of a breakdown of this magnitude are clear from the opening passage of 'The Book of Memory':

> [A.] finds a fresh sheet of paper and lays it out on the table before him. He writes until he has covered the entire page with words. Later, when he reads over what he has written, he has trouble deciphering the words. Those he does manage to understand do not seem to say what he thought he was saying. (Auster, 1982: 75)

A.'s 'aphasic' episode here is figured as a slippage between his use of a word and what he meant it to mean. The result is a fall (like Adam's) into a dizzying chasm of the same order A. experienced in the 'wordless panic' of his empty and lonely room.

Elsewhere in 'The Book of Memory' A. is 'hunched over a small rectangle of wood, concentrating on an even smaller rectangle of paper', which he relates directly to his walks through foreign cities (Auster, 1982: 98). The relationship between the two becomes clear in the following passage, particularly in the context of the relationship of steps to thoughts to words in 'White Spaces':

> Sometimes it feels as though we are wandering through a city without purpose. . . . But just as one step will inevitably lead to the next step, so it is that one thought inevitably follows from the previous thought, and in the event that a thought should engender more than a single thought . . . it will be necessary not only to follow the first thought to its conclusion, but also to backtrack to the original position of that thought in order to follow the second thought to its conclusion . . . and so on in this way, if we were to try to make an image of this process in our minds, a network of paths begins to be drawn, . . . as in the image of a map (of city streets, for example, preferably a large city . . .), so that what we are really doing when we walk through the city is thinking, and this journey is no more or less than the steps we have taken, so that, in the end, we might safely say that we have been on a journey, and even if we do not leave our room,

it has been a journey, and we might safely say that we have been
somewhere, even if we don't know where it is. (Auster, 1982: 121–2)

In this passage Auster draws together the themes of the room, the
metropolis, memory, language and writing into a single account that
reveals not only his process of artistic production, but also the way that
he – in the room and in the metropolis – can connect to his wider
environment. Footsteps are related to thoughts; in 'White Spaces' they
relate to words, and in Dublin they related to the trace of a youthful and
tumultuous 'inner terrain'. So each sequence of steps forms sentences
and then a 'network' of thoughts. Thus the urban-wanderer-writer
begins to trace out a map of ideas generated in metropolitan space and
constrained by the limits and patterns of that space (the street grid, for
example). It is these patterns that emerge in part as the urban literary
text and give the text its particularly metropolitan qualities. However,
when it comes to deciphering the metropolis, the limitations of this
position become apparent, as will be discussed in Chapter 2, with the
onset of instability in any part of the network of relationships between
these elements.

   On the face of it there appears to be a tension between two of the
central positions in the texts explored in this chapter. On the one hand
Auster is proposing that language is a way of forming a relationship
with the metropolitan world. The individual – here the poet, but
elsewhere in Auster's work, writers and artists of many kinds –
attempts to name the objects around him, and so bring the word and
the world into a closer relationship. By doing so the individual explores
her or his relationship to the environment, and so begins the process
of 'placing oneself in the world'. Auster describes the way that the
Objectivist poet Charles Reznikoff sought to do this by 'standing at
the interval of silence' between the metropolis and the words of a
metropolitan language in his 'spare city lyrics', which by their linguistic
proximity to their subject become 'transcriptions of immediate sensual
data' (Auster, 1997: 45). On the other hand, Auster seems to be
proposing that the artist's place is in solitude, isolated from the world
in his room like Hölderlin, Van Gogh or Anne Frank. Hölderlin and
Van Gogh went mad, and Anne Frank's isolation weighs so heavily on
the consciousness of the reader that the very thought of her solitude
becomes suffocating. If, like A., the poet were to leave his room, he
invites the possibility of a 'wordless panic' that has the horrors and
dimensions of a black hole. To fall into this abyss would be catastrophic

for the poet, as it would disconnect him from both his medium and his environment at once.

Auster begins to renegotiate the central terms of this dilemma by exploring the complex relationship between memory, language and writing in both his poetry and *The Invention of Solitude*. He reconsiders these practical and aesthetic phenomena under the condition of solitude. Paradoxically, he finds that solitude promotes connections between the writer and the world. Auster makes the extension from the isolation of the room to the connection of the 'everything else of the world' through the writing process and its comparison with the freedom of urban wandering. As emerges in the passage above, the steps taken through a city are comparable to the chain of thoughts that constitute a story, such that the process of writing is experienced as a journey. Auster told Mark Irwin that his writing practice is like the immense wanderings of an explorer. Writing is like a 'journey into the unknown, and yet the whole time I'm just sitting there in my room. The door is locked, I never budge, and yet that confinement offers me absolute freedom – to be whoever I want to be, to go wherever my thoughts take me' (Auster, 1997: 328). The freedom that writing offers Auster means that solitude does not have to be an entirely negative condition for him, but can instead be a necessary part of being human (Auster, 1997: 313). The social exchange of language, for Auster, is a way of being in the world precisely because by speaking the language of men, the poet is able to take his 'stand among other men' (Auster, 1997: 118–19). As such, language is the negotiation between the singular self and plural multitudes of the metropolis. Language then becomes an essential part of the equation relating the individual, who in Oppen's words is 'bewildered / By the shipwreck / Of the singular', to what Auster calls 'the blinding / enumeration of stones' of the metropolitan populace.

Finally in Auster's thinking, language emerges as a way of ordering, classifying and harmonising memory. For Auster, the act of writing is an act of memorialisation, because, as we have already seen, 'the act of writing' is 'an act of memory'. While Auster proposes this in respect of poems written about the paintings of Van Gogh, it is the act of 'writing' his father that both memorialises him and at the same time exposes the inadequacies of language.

The following meditation on the nature of writing explains how the writer draws on memory and language to transcribe or 'write' the world:

As he writes, he feels that he is moving inward (through himself) and at the same time moving outward (towards the world). What he experienced ... was this: ... even alone, in the deepest solitude of his room, he was not alone, or, more precisely, that the moment he began to try to speak of that solitude, he had become more than just himself. Memory, therefore, not simply as the resurrection of one's private past, but an immersion in the past of others, which is to say: history – which one both participates in and is a witness to, is a part of and is apart from. ... And yet, the telling of it is necessarily slow, a delicate business of trying to remember what has already been remembered. The pen will never be able to move fast enough to write down every word discovered in the space of memory. Some things have been lost forever, other things will perhaps be remembered again, and still other things have been lost and found and lost again. There is no way to be sure of any of this. (Auster, 1982: 139)

Elsewhere Auster has encapsulated this experience in the following terms: 'I felt as though I were looking down to the bottom of myself, and what I found there was more than just myself – I found the world' (Auster, 1997: 315–16). In the moment of his most extreme solitude A. realises that by attempting to write the world he also moves out into it and discovers that he is more than just himself. Crucially, A. finds the world in himself simultaneously through memories of his own life and his immersion in the histories of other writers.

Auster explained to Larry McCaffrey that the isolated individual is connected to the world because it

isn't possible for a person to isolate himself from other people. No matter how apart you might find yourself in a physical sense ... you discover that you are inhabited by others. Your language, your memories, even your sense of isolation – every thought in your head has been born from your connection with others. (Auster, 1997: 315)

The discovery of the world within the self at the same time that the self is in the world, is reflected in Rimbaud's aphoristic 'Je est un autre' (I am an other) which Auster invokes to describe his relationship as an author to the world (Auster, 1997: 277). The aesthetic truth of this is demonstrated by the literary influences Auster draws on and acknowledges as inhabiting both his own sense of identity as a writer and the text of *The Invention of Solitude*. In interview Auster has said that *The Invention of Solitude* (although it is equally true of many of his books) is a book about being alone, and at the same time it is about community (Auster, 1997: 316). It is about community because it 'has

dozens of authors', and through proliferating 'references and quota-
tions' in the text these other writers speak to us, from across time,
through Auster (Auster, 1997: 316).

Ultimately, then, the poet's retreat to his room is a way of engaging
with the metropolis while protecting the artistic self from the
bewildering and overwhelming complexities of contemporary city
life as it is experienced in Auster's New York. At this point in the
development of his sense of the metropolis Auster suggests that for
the artist to protect himself from wordless panic he must remain in
his room, as to leave the room would create the risk of returning to a
linguistic abyss. By shielding himself in this way, A. hopes to retain a
coherent hold on the relationship between the world and language,
even though that world has atrophied to the small space between the
four walls of a room. But in doing so he manages to maintain enough
of a grasp on language to avoid the psychosis that causes language to
disintegrate. As later chapters will demonstrate, in subsequent works
Auster's writer-characters are often able to step out of the suffocating
room to find new and more fulfilling connections to the world.

Notes

1   After a number of revisions by Auster this interview was published in
    Mississippi Review, and is reprinted in Auster, 1997: 287–326.
2   In his influential study about language disorder Freud described aphasia
    as brain damage causing a 'complete loss or severe reduction of articulate
    speech whereas . . . the intellect remained unimpaired' and an 'inability to
    understand language, i.e., sensory aphasia, word deafness' (Freud, 1953:
    2–3).
3   Poe's urban hero, Dupin, is also a poet who uses his poetical imagination
    to solve crimes, with far greater effect than the scientific rationality of the
    institutions of state. Baudelaire translated these tales into French and was
    much interested in the emergence of the detective in literature. See also
    Benjamin, 1997: 42–4.
4   References and materials in the Auster Archive, the Berg Collection, New
    York Public Library. Materials include artwork for covers and proof copies
    of content.
5   Louis Zukofsky was also included in an original essay entitled 'The Poem
    as Object' (Auster, undated a). However, Zukofsky was omitted when this
    was published as three separate essays on each of the other central figures.
    Reznikoff is discussed at length in 'The Decisive Moment', while Rakosi
    and Oppen are handled more briefly in 'Resurrection' and 'Private I, Public
    Eye' respectively (collected in Auster, 1997:). The name and the personnel

of the group come from a 1931 Objectivist issue of *Poetry* edited by Louis Zukofsky. Auster names the Objectivists as a particular influence in an interview with Joseph Mallia (Auster, 1997: 275).

6 'White Spaces' is suggestive of the metaphorical journeys taken by the artist through language, traversing empty spaces that are given meaning and shape through the artist's imagination and words, in the same way that a dancer 'actualises' the performance space with movement. This supposition is supported by the names that earlier revisions and published versions of the text carried. One such title was 'Happiness – Or a Journey through Space'; the subtitle described this work as a 'text for reading aloud while someone dances' (TS, Berg Collection, dated 'turn of the year 1978–9', n.p.).

7 When writing 'The Book of Memory', Auster employed a cartographic approach to the organisation of the material which has parallels with his description of memory here. He told Michel Contat, 'I was struggling to find the structure. . . . "The Book of Memory" was very complicated. . . . I was very confused, and I just had to make this map, to see how everything fit with everything else'. This is accompanied by the diagram Auster worked from in producing the book. At the centre is the word 'ROOM'. Radiating out from this central theme and space are four different themes of enquiry: father figures, writing, exile and New York (Auster/ Contat, 1996: 173).

2
Streets

The New York Trilogy is a volume of three interconnected novels – *City of Glass* (1985), *Ghosts* (1986) and *The Locked Room* (1986) – originally published separately, but brought together as a single edition in 1987. Each book of the *Trilogy* is a detective story, but each takes the themes and the structural conventions of the genre and subverts them. The first story, 'City of Glass', follows a detective writer, Daniel Quinn, who inadvertently becomes a detective in the name of his author, Paul Auster. Quinn is hired to protect Peter Stillman from his father, also called Peter Stillman, who carried out language experiments on him when he was a child. The story of Quinn's detection explores loss and isolation (Quinn's wife and son are dead), the labyrinthine streets of New York, the capacity of language to obscure meaning and under-standing, and the problems of writing in the metropolis. 'Ghosts' is a detective story stripped back to its minimum requirements: a detective and a criminal. The detective, Blue, is set the task of watching Black by the client, White. As the 'investigation' progresses, it becomes clear that Blue's isolation is forcing him to consider his increasingly unstable sense of self rather than what Black is up to. In the final story, 'The Locked Room', Auster takes one of the oldest motifs of the detective form – the room which is the scene of a crime and is locked from the inside – and alters it to once again examine notions of identity. Here, the unnamed narrator attempts to track down his childhood friend, Fanshawe, now a writer, becoming Fanshawe's literary executor and marrying his (Fanshawe's) wife along the way.

This chapter takes in turn the three main themes of New York, language and writing. New York City is explored for the ways in which the characters, but particularly Quinn in 'City of Glass', relate to the urban experience. Auster's persistent theme of language is examined

for its capacity to both engage with and represent the metropolitan
condition in all three stories. Finally, the idea of writing is once again
examined, but here with an emphasis on the instabilities of literary
form.

New York City

Paul Auster has said: 'I tend to think of myself more as a storyteller than
a novelist. I believe that stories are the fundamental food for the soul.
. . . It's through stories that we struggle to make sense of the world'
(Auster, 1997: 336). The stories in *The New York Trilogy* attempt to
make sense of the urban world by exploring its effects on the individual
consciousness when the conditions of isolation and loneliness are at
their most extreme. As a storyteller and a writer of fiction, Auster
apprehends New York City on an imaginative level, subjecting his
characters to extreme conditions and exposing them to unlikely, but
still conceivable, situations.

Both Auster's perception of the urban condition, and these stories
themselves, are influenced in many ways by Nathaniel Hawthorne's
early story 'Wakefield' (1835).[1] Wakefield tells his wife he is going away
on business and then disguises himself and takes lodgings nearby. He
allows time to pass, and it becomes more difficult to return home. He
sees his wife in the street and brushes against her, but in the hectic city
street she does not notice him. She eventually assumes herself to be a
widow. Twenty years later Wakefield returns to the threshold of his
house on a whim, and here the story ends. Hawthorne summarises
Wakefield's predicament in this way:

> Amid the seeming confusion of our mysterious world, individuals are so
> nicely adjusted to a system, and systems to one another, and to a whole,
> that by stepping aside for a moment, a man exposes himself to a fearful
> risk of losing his place forever. Like Wakefield, he may become, as it were,
> the Outcast of the Universe. (Hawthorne, 1987: 133)

The fate of each central character in the *Trilogy* is to become just such
an 'outcast'. Among the stories, 'Ghosts' follows 'Wakefield' most faith-
fully and includes a brief telling of this tale. But all three of the stories
pursue the urban concerns of the anonymous crowd, alienation and
the fragile stability of identity in the complex urban realm. However,
Auster's contemporary metropolis, as we shall see, does not necessarily
provide the opportunity for the same urban reunion Hawthorne

proposes for Wakefield. Through the textual and narrative references to 'Wakefield', and the intertextual allusions to works by Edgar Allan Poe, Henry David Thoreau and Herman Melville,[2] Auster signals a heritage of literary representations of the city, and particularly New York.

The streets of New York are the setting of these stories. On the city streets Auster's characters experience loneliness, disconnection and personal disintegration. For each of them, solitary urban experience becomes the 'raw data' (to echo Rakosi) of their urban record. These records then go on to form the bases of the narratives which constitute the *Trilogy*.

In an interview with Allan Reich, Auster described how *The New York Trilogy* traces a causal path from disorientation, through introspection (the period of solitude during which external contact is lost), to ultimate alienation (Reich, 1988: n.p.). It is Quinn's loneliness that drives him on to the streets of the city. His disorientation and solitude in 'City of Glass' are triggered by the deaths of his wife and infant son five years earlier. When he remembers the funeral, he thinks to himself, '[t]hat was isolation, . . . [t]hat was silence' (Auster, 1988: 35).[3] He can still feel how it felt to hold his three-year-old son as 'a physical sensation, an imprint of the past that had been left on his body' (Auster, 1988: 5). Quinn's tragedy leads him to cast off the other people who had constituted his social world. His friends, for example, are unaware that he writes pseudonymous detective fiction because 'the fact was that he no longer had any friends' (Auster, 1988: 5). By divesting himself of one layer of social contact after another, and by withdrawing from his previous life, Quinn has managed to create for himself an almost entirely solitary existence in the centre of New York City. In the heart of Manhattan, Quinn creates a self-imposed exile echoing that of Hölderlin described in *The Invention of Solitude*.

In 'Ghosts', Blue is similarly disconnected from the social world, which carries on around him but in which he plays no part. The 'case' confines Blue to his room in Brooklyn, watching Black across Orange Street. While limiting his attention to his room and to Black, Blue feels content, but when he turns his thoughts outward, to his fiancée in particular, his position in the world becomes less stable. At these moments, when thinking of the future Mrs Blue, 'his calm turns to anguish, and he feels as though he is falling into some dark, cave-like place, with no hope of finding a way out. . . . [P]erhaps a moment of real contact would break the spell' (Auster, 1988: 145). Social contact may indeed break the cycle of Blue's solitude, but he does not take the opportunities to quit the case and return to his previous life.

The quality of the self-imposed urban exile that Quinn and Blue experience is invoked in 'The Locked Room' as a part of what it means to become a writer, and the conditions of possibility for writing. Fanshawe's personality, since adolescence, has marked him out as a writer. From the age of thirteen he was in a 'kind of internal exile' that pushed him towards a 'stubborn marginality' (Auster, 1988: 216). In adulthood, the 'severity of his inwardness' seemed to demand that he be a writer (Auster, 1988: 214). The Narrator, too, seems to exist in New York in a social and familial vacuum. Between his childhood associations with Fanshawe and his subsequent relationship with Fanshawe's wife, Sophie, there is no evidence of a family or a circle of friends. The three central characters of this novel all find themselves, through stubborn application to their task regardless of the consequences, occupying a physically and socially marginal space.

On the streets, Quinn achieves some respite from his isolation amongst the crowds, and a place where, paradoxically, he can lose rather than find himself. Once on the streets Quinn is alienated by the complexity and intensity of his metropolitan experiences, and by his feelings of insignificance. His urban wanderings reveal the extent to which he has become dislocated from the texture of everyday life. 'New York was an inexhaustible space, a labyrinth of endless steps', we are told of Quinn's walks:

> and no matter how far he walked, no matter how well he came to know its neighborhoods and streets, it always left him with the feeling of being lost. Lost, not only in the city, but within himself as well. Each time he took a walk, he felt as though he were leaving himself behind . . . and this, more than anything else, brought him a measure of peace, a salutary emptiness within. . . . New York was the nowhere he had built around himself, and he realized that he had no intention of ever leaving it again.
> (Auster, 1988: 4–5)

Quinn experiences the streets of New York as a series of equal and indiscernible spaces. As a form of analytical engagement his aimless wandering predictably presents him with a cityscape that is a nowhere, but which could equally be an anywhere. This interpretation of Quinn's predicament is reinforced by an early handwritten and unpublished story called 'Invasions'. Here Auster describes a subjective experience of New York City which emphasises the insignificance of the human form:

New York, a city of impenetrable facades. . . . Everywhere it eludes the
grasp, sealing itself off from the mind, forbidding the secret knowledge
that would allow it to be defined. The redundancy of its parallels and
intersections. . . . I move through it like a somnambulist. Faces might
appear, large crowds might grow, but they cannot alter or penetrate the
facades that surround them. The city . . . reduces its inhabitants to objects.
Each person, entitled to just a single perspective, creates a city which is
merely a function of his imagination. Properly speaking, New York does
not exist. (Auster, undated b: 7–8)

This fragment demonstrates a response to the physical and discursive realities of New York City that emphasises an extreme social
and neurotic subjectivity. The façades of the buildings represent
impenetrable urban forces, the remoteness of their 'secret knowledge'
denies interpretation, and the rational logic of its street grid contains
the imagination, limiting personal agency. The result, as with Auster's
earlier poetry, is an alienated individual, reduced to the status of
an 'object' in the city's vast structures. Because Quinn too wanders
aimlessly in a city which reduces his human form to an irrelevance, he
achieves a subjective sense of the city that enhances his feelings of
anonymity. His New York is represented as an incomprehensible
labyrinth where individual spaces are indistinguishable, which provides little in the way of coordinates for the individual to navigate by,
and so produces an arena in which the individual easily becomes lost
in the 'nowhereness' of everywhere. Quinn is clearly seeking this
outcome from his wandering, and its result is to evacuate his sense of
self. By replacing the inwardness of self with the outwardness of the
city Quinn establishes a distance between his physical and mental
selves. The 'salutary emptiness' left by the city's motion creates the
conditions for the individual to become a mere reflection of the urban
process, and the resulting void of selfhood can be colonised by the city's
multiplicities. Yet Quinn's 'excursions' do achieve an understanding
of how to connect the 'inner' to the 'outer', so that:

on his best days he could bring the outside in and thus usurp the
sovereignty of inwardness. By flooding himself with externals, by
drowning himself out of himself, he had managed to exert some small
degree of control over his fits of despair. Wandering, therefore, was a
form of mindlessness. (Auster, 1988: 61)

The city floods Quinn's consciousness and usurps the authority of
his inner self. If a part of Auster's project is to locate the individual in

the world, then Quinn stands as an exemplar of a failure to find one's place, and to find a way of being in the world. Fredric Jameson would read Quinn's relationship to his metropolitan environment as a failure to 'cognitively . . . map [his] position in a mappable external world' (Jameson, 1991: 44). Steven E. Alford sees Quinn's wanderings as an attempt to map a spatial relationship between the self and the metropolis. However, the main protagonists in the *Trilogy* all fail to create a stable connection with their metropolitan environment. Indeed, as Alford puts it, Quinn's 'desire to lose his self in the streets of Manhattan . . . point[s] to a figure who suffers from a genuine mis-understanding of his place in the world, of the space that he occupies', and he, Blue and the Narrator all experience 'a lack of understanding that space and the self are coeval' (Alford, 1995b: 631).

When Quinn's self and the space that he occupies are not 'coeval', it follows that his interior self must be elsewhere. While I have shown how Auster represents Quinn evacuating his interiority in favour of the impersonal narratives of the city, Auster chooses a quotation from Baudelaire to describe Quinn's relationship to the urban environment that is able to do this to him. As Baudelaire's name is synonymous with the urban wander-observer, it is appropriate that Quinn, a modern-day *flâneur*, should record the words in his notebook:

> Baudelaire: Il me semble que je serais toujours bien là où je ne suis pas. In other words: It seems to me that I will always be happy in the place where I am not. Or, more bluntly: Wherever I am not is the place where I am myself. Or else, taking the bull by the horns: Anywhere out of the world. (Auster, 1988: 110)

Quinn clearly wants to escape himself, and so his sense of self and the space that his physical self occupies are not 'coeval'. The disorientation that he experiences from this point on in the book – until his eventual erasure from it – is in part due to his failure to create a meaningful connection between his inner self and the material world, and so establish his place as a unified self within it.

Language

Language is what places us in the world. It is the way in which the intangible interiority of selfhood negotiates with the tangible exterior reality of the world. Language is also the medium we use as isolated individuals to form connections and bonds in a social realm, which consists of fleeting and inconsequential contact. The disorienting nature of the darkly urban world that Auster represents in *The New York Trilogy* – like his poetry – calls into question the capacity of language to provide a stable mediation of the metropolitan world for the individuals who inhabit it. Through the experiences of Quinn, Blue and the Narrator in New York's overwhelming environment, Auster explores what potential calamities can befall the individual when language begins to fail them, and the word and the world no longer correspond.

Language is examined in 'City of Glass' for its capacity to represent the metropolitan spaces and the urban experiences of New York. Auster allies this concern with the biblical concerns of language described in Genesis, and their potential relationship to the history of America through the Edenic visions of the early settlers. Stillman Jr. has been imprisoned by his father in an attempt to isolate his young son from the influence of the fallen world, and to recover the innocent language of Adam. Stillman Sr.'s final project is to find a language adequate to the contemporary urban experience. He collects debris from the streets of New York and catalogues the objects in his notebook because, as he tells Quinn, he is 'inventing a new language' (Auster, 1988: 76) able to describe objects that no longer fulfil their function. As William G. Little notes, Stillman is directly relating 'the corrupt nature of the sign – its inability to represent properly – to a lament about the fractured, disunited state of modern existence' by pointing to the inadequacy of language to describe the contemporary New York cityscape in the true terms of its decay, degradation and personal isolation (Little, 1997: 157).

The origins of Stillman's work in New York, his experimentation with Stillman Jr. as a child, and his doctoral thesis upon which they build, are the biblical tales of Eden and Babel, and how they relate to American national identification with the Garden of Eden. The first part of Stillman's book, 'The Myth of Paradise', focuses on how the American continent was perceived by its discoverers to be a new Eden (Auster, 1988: 41–2). The second part, 'The Myth of Babel', explores the fall of Adam through Milton's *Paradise Lost*. Stillman describes language's prelapsarian state, when Adam's 'tongue had gone straight to the quick of the world' and the names given had revealed an 'essence', such that a 'thing and its name were interchangeable' (Auster, 1988: 43). 'After the fall', however:

> this was no longer true. Names became detached from things; words devolved into a collection of arbitrary signs; language had been severed

from God. The story of the Garden, therefore, records not only the fall of
man, but the fall of language. (Auster, 1988: 43)

Stillman's experiment in isolating his son was an attempt to recover the
Adamic prelapsarian language of God. Stillman Jr. was locked in a
darkened room and kept in absolute silence from the age of two until
he was eleven (Auster, 1988: 26–7). Stillman Jr. does not fully recover
from his disconnection from human contact, and his speech patterns
are odd, veering between first and third person, between tenses, and
incorporating weird grammatical forms, infantile idioms and made-up
words. Peter describes his imprisonment in this way:

> Dark, dark. They say for nine years. Not even a window. Poor Peter
> Stillman. And the boom, boom, boom. The cacca piles. The pipi lakes.
> The swoons. Excuse me. Numb and naked. Excuse me. Anymore.
> (Auster, 1988: 16)

This passage is suggestive of a number of elements in the *Trilogy*.
It prefigures Quinn's destiny at the end of the story, where he too is
confined to a bare room, naked and struggling with language. It also
points to an image of the dark language void that is symptomatic of
linguistic and social failure. Finally, it suggests the popular image
of the poet, trapped in his room and drawing words out of himself
in an attempt to describe the world.[4] Peter's 'aphasic-type' relationship with the world prompts Quinn to question exactly how one can
engage with the material world when the collective experience of
language has been lost. Quinn wonders 'if these were the same trees
that Peter Stillman saw. . . . And if a tree was not a tree, he wondered
what it really was' (Auster, 1988: 36). Quinn, for the time being, is able
to bridge the gap between 'social space' and 'private, inner space' with
socially meaningful words. But, as with Stillman Jr., as the relationship
between the word and the world breaks down, so does Quinn's
relationship with the wider social world.

Quinn's linguistic anxiety finds its echo in Blue's efforts in 'Ghosts'
to report the events of his case. Previously, reports have been second
nature to Blue; he records 'the outward facts, describing events as
though each word tallied exactly with the thing described, and to question the matter no further . . . actions hold over interpretation' (Auster,
1988: 146). This is because, for Blue, words are transparent, like
'windows that stand between him and the world'. However, he soon
discovers that words do not always 'work' because 'it is possible for them
to obscure the things that they are trying to say' (Auster, 1988: 147–8).

In 'The Locked Room' the Narrator violently confronts an American, chosen arbitrarily to represent Fanshawe, on the streets of Paris – a man called Peter Stillman. The Narrator confers on himself the power to rename the world and exults in the fantasy of his assertion, because he is 'the sublime alchemist who could change the world at will' (Auster, 1988: 296). The streets of Paris, as I will show shortly, have undermined the Narrator's stability and he now believes he has the power to change the world through a linguistic alchemy.

These three linguistic predicaments resonate with Reznikoff's poetics of urban representation. For our writer-detectives, too, '[s]eeing . . . always comes before speech' and, like the poet, they discover that 'we do not find ourselves in the midst of an already established world, . . . we do not automatically take possession of our surroundings', but instead embark upon an 'inscription of the visible into the brute, undeciphered code of being' (Auster, 1997: 34–5). For Reznikoff, Auster and the characters of the *Trilogy*, the alienating urban experience must be translated into language before it can be deciphered. However, each needs first to fashion a vocabulary appropriate to the complexities of the metropolitan environment.

Quinn attempts to 'take possession of' his 'surroundings' by reinterpreting his record and seeking out clues in the text. It is, after all, an account of Stillman's urban wanderings, and has acquired many of the qualities of the events it documents. When Quinn maps out Stillman's steps he is shocked to discover that the pattern revealed is one of letters; one for each day to spell out 'THE TOWER OF BABEL' (Auster, 1988: 70). This discovery drives Quinn into a 'neverland of fragments, a place of wordless things and thingless words' (Auster, 1988: 72). It is also resonant of Quinn's own fate in Stillman's room, where he attempts to speak his words directly into the fabric of the city.

Stillman's pedestrian inscriptions textualise urban space and reaffirm Michel de Certeau's comparison of language and the invisible patterns individuals trace on the streets. In 'Walking in the City' he describes the ways in which pedestrian footsteps form patterns, which are themselves comparable to elements of a linguistic system. Idle footsteps, he says, generate a 'chorus', the concept of 'pedestrian speech acts' adds a sense of coherence or legibility, and these combine to constitute 'walking rhetorics' and, lyrically, 'the long poem of walking' (de Certeau, 1984: 97–102). Auster suggests, through the erasure from the text of both Stillman Sr. (when he plunges from the Brooklyn Bridge) and Quinn (as a result of an inappropriate linguistic and urban strategy), that the practice of reading the urban text is not an easy one, and is frequently unable to reconcile the disjunction between the individual and the contemporary metropolis. While ethereal texts can be written upon the urban fabric, as de Certeau suggests, for Auster they are only capable of communicating the constant cycle of deferrals of language that the Tower of Babel symbolises. In the case of Stillman and Quinn, the urban poem is one that promotes confusion and evades interpretation. The capacity of language to negotiate urban phenomena becomes less, not more, apparent to Quinn in his pursuit of the case.[5]

The importance of this episode in Quinn's narrative lies both in his location and his mode of analysis or 'detection'. For the first time in a considerable while he is in his room, at his desk and pursuing the activities of a writer. This practice leads him to his only real break-through in the case. By shifting his attention away from observation and towards interpretation (the activity of the writer) he deduces Stillman's malevolent purposes. Quinn uses his powers of interpretation to decipher the letters from Stillman's tracks and the words from the letters (the first and last of which are missing). This suggests that urban events become legible when the perspective adopted is one of critical distance. Quinn is able to bring his faculty of interpretation to bear on the metropolis when he can consider it as a text, from above, as it were. This view offers a degree of legibility and clarity that is not afforded in the immediacy and confusion of the streets.

These events suggest that Quinn has found a way of occupying the role of detective more effectively than he has so far, and that his place in the world is becoming more secure as his capacity to 'read' it improves. But if Quinn has found a strategy to successfully fill the role of the detective, why does his subsequent detection fail him so profoundly? This failure to 'read' his urban predicament is demon-strated when he records an extended wander around lower Manhattan. Quinn records the trace of his own steps with the same exactness that had earlier uncovered Stillman's purpose, but no readable pattern is revealed this time. The difference between these two events and their subsequent interpretation can be found in the encounter Quinn has with the 'Paul Auster' character. 'Auster' comfortably occupies a homely and domestic retreat on the busy and prosperous Upper West Side. The contrast with Quinn's home life, just a few blocks away, provokes a deepening realisation of his disconnection and isolation. As we will see, this event has a profound importance for Quinn's destiny and the reader's comprehension of the narrative.

It is Quinn's catastrophic inability to 'read' his urban predicament which both triggers and maintains his inexorable slide into vagrancy. When for the first time in 'City of Glass' Quinn becomes the recorder of his urban environment, as opposed to the recorder of 'the Stillman case', it is the nature of social decay on the streets of New York that he records. 'Today, as never before:', he writes in his notebook, 'the tramps, the down-and-outs, the shopping bag ladies, the drifters and the drunks. They range from the merely destitute to the wretchedly broken. Wherever you turn, they are there, in good neighbourhoods and bad' (Auster, 1988: 108). Vagabonds are simultaneously truly lost in the city, synonymous with it and utterly anonymous to the urban population they live amongst. As Quinn notes, the derelicts' anonymity makes them almost invisible, but his careful urban observation redefines them against the cityscape they inhabit. These people have suffered, as Quinn himself will in the following pages, a series of personally catastrophic events. Once Quinn takes the decision to stake out the Stillman apartment, he triggers the final break with social contact that began with the death of his wife and son.

As Quinn prefigures his own destiny with his record of urban dereliction, so Blue inadvertently plays the role of his alienated self in the disguise of Jimmy Rose. Blue dresses himself as a tramp to speak with Black in an attempt to crack the case. Jimmy Rose is described as 'a wise old fool, a saint of penury living on the margins of society. . . . [S]ince everything has happened to him already, nothing can disturb him anymore' (Auster, 1988: 171). Auster has described how he based this figure on a real tramp, Joe Reilly, who begged for change outside his apartment block. After suffering a series of reversals in his life, Reilly very quickly found himself friendless, homeless and broke (Auster, 1998a: 63–8). These are the conditions of possibility for dereliction, and this is where Quinn rapidly finds himself.

Quinn's desire to record the margins of New York's society marks a departure in his role in relation to the 'case' and a pivotal moment in 'City of Glass'. After Stillman Sr.'s disappearance Quinn takes up a position in an alleyway where he can observe the Stillman apartment and so protect young Peter from his father's malevolent intentions. This is a change of role for Quinn from pursuit to observation, and a change of emphasis from an active role (searching for clues) to a passive one (merely recording what goes on around him). Quinn embarks on a new phase when he enters the alleyway, and it will trigger his fall from a general sense of despair into an abyss of darkness, dereliction and erasure. It also marks a point of departure in the narrative address of the book, admitting a new and unnamed narrator into the narrative, and an additional layer of interpretation of Quinn's experiences, their record in his red notebook and the way they are related in the story.

From this point in the narrative, Auster opens up a number of debates about representation of the metropolitan environment, the adequacy of language to represent it and the role of the author in doing so. Quinn's surveillance of the apartment from an alleyway is his final act of folly on the route to dereliction. Once established in his spot, Quinn embarks upon a strategy designed to optimise his chances of protecting Stillman. He organises his routine so that he needs as little as possible to eat, and consequently needs to leave his watch as little as possible to shop. This strategy has two related outcomes. On the one hand, Quinn ensures that his descent into dereliction proceeds unchecked by maintaining his social contact at the absolute minimum. On the other, he diminishes his physical self through fasting, thus further reducing his presence in the cityscape (Auster, 1988: 114).

Auster examines the implications of hunger for rational and artistic thought in his 1970 essay, 'The Art of Hunger'. Auster describes how the hero of Knut Hamsun's novel *Hunger* (1890) drives himself into a spiral of descent through starvation. Like Quinn, Hamsun's anonymous central character withdraws into a 'near perfect solitude' to become 'both the subject and the object of his own experiment' (Auster, 1997: 12). According to Auster, by peering 'into the darkness that hunger has created for him' he finds 'a void of language', where reality 'has become a confusion of thingless names and nameless things' (Auster, 1997: 15). Hamsun's tragic hero and Quinn pursue their misguided endeavours until the connection between the self and the world is broken, by which time it is too late to return to normal life. There is an artistic precedent for the 'aesthetics of hunger' (Auster, 1997: 19) that Auster touches on briefly, which is explored by Kafka in his story 'A Hunger Artist'.[6] Hunger also haunts Bartleby's demise in Herman Melville's story 'Bartleby the Scrivener' (1853) – a narrative that has deep implications for the outcome of Quinn's predicament in 'City of Glass', and one of the more evident influences on Auster's work.[7] Of Kafka's character, Auster says: 'the art of hunger can be described as an existential art. It is a way of looking death in the face, . . . death as we live it today. . . . Death as the abrupt and absurd end of life' (Auster, 1997: 20). But before death, when the process of hunger and disconnection is at its most pronounced, Auster describes the effects on Hamsun's writer-character, a description equally applicable to Quinn. 'He loses everything – even himself', Auster says. At 'the bottom of a Godless hell, . . . identity disappears. It is no accident that Hamsun's hero has no name: as time goes on, he is truly shorn of his self' (Auster, 1997: 14–15). Throughout this chapter I have argued that the experience of the metropolis reduces the human form to an insignificant scale. Here, through starvation, Quinn is complicit in the process of reducing the importance of the individual in an urban analysis by literally and symbolically diminishing his presence in the cityscape, while at the same time promoting his own invisibility through his vagrancy and dereliction. Blue's presence as a character in his own narrative is diminished by his reductive name and Auster's stereotypical representation of him as a detective. Similarly, the Narrator remains anonymous throughout 'The Locked Room'.

Quinn's anonymity and physical reduction serve to make him invisible, 'as though he had melted into the walls of the city' (Auster, 1988: 116). As we have already seen, Reznikoff's concern, as an urban poet, is to minimise the poet's presence in the cityscape he presents. 'The Reznikoff equation, which weds seeing to invisibility,' Auster insists, 'cannot be made except by renunciation. In order to see, the poet must make himself invisible. He must disappear, efface himself in anonymity' (Auster, 1997: 38). The parallels between Quinn's position of anonymity and erasure, and Reznikoff's aesthetic of effacement, are clear. Quinn's record in the notebook is now one exclusively of his life on the streets of New York, and his invisibility in the fabric of the city offers a relationship to the city that Reznikoff strives for in his poetry.

When he then discovers that his apartment has been let and his possessions disposed of, Quinn finally realises that he no longer has a place in the social world. As Richard Swope notes, 'the apartment that acted as a spatial anchor for his sense of identity has also vanished' (Swope, 2002: para. 13). At this point Quinn concedes that he 'had come to the end of himself . . . , he was gone, everything was gone' (Auster, 1988: 125). With all social contact stripped from him, and the last remnants of his 'real' self evacuated, the void of Quinn's identity is finally occupied by the urban stereotype of the street bum. In failing to locate himself adequately in the social world of New York, Quinn has effectively been erased from the physical cityscape.

Quinn's narrative draws to a close when he returns to the Stillman apartment. Here he finds a back room with a single window onto the airshaft, strips naked (like Adam in Eden) and settles down with his notebook (Auster, 1988: 126). This room resembles Bartleby's office in Melville's story and his cell in the New York dungeons, and echoes an incident at the beginning of the case when 'suddenly, with great clarity and precision, [Quinn] saw Bartleby's window and the blank brick wall before him' (Auster, 1988: 51–2). This prescient vision alerts the reader to the potential outcomes of Quinn's predicament. Unlike Bartleby, though, Quinn is sustained by the mysterious appearance of food in the room. However, Quinn finds that he can utilise his time more effectively writing in his notebook rather than eating. In these entries Quinn enters into the final struggle with the means to rearticulate his relationship with the world. As the pages of the notebook dwindle, Quinn becomes aware that his capacity to relate his story is diminishing. The case is 'far behind him now', and he writes 'about the stars, the earth, his hopes for mankind' (Auster, 1988: 130). Quinn's relationship to words changes; they are now a part of the material world, related in their prelapsarian sense to the things they represent.[8] This is, of course, because Quinn is no longer a part of the social world, and his presence in the material world is fading rapidly. As a conse-quence, 'his words had been severed from him, . . . now they were a part of the world at large, as real and specific as a stone, or a lake, or a flower' (Auster, 1988: 130).

Quinn anticipates the end of the notebook by exploring modes of representation that go beyond the visible inscriptions of writing. Advancing the practices of Stillman Sr. of inscribing onto the material world, he 'wondered if he had it in him to write without a pen, if he could learn to speak instead, filling the darkness with his voice, speaking the words into the air, into the walls, into the city. . . . The last sentence of the red notebook reads: "What will happen when there are no more pages in the red notebook?"' (Auster, 1988: 131). These questions strike at the very heart of Auster's quest in the *Trilogy*: how do we locate ourselves in the world when language has failed us? Further, what happens to characters when the writer stops writing their stories, and how does the writer, as an artist, relate to the material and social realms when the relationship between the word and the world is so problematical?

These questions do not find easy answers through Blue's 'detection' in 'Ghosts'. Auster sets out his linguistic intentions from the outset. With central characters and the 'cases' all named after colours, Auster signals that this 'investigation' too will incorporate a search for a language adequate to the detective's purpose. 'Colors are irreducible as words', Auster told Allan Reich; '– how do you define blue? Or red? You can't – and I wanted irreducible figures in the book' (Reich, 1988: n.p.). Blue has his emerging problem with 'transparent' words for his reports. Also, his social isolation prompts instability in his relationship with the material world, just like Quinn's struggle with 'nameless things and thingless names'. Initially Blue feels that he has a fairly secure relationship with his environment. With the social world removed from him and reduced, however, to just himself and Black, Blue begins to question his connections with the material world. With only the insubstantial and indistinct figure of Black as a reference, Blue's ontological position becomes unstable.

Within the hermetic existence of his room, Blue is able to will stability into his relationship with a small and very narrowly defined world. Blue 'sees the lamp and says to himself, lamp. He sees the bed and says to himself, bed. . . . It will not do to call the lamp a bed, he thinks, or the bed a lamp. No, these words fit snugly around the things they stand for, and the moment Blue speaks them, he feels a deep satisfaction, as though he has just proved the existence of the world' (Auster, 1988: 148). However, Blue's ontological stability, grasped by naming aloud the objects close at hand, does not stand up to the complexities of the world outside the window. Like Quinn, Blue allows his interiority to become a vacuum. He chooses to live life on the surface, leaving his interior to be occupied by the narratives of his environment – in his case the stories of his previous cases, the fictions of detective magazines and films, and the story of his relationship to the 'Black case'. But ultimately Blue's unstable and deteriorating relationship with the material and the social world leads to confrontation, violence and an inconclusive resolution.

The relationship of the central characters to language in 'The Locked Room' goes through a number of transformations. At first, when the Narrator is getting to know Sophie he claims for language an erotic and seductive power (Auster, 1988: 226). For Fanshawe, in his early writing, language has a prelapsarian quality, brought about by an understanding of the world and his place within it. However, the world that he is inhabiting is not the complex world of New York City, but the natural environment of rural France. Here 'Fanshawe's eye has become incredibly sharp, and one senses a new availability of words inside him, as though the distance between seeing and writing had been narrowed, the two acts now almost identical, part of a single unbroken gesture' (Auster, 1988: 277). The Narrator tells us that this is the point at which Fanshawe's work matures – from promising to fulfilled. He also tells us that while Fanshawe's poetry is written in the country, his well-received plays and novel are written in New York (Auster, 1988: 278). What Auster proposes here has far-reaching implications. Fanshawe's relationship with language goes through three distinct stages: first he reaches an accommodation with language while in rural France; this faculty remains with him when he returns to New York, where he writes his *magnum opus*; but while still in New York he becomes alienated from his work and his environment, and language fails him to the extent that he 'came close to a kind of horror' (Auster, 1988: 309). This suggests that the subjective failure of language for Fanshawe is the result of a complex of reasons which, while they are to do with the alienation and disconnection of the city, are not rooted wholly in the disorientating complexities of the modern metropolis. For Fanshawe, then, like Quinn and Blue before him, urban disconnection is triggered by a personal and emotional event which, crucially for us here, takes place in the metropolis. It is the combination of catastrophe and the urban experience which sends these characters sliding into the darkness of the void.

As the story of 'The Locked Room' progresses and the Narrator's obsession with Fanshawe deepens, the psychosis into which he descends begins to erode his own language function. As when Blue attempts to write reports, words begin to obscure the Narrator's intentions. Instead of seducing Sophie with words, he uses them to evade her questioning, forcing her away from him. By going to Paris, the Narrator, like Blue, abandons the one emotional connection able to offer the hope of stability. Once there, he feels unable to call Sophie, and the acceptance of this fact brings with it the acknowledgement that words are constantly failing him. The Narrator is losing contact with his interior self to the extent that the 'sky was growing dark on the inside . . . the ground was trembling' (Auster, 1988: 290). In Paris the Narrator is geographically as well as mentally distant from the stabilising force of Sophie, and so susceptible to an accelerated descent into disorientation, alienation and madness – assisted by the incomprehensible forces of a foreign metropolis. It is at this stage that he begins 'to lose track' of himself and 'come apart' (Auster, 1988: 293). The Narrator finally loses his struggle to retain a unified sense of self, and as a consequence the relationship between language and the metropolitan realm disintegrates too. By employing 'some muddled chain of reasoning', the Narrator attaches the name Fanshawe to the random figure of an American stranger (Auster, 1988: 293–4). At this point in his narrative, the Narrator is picking through a rubble of referents and reconstituting the chain of signifiers in an arbitrary way through 'randomness' and 'pure chance' (Auster, 1988: 298). Such a practice, of course, is unable to return order to the chaos of a disintegrating relationship between word and world. There is a chase through the empty Parisian streets, and before the violent confrontation that ends the Narrator's search for the real Fanshawe, the Narrator (like Quinn and Blue, before him) feels as though he is no longer inside himself; the 'sensation of life' is displaced by a 'miraculous euphoria, . . . the undeniable odour of nothing' (Auster, 1988: 299).

Fanshawe eventually 'reveals' his disembodied self at the end of the novel. The audience with Fanshawe in Boston divulges little, but generates a new quality of confusion and disorientation in the Narrator. Fanshawe provides a notebook, to explain his actions over the years. However, unlike the letters written in France and the literary work that followed, the words do not have a simple and direct relationship with what they are meant to describe. The Narrator describes the experience of reading the notebook at length. 'All the words were familiar to me', he records:

> and yet they seemed to have been put together strangely, as though their final purpose was to cancel each other out. . . . Each sentence erased the sentence before it, each paragraph made the next paragraph impossible. . . . He had answered the question by asking another question, and therefore everything remained open, unfinished, to be started again. I lost my way after the first word, and from then on I could only grope ahead, faltering in the darkness, blinded by the book that had been written for me. (Auster, 1988: 314)

All the essential elements of destabilised identity are here again: disorientation, the lack of metropolitan social coordinates, the void and the darkness that symbolises it. Fanshawe's notebook mirrors language's constant deferral through constant questioning of the authority of his words, repeatedly cancelling out meanings and proliferating layers of interpretation. The symbolic darkness of the abyss returns to further disorient the Narrator and to relate his sensory incoherence to the failing (or aphasic) relationship between Fanshawe's words and the things that they relate to. Finally, the

Narrator destroys the notebook standing by the tracks in Boston. 'One by one, I tore the pages from the notebook', he writes, 'crumpled them in my hand, and dropped them into a trash bin on the platform. I came to the last page just as the train was pulling out' (Auster, 1988: 314). This final passage has two important implications for the narratives that precede it. One is the capacity of language to obscure, and the other is the capacity of the story to confound readers' expectations. Auster is at his most ambiguous here (in a book crowded with ambiguities); he neither resolves the 'Fanshawe case' or concludes the Narrator's fate. Ultimately, we do not know whether he catches the train back to Sophie, Ben and his baby son in New York, or remains in Boston.

Alford notes that Quinn, Stillman, Blue, Fanshawe and the Narrator all move beyond 'the constitutive purview of language' (Alford, 1995b: 621). He argues that Quinn ceases to exist when the red notebook runs out (Alford, 1995a: 23; Alford, 1995b: 614), while Alison Russell argues that 'characters "die" when their signifiers are omitted from the printed page' (Russell, 1990: 75). However, in 'The Red Notebook' (1992, reprinted in *The Art of Hunger*[9]), Auster insists that 'books are never finished, . . . it is possible for stories to go on writing themselves without an author' (Auster, 1997: 378). In 'Portrait of an Invisible Man', for example, Auster says of the story of his father, and of the story of writing the story of his father, 'once this story has ended, it will go on telling itself, even after the words have been used up' (Auster, 1982: 67). Similarly, in 'The Locked Room' the Narrator explains that he must set down his story in order to escape Fanshawe's grip. But, he tells us, stories 'without endings can do nothing but go on forever' (Auster, 1988: 235). Both of the previous stories end without resolution; their narrators cannot attest to the whereabouts of Quinn and Blue. Without language their story ceases to be told, but they persist beyond language's purview, when the words have been used up. Irresolution also acts in these texts to highlight the uncertainty of accounts mediated by language, and to emphasise that literature captures the moment of a story, but that the story has a life of its own stretching before the beginning of its telling and beyond its end.

Writing

Like Baudelaire and Reznikoff before him, Auster contemplates the presence of the poet-recorder within the urban text, and the impact of the environment on the recorder's physical and mental coherence. The

personal consequences for Auster's characters of taking on the role of
the urban observer-recorder and poet encompass a combination
of Reznikoff's poetic paradox of effacement and Hamsun's and Kafka's
aesthetic propositions of starvation, suffocating and extreme solitude,
and anonymous violence. The way in which the characters experience New York is further reflected in the representation of that
experience through the destabilisation of a number of key literary
conventions.

Auster emphasises the characters' urban instability by disorientating
and confusing the reader. He achieves this by destabilising elements
of novelistic convention. Authorship, narration and genre – conventionally stable elements of the detective form – are disrupted and
inverted to problematise the normal relationship between the reader
and the text. Thus the experience of urban instability is communicated
to the reader through a narrative form normally associated with the
resolution of urban mysteries. The detective motif is a particularly
urban one with a rich literary tradition, and Auster adopts it here to
explore the role of the urban writer-observer.[10] Through what has
become known as the 'metaphysical detective' or 'anti-detective' form,
Auster subverts the conventions of the detective fiction to exemplify
and emphasise the destabilising nature of the urban experience. At
the same time the process of detection is turned in on itself so that the
object of the detective's investigation becomes his own identity.

By failing to resolve his detective fiction, Auster draws attention to
the way in which he manipulates the form, and the way in which he
contributes to the new 'metaphysical detective' fiction first described
by Michael Holquist. Holquist was one of the earliest critics to note
the emergence of a detective fiction which creates more mystery than
it solves. In 1971 he wrote of how 'the new metaphysical detective story
finally obliterates the traces of the old which underlie it' (Holquist,
1971: 153). These new stories subvert many of the conventions which
had in the past made the detective form stable and predictable, to the
extent that '[i]nstead of reassuring, they disturb' (Holquist, 1971: 155).
Russell notes that Auster's stories similarly 'employ and deconstruct
the conventional elements of the detective story, resulting in a recursive
linguistic investigation of the nature, function and meaning of
language' rather than the traditional resolution of a crime (Russell,
1990: 71). We have seen already how language and identity become
the objects of the detective's quest, and how they are constantly
destabilised in this text. We need now to look at the structural elements

of the fictions which constitute the *Trilogy* to establish how these contribute to the sense of instability experienced by the reader. The failure of resolution and the layering of ambiguities into the narratives and subnarratives of the three stories are structural devices Auster employs to destabilise the reader's experience of *The New York Trilogy*. Along with resolution, Auster also problematises authorship and genre. These disruptions mirror the disorientation of Quinn, Blue and the Narrator in the narratives themselves. That is to say, the failure of the characters' urban tools or tactics for living is equivalent to the failure of the reader's literary tools or reading strategies. For example, Anne M. Holzapfel describes how 'readers themselves, in their attempts to give meaning to the text, cannot avoid repetitions, doublings, mirror images and labyrinths. In order to attain meaning, they, like the detective, have to read the signs on another level' (Holzapfel, 1996: 25). Like the detective figures, the reader is forced to search for clues in the text. The layering of authorship, the undermining of genre conventions and the deferral of resolution constantly move the ground beneath the reader's feet. The experience of instability within these aspects of literary practice also parallels the way that Auster represents the instability inherent in language in these narratives. Meaning is constantly deferred as the stories are subjected to proliferating narrators, unexpected twists and any number of possible endings.

Authorship in these narratives operates on two levels. First, it is a concept that relates the name of the person on the front of the book to the person of a writer. Secondly, it relates the characters to a force that motivates and controls their movements. These two concepts come together in the person of Quinn, who is at once a fictional detective, a pseudonymous detective novel writer and the 'tiny life-bud buried in the breathing self' that is the man called Daniel Quinn (Auster, 1988: 8). By taking a case in the name of Paul Auster, Quinn masquerades as the author of his own book. At the same time, the Paul Auster detective persona is added to the 'triad' of selves that Quinn has already constructed through his detective writing. Quinn writes about a fictional detective, 'Max Work', under the pseudonym, 'William Wilson'. This name is a rich source of circular puns – William Wilson, for example, can become Will, I am, the son of Will. Also, the act of authorship, of creating a character and navigating them through their story, is an act of will by the author on behalf of the character. Finally, 'William Wilson' is, of course, the name of a short story by Edgar Allan

Poe in which a schoolboy and his double (or alter ego) compete until
they destroy each other. Max Work also constitutes Quinn's 'work',
and so the pattern of punning on names in each of these stories is set.
Auster describes the relationship between the writer, the pseudonymous author and the detective character in 'City of Glass' in this way:

> In the triad of selves that Quinn had become, Wilson served as a kind of
> ventriloquist. Quinn himself was the dummy, and Work was the
> animated voice that gave purpose to the enterprise. . . . And little by little,
> Work had become a presence in Quinn's life, his interior brother, his
> comrade in solitude. (Auster, 1988: 6)

Two aspects of this passage are important. First, the conventional
ventriloquism of authorship would have Quinn manipulating Wilson,
and Wilson giving words to the character, Work. Secondly, the direct
relationship between Quinn and the character that he gives voice to,
along with that character's name, suggest that Quinn generates his
sense of self from the personality of his character, and hence the words
that he, Quinn, puts into his mouth. The result is that Quinn does not
think of himself as real; he lives instead 'at one remove' such that he
'seemed to vanish, the more persistent Work's presence in the world
became' (Auster, 1988: 9). However, Quinn finds himself unsuited
to the task of detection, which Work would have taken in his stride.
This suggests that Quinn is a dysfunctional detective, unable to decode
the clues in the 'case', often unable even to identify them as such.
Auster makes the distinction between the two clear: '[w]hereas Quinn
tended to feel out of place in his own skin, Work was aggressive, quick
tongued, at home in whatever spot he happened to find himself'
(Auster, 1988: 9).

The triad becomes a quartet when Quinn takes the 'Stillman case'
in Paul Auster's place. Auster is both Quinn's author (in much the
same way that Quinn is Work's author) and a character in the book.[11]
That Quinn is authored becomes apparent when the conventions of
the detective form require him to meet his client, Peter Stillman Jr.
Although Quinn has no intention of keeping the appointment, he finds
himself 'doing a good impression of a man preparing to go out'. He
'tends toward a jacket and tie', and puts them on 'in a kind of trance'.
Finally, with his hand on the doorknob the truth dawns on him: ' "I
seem to be going out," he said to himself. "But if I am going out, where
exactly am I going?" ' (Auster, 1988: 12). Quinn is 'willed' to the
appointment by his author, who places his hand on the doorknob and

propels him to the Stillmans' apartment. Brian McHale calls this literary device 'metalepsis'. This, he explains, is a process in which characters disturb 'the ontological hierarchy of levels through their awareness of the recursive structures in which they find themselves' (McHale, 1987: 121). By foregrounding the relationship of the author to his characters in this way, and the connections between different fictional realms, Auster draws the reader's attention to the textuality of storytelling and narrative.

Quinn's relationship to his author's will is fairly immediate, and his presence in the text is strongly determined and substantial. Peter Stillman Jr., in contrast, has a less determined physical presence in the narrative. The proximity of the character to the intentions of his author has a direct relationship with the presence and materiality of that character within the text. Peter's actions are described as 'machine-like, fitful, alternating between slow and rapid gestures, rigid and yet expressive, as if the operation were out of control, not quite corresponding to the will that lay behind it. . . . It was like watching a marionette trying to walk without strings' (Auster, 1988: 15). The similarity of Stillman's movements to those of an uncontrolled marionette is in contrast to Quinn's movements under the firm control of his author's unseen hand. Stillman Jr.'s awkward movements are in part a result of Quinn's presence. Stillman has called for Paul Auster, his author, and the will that should motivate his actions, but he has been sent Quinn – the wrong author, and a mere character at that. As a consequence of the narrative distance between the character, Stillman Jr., and his author, Paul Auster, Stillman inhabits the book in a spectral way. In the interview with Quinn his appearance is insubstantial and transparent. His clothes are white, his skin pale and his hair thin – 'the effect was almost transparent. . . . As their eyes met, Quinn suddenly felt that Stillman had become invisible' (Auster, 1988: 15). Lavender refers to Stillman as a 'narrative anaemia', whose incomplete relationship with his author distances him both from Auster's will and the signifying terms of language that can give him status within the text (Lavender, 1993: 226–7). As a result of his distance from his author and from language, Stillman Jr. walks clumsily off at page twenty-four and disappears.

In 'The Locked Room' Auster proposes that where the writer is not physically present, his presence can be accessed through his work, in a way similar to Quinn's relationship to his 'Work'. Fanshawe's presence is always associated with the manuscripts of his poetry, plays and novels, which collected together in two suitcases 'were as heavy as a man' (Auster, 1988: 208). As a consequence, his presence in the text has a spectral quality, similar to that of Stillman Jr. In a sense, because he is never physically manifest in the narrative, Fanshawe only exists in the text as a text, to be read and interpreted. The Narrator's materiality in the text, then, is dependent on his relationship with language. As the Narrator's obsession with Fanshawe deepens and his relationship with Sophie becomes more distant, the Narrator accepts that he is using language to evade meanings and to obscure his intentions. Auster symbolises the Narrator's emotional evasion and concealment from Sophie as a form of insubstantiality. 'You're so close to being gone already', she tells him as he is about to leave for Paris, 'I sometimes think I can see you vanishing before my eyes. . . . You're going to vanish, and I'll never see you again' (Auster, 1988: 286). Like Stillman Jr., the Narrator also experiences an episode of symbolic transparency. However, the Narrator's relationship to his author is closer than Stillman's, Quinn's and Blue's, and, therefore, he is more able to enter into the struggle with language and attempt to recover his materiality.

Narrative models, like the detective form itself, are constantly subverted to surprise and disorient the reader throughout *The New York Trilogy*. Auster presents narrative as a puzzle which is as challenging as the cases that his 'detectives' undertake. The most important 'clue' and piece of evidence in this submystery is the meeting between Quinn and the character 'Paul Auster' at his apartment on Riverside Drive on the Upper West Side. As Brooker notes, for Auster, 'the fall of the author into his own work is a repeated event' (Brooker, 1996: 144).[12] Quinn tracks down the 'real' Paul Auster in the hope that he is the detective for whom the case was originally destined, and that he can help to 'solve' it. But 'Auster' is a literary essayist (as both Quinn and the real Auster were), and he is able to offer only a friendly chat and a brief respite from Quinn's lonely pursuit of Stillman Sr. 'Auster' lives with his wife, 'Siri', and son, 'Daniel' (more autobiographical references). Here, the man who would be Quinn's author presents the narrative structure of Cervantes' *The Adventures of Don Quixote* as a possible model for Quinn's story.[13] 'Auster' explains to Quinn his 'imaginative reading' of 'the book inside the book Cervantes wrote, the one he imagined he was writing' (Auster, 1988: 97). The twist 'Auster' introduces is that Quixote is sane and has tricked his friends into recording his adventures for posterity, possibly even posing as Cid

Hamet Benengeli and translating his own story back into Spanish. This reading of events still allows Cervantes to be truthful when presenting himself as no more than an editor of the translation.

The are many linguistic and textual 'clues' linking 'City of Glass' and *Don Quixote*. Quinn's initials are the same as Don Quixote's and their predicaments have striking similarities (the delusional detective/ knight fulfilling the fantasies of genre fiction). In the early part of the story we also discover that 'Auster' has been recommended by a retired police officer called Saavedra – which is Cervantes' family name. As Quinn is leaving 'Auster's' apartment they agree to talk on the phone. 'Auster' asks: ' "Are you in the book?"' ' "Yes"', Quinn replies, ' "The only one"' (102–3). Reading the 'clues' (as a good detective should), Auster hints that the reader should be guided by the literary 'map' of actors and narrators proposed in the book of Don Quixote.[14] However, this map only continues the series of deferrals started with language, and is as unstable as the linguistic and urban maps that Quinn, Blue and the Narrator employ.

The 'straightforward' narrative address that typifies detective fiction is present in the *Trilogy* only in the matter of style. The authority of the narrative voice of each of these stories is undermined by numerous interventions and shifts in the narrative point of view, along with tense and temporal instability. In 'City of Glass' and 'The Locked Room', interventions by 'authorial' voices shift the address between first and third person, blurring the boundary between them. These intrusions contribute to the impression of proliferating narrators, and they problematise the notion of a unified and identifiable author (as in 'Auster's' model of *Don Quixote*). In 'Ghosts', shifting tenses and temporal viewpoints combine to expose the mechanics of narrative strategy in the telling of stories.

The conventions of narrative and authorship are further problematised when the authorial veil is lifted for the first time. The omniscient third-person narrative of 'City of Glass' is interrupted by the following intervention:

> The account of this period is less full than the author would have liked. . . . Even the red notebook, which until now has provided a detailed account of Quinn's experience, is suspect. We cannot say for certain what happened to Quinn during this period, for it is at this point in the story that he began to lose his grip. (Auster, 1988: 113)

To emphasise the connection between Quinn's sense of self and stable narrative structure, Auster warns of misreadings at just the point where

Quinn's sense of coherence, as both a person and a recorder, begins to fail. Quinn's urban record becomes incoherent just as his sense of self is occupied by the archetype of the New York vagrant. At the same time Auster shifts from a third- to a first-person address. In the interview with Gregory and McCaffrey Auster describes how, for him, the distinction between first- and third-person narrative is not as great as it might seem. '[T]here's a vast range between those two categories', he insists, 'and it's possible to bring the boundaries of first-person and third-person so close to each other that they touch, even overlap' (Auster, 1997: 316). The new, first-person narrator states: 'I have followed the red notebook as closely as I could, and any inaccuracies in the story should be blamed on me. There were moments when the text was difficult to decipher, but I have done my best with it and have refrained from any interpretations' (Auster, 1988: 132). This narrator moves into the position previously occupied by Quinn, but one further 'reading' removed from the events. He disingenuously claims 'authority' for his telling of the story because of avoidance of interpretation. However, it is this new narrator who is now attempting to decipher the urban text, again through the pages of the notebook, just as Quinn did with Stillman's footsteps. Like Quinn, he follows the clues and then views the totality from above, only to find that true insight is resisted by the deferrals of language and text.

The third-person narrative of 'Ghosts' conforms to the economic style of detective fiction.[15] However, the way Auster plays with time across the telling of the story undermines the authority of the primary narrative address. 'The place is New York, the time is the present, and neither one will ever change', we are told at the beginning (Auster, 1988: 135). The temporal specificity of the story is sufficiently exact to identify the actual day '3 February 1947' (Auster, 1988: 136) – Auster's date of birth. However, this temporal exactitude is undermined in the closing passage. The narration is not taking place in the 'present' of 1947, as these events 'all . . . took place more than thirty years ago, back in the days of our earliest childhood' (Auster, 1988: 195). Auster intervenes once again to expose the mechanics of storytelling and show how, just as the juxtaposition of first- and third-person narration can bring instability to a text, so the tense of the address can unbalance the reader. The reader's last sight of Blue comes close to the end of the story:

> But the story is not yet over. There is still the final moment, and that will
> not come until Blue leaves the room. Such is the way of the world: not one
> moment more, not one moment less. When Blue stands up from his

chair, puts on his hat, and walks through the door, that will be the end of it. (Auster, 1988: 195)

But this is emphatically not 'the end of it'. Here the instability of literary form is exposed. The genre requires an ending, and Auster anticipates this on the reader's behalf, delivering a stereotyped ending before Blue's narrative has actually come to an end.

It is in 'The Locked Room' that the most profound and important narrative intervention takes place. Here, yet another narrative voice claims authorship of all three stories. In doing so, this 'real' narrator disrupts not just the sense of a single narrator figure, but also the notion of a unified figure of an author. 'These three stories are finally the same story', he concedes, 'but each one represents a different stage in my awareness of what it is about' (Auster, 1988: 294).[16] The presence in the text of an author figure, rather than that of a narrator, is related to the presence of an 'Auster' character in 'City of Glass'. In both instances, the presence of the voice or figure acts, as Auster himself put it, to 'expose the plumbing' of authorship (Auster, 1997: 308).

In his 1960 essay 'Authors and Writers', Roland Barthes describes the relationship between the author, his literary role and the language he deploys: 'Language is neither an instrument or a vehicle: it is a structure . . .; but the author is the only man, by definition, to lose his own structure and that of the world in the structure of language', (Barthes, 1993: 187). For Barthes, then, the author is lost in the structure of language when his name appears on the cover of a book. The linguistic function of the author's name on the book acts to associate him with the text, and with other texts bearing the same name. As a result the author's name becomes a linguistic construct that obscures his materiality behind a series of signifiers. Besides his real name, the linguistic construct is comprised of his work, his image (his photo on the dust jacket), his autobiographical detail and his physical self (for promotional events etc.) (Barthes, 1993: 186–7). Similarly, in 'What is an Author', Michel Foucault collectively terms these characteristics the 'author function' (Foucault, 1991: 107). This function, he insists, 'does not refer purely and simply to a real individual, since it can give rise to several selves, to several subjects – positions that can be occupied by different classes of individual' (Foucault, 1991: 113). Consequently, the 'author function' is not the spontaneous association of an individual to a text, but 'the result of a complex operation which constructs a certain rational being that we call "author"' (Foucault, 1991: 110).

Auster has referred to the 'person' of the 'author function' as 'my author self, that mysterious other who lives inside me and puts my name on the covers of books' (Auster, 1997: 308).[17] Auster self-consciously plays with the categories of the 'linguistic construct' of 'author function' in 'City of Glass'. By falling into his own work as a character (a conspicuously autobiographical one as well), Auster draws attention to the fact that the figure whose picture appears on his dust jackets is both a real person and a character created by the world of publishing. It also indicates the way in which authors often draw upon their own experiences of real people to create characters. Ultimately, the exchange between the real and the fictional demonstrates, once again, the linguistic nature of identity and the textuality of storytelling.

The general disorientation that the reader experiences through the shifts in narration and the disunity of authorship is further exploited by Auster through the disruption of some of the most rigid conventions of the detective genre. These can be reduced to the crime (or missing person), the detective (and his search for clues) and the solution. Where these have customarily offered clarity and explanation to the reader, at least by the end of the story, in Auster's detective fiction the form becomes characterised by distortion and confusion. This, as we have already seen, has been termed 'metaphysical detective fiction'. Benjamin lists the essential elements at the heart of the conventional detective story as 'the victim and the scene of crime', 'the murderer', 'the masses' and the intellect of the detective that breaks through the 'emotion-laden atmosphere' (Benjamin, 1997: 43). At the conclusion of the story the mystery of how the crime was carried out and by whom should be resolved, the perpetrator bought to justice, and order restored to the world.[18]

Crime as a central concern and a concept is undermined in *The New York Trilogy* by the indeterminate nature of the events that are the original object of the detective's investigation. In 'City of Glass', Stillman Sr.'s intentions remain ambiguous until the end. The story of 'Ghosts' is all investigation and no crime, while in 'The Locked Room' the Narrator seeks a missing person who does not want to be found. If the object of the Narrator's 'investigation' is the corporeal Fanshawe, it quickly becomes the search for an essence that constitutes Fanshawe, but this mystery has little chance of a solution. At the beginning of the search, the Narrator is willing to admit that 'each life is no more than the sum of contingent facts, a chronicle of chance intersections, of flukes, of random events that divulge nothing but their

own lack of purpose' (Auster, 1988: 217). This leads him to conclude
that every 'life is inexplicable, . . . no matter how many details are given,
the essential thing resists telling' (Auster, 1988: 247). The Narrator's
position in relation to the subject of his writing is that the essential
thing – Fanshawe, a man's life, the material world – resists representation through language in a way similar to that experienced by the
Objectivists attempting to translate the data of the eye into a poetical
language for the city. The closing passages of this story invert the motif
of a room locked from the inside, in which a crime (murder) has been
committed.[19] In the *Trilogy* the mysteries, like the narrators, proliferate
until they encompass the metaphysical concerns of language and
identity.

The detective conventionally conforms to a number of stereotypes.
The Max Work character of Quinn's fiction is the archetype of the
quick-witted, analytically adept, strong-jawed detective who always gets
his man, and invariably gets the girl too. For Quinn, the detective 'is
the one who looks, who listens, who moves through this morass of
objects and events in search of the thought, the idea that will pull all
these things together and make sense of them' (Auster, 1988: 8). Yet
in these stories the traditional purposes of convention are not
maintained. As Auster told Joseph Mallia: 'the detective really is a very
compelling figure, a figure we all understand. He's a seeker after the
truth, the problem-solver, the one who tries to figure things out. But
what if, in the course of trying to figure it out, you just unveil more
mysteries?' (Auster, 1997: 280). Quinn and Blue clearly occupy the
role of detective in their stories. The Narrator also enacts the detective
function. He takes up the search for Fanshawe where a private
detective, one named Quinn and employed by Sophie, had failed. Once
on the case, the Narrator describes his pursuit of Fanshawe to Paris in
terms of a detective hunting for clues to the 'one path' leading to the
solution (Auster, 1988: 282). However, in Paris the Narrator concludes
that there 'were no leads, no clues, no tracks to follow' (Auster, 1988:
289). In short, the process of detection – the analysis of evidence, the
interpretation of clues – is unable to provide any stable sense of who
or where Fanshawe is and, as the Narrator is dependent on comparison
with Fanshawe to negotiate his sense of self, his own identity becomes
incoherent.

As noted earlier, the detective novel is the most urban of texts. The
complexity of the labyrinthine streets, the density of the population
and the anonymity of the individual in the crowd make it the ideal place

to commit a crime, and the most unpromising of environments for its solution. This metropolitan environment is one dependent on reading and interpretation. In the city evidence is everywhere, but concrete significations are in short supply. The detective mystery too requires the identification and deciphering of encoded information, in the form of clues. For Quinn, the abundance of clues is a compelling aspect of the detective mystery. In these books every event is potentially crucial, such that '[e]verything becomes essence; the centre of the book shifts with each event that propels it forward. The centre, then, is everywhere, and no circumference can be drawn until the book has come to its end' (Auster, 1988: 8). However, in the *Trilogy* evidence goes by the way, clues lie uninterpreted, or misinterpreted, the book does not come to its end, the circumference is never drawn, and so the centre remains everywhere. As Auster says himself, he is using the genre conventions of detective fiction 'to get to another place . . . altogether' (Auster, 1997: 279). By subverting the conventions of the crime and the detective, the other place that Auster gets to is the struggle with language and the struggle to identify not the criminal, but the self.

The final element of detective fiction that Auster undermines is the certainty of resolution. Without it the mystery or crime cannot be solved, the perpetrator cannot be brought to justice, and the circumference of the book cannot finally be drawn. However, *The New York Trilogy* eludes such possibilities as its narrators multiply, its mysteries proliferate and its solutions consistently fail to emerge from a morass of irrelevant or contradictory information.

In 'City of Glass', Quinn's fate remains unknown because the pages of the notebook run out. 'At this point the story grows obscure', the narrator writes, '[t]he information has run out, and the events that follow this last sentence will never be known' (Auster, 1988: 131). The interpreter of the red notebook is left to speculate on what happened to Quinn:

> it is impossible for me to say where he is now. . . . The red notebook, of course, is only half the story, as any sensitive reader will understand. . . . [M]y thoughts remain with Quinn. He will be with me always. And wherever he may have disappeared to, I wish him luck. (Auster, 1988: 132)

The resolution of 'Ghosts' is similarly undetermined. We have seen how the omniscient, third-person narrator manipulates the arts of storytelling and genre convention by 'predicting' Blue's last actions in the story, as he puts on his hat and leaves the room. The narrator then addresses the reader in a way that mirrors the shifts between third and first person in 'City of Glass'. Once Blue has left the room, we are told that '[w]here he goes after that is not important' (Auster, 1988: 195), and the reader is drawn into a conspiratorial 'we' before the person of the narrator emerges at the very end of the story. 'I myself prefer to think that he went far away . . .,' he says:

> Let it be China, then, and we'll leave it at that. For now is the moment that Blue stands up from his chair, puts on his hat, and walks through the door. And from this moment on, we know nothing. (Auster, 1988: 195–6)

In 'The Locked Room' resolution is deferred by the failure of the notebook to reveal Fanshawe's actions, intentions and motives. The deferral of language is duplicated in the ambiguity of the last sentence of the *Trilogy*, leaving the reader unsure of the Narrator's actions. The detective's investigation into his selfhood and his identity remains unresolved; language does not have the capacity for the Narrator to locate either himself or Fanshawe in the world. Two simple possibilities present themselves: either he remains in Boston, where his disconnected and disorientated relationship with the physical and social world will continue to drag him into the darkness of the abyss; or he returns to his family in New York, where, through Sophie, he can build a sustainable but fragile relationship with people and his material metropolitan environment.

Auster does not encourage the reader towards the greater likelihood of either of these possibilities, each being equal and valid in its own right. It is, however, a concern that the text prompts us to examine, not least for the sake of natural curiosity and a sense of disappointment that our readerly expectations have been deceived. The implications of the first position are clear: the Narrator's story would constantly turn in on itself, and he would be condemned to repeat indefinitely Quinn's misreadings and failures (these stories are all the same, after all). Equally, the Narrator may board the train and return to Sophie. The cycle of loneliness and alienation, disconnection and erasure would then be broken, and some major implications for *The New York Trilogy* as a text would begin to emerge.

The Narrator's options – confusion on the metropolitan streets or domestic stability with Sophie in their new Brownstone home in Brooklyn – both represent ways of being in the world. The outcome of the first option, when taken by Quinn, has been considered in detail above. If the Narrator were to take this course his future would be an uncertain one. The dereliction that Quinn experiences carries with it the potential of an early or violent death, through starvation or exposure, or by being 'beaten or burned or tortured' (Auster, 1988: 109). The place that these tragic figures occupy (Quinn possibly amongst them) is a result of complete disconnection from the metropolitan social world, leading to the interior confusion and disorientation of madness. These characters do not come to occupy this place in the world through conscious effort; they have instead stumbled into it by misfortune and misreading. Equally, Quinn, Blue and the Narrator occupy this place in the world without meaningfully comprehending how they are related to the world as individuals. Quinn attempts to prove to himself that he still exists through conversations about baseball with the counterman in the Heights Luncheonette (Auster, 1988: 36). Blue also attempts to reconnect with the metropolitan social world by going to ball games at Ebbetts Field and having an occasional physical relationship with 'a blowsy tart named Violet' whom he meets in a bar near his Orange Street room (Auster, 1988: 158–60). But he too remains detached from all but the most meagre of coordinates. All he has is Black and Black's room, which Blue thinks of as 'a no man's land, the place you come to at the end of the world' (Auster, 1988: 185). Clearly, if Blue wants to place himself in relation to the physical and social world, the very end of the world itself does not represent a particularly secure point of reference.

Auster's vision of New York for Quinn and Blue, then, is overwhelmingly pessimistic, nihilistic even. But is this bleak reading of the *Trilogy* the only one available to us? As I have suggested, some glimmers of hope do emerge in the shape of particular people and places in the metropolis. These spaces, and the people who inhabit them, stand as antipodes to the alienation of the streets of New York, or the isolation and loneliness of the writers' rooms Quinn and Blue inhabit. Sites of familial calm and stability, such as the apartment of 'Paul Auster' and his wife 'Siri', operate as oases of hope for alienated characters. The 'Auster'/'Siri' relationship in 'City of Glass' bears a close resemblance to the Narrator/Sophie relationship in 'The Locked Room'. Auster has described 'City of Glass' as a 'homage' to his second wife, Siri Hustvedt (Auster, 1997: 278). Quinn, he says, is what he might have become if he had not met her. But the Narrator is more able to enter the struggle to secure a place for himself and seek a metropolitan redemption than Quinn and Blue are because he is more aware of his predicament and is 'closer' to his author. The Narrator's hopes for recovery from the traumas of alienation lie in his relationship with Sophie. Along with the protection offered by a stable family and home life, it is Sophie's way of being in the world that the Narrator finds both compelling and sustaining. 'Siri' has a similar quality that relates her presence to the physical world in a very particular way. Quinn describes her as 'radiantly beautiful, with an invisible energy and happiness that seemed to make everything around her invisible' (Auster, 1988: 101). Equally, Sophie's view on the world allows her to form a relationship with it that is far more stable than the Narrator's by being both analytical and emotional at the same time. Sophie, he tells us, is 'both sensual and watchful, as though she looked out on the world from the heart of a deep inner vigilance' (Auster, 1988: 201). Chapter 3, in particular, explores the way women artists in Auster's later fiction adopt more effective metropolitan strategies than many of the troubled male characters. Indeed, the sensuality of the women in the *Trilogy*, 'Siri' and Sophie, stands in contrast to the ontological rigidities employed by Quinn and the Narrator in the pursuit of Stillman Sr. and Fanshawe. Before embarking on the 'Fanshawe case' the relationship that the Narrator forms with Sophie gives him a revelatory insight into how it is possible to locate himself in the world, and a potential return at the end of the story to recover that place. Sophie, he says, changed everything for him:

> By belonging to Sophie, I began to feel as though I belonged to everyone else as well. My true place in the world, it turned out, was somewhere beyond myself, and if that place was inside me, it was also unlocatable. This was the tiny hole between self and not-self, and for the first time in my life I saw this nowhere as the exact centre of the world.[20] (Auster, 1988: 232)

Like Quinn and Blue, the Narrator is trying to negotiate the space between the self and the not-self, or the self and the everything else. Unlike Quinn, though, the Narrator is attempting to negotiate the space with a significant point of social reference in Sophie. And unlike Blue, that reference is more than just a shadowy outline. Here at last, with Sophie, is the refuge from the confusing and alienating maelstrom of New York. The knowledge of how he might relate to the world, through Sophie, allows the Narrator a fleeting chance at the stable sense of self that Blue and Quinn have abandoned through their isolation. The possibilities which emerge from the narrator's relationship with Sophie suggest that there is a route out of the isolation.

If telling stories is the way that we make sense of the world, then telling metropolitan stories is how Auster attempts to make sense of New York City. The stories that comprise the *Trilogy* emphasise Auster's understanding, at this stage in his writing career, of the confusing nature of contemporary city life. Simultaneously he holds up the modest hope of stabilising and redemptive relationships and spaces able to ground the individual enough to begin forming a coherent sense of self. The presence of Sophie in the Narrator's life provides a significant insight into how to break the destructive cycle of isolation and alienation. This emotional and familial contact brings some stability to the Narrator's life and a route out of the abyss.

However, the presentation of New York as a sprawling, alienating labyrinth punctuated with oases of optimism reflects a motive which Auster identifies in his own work. His writing, he told Mark Irwin:

> has come out of a position of intense personal despair, a very deep nihilism and hopelessness about the world, the fact of our own transience and mortality, the inadequacy of language, the isolation of one person from another. And yet, at the same time, I've wanted to express the beauty and extraordinary happiness of feeling alive in your own skin. To manage to wrench words out of all this, no matter how inadequate they might be, is at the core of everything I've ever done. (Auster, 1997: 335)

It is through these painfully wrought words, and through the redemptive power of art, that New York is recovered, at least in some small way, from 'ultimate alienation' as the predominant metropolitan experience.

Notes

1 On the influence of Hawthorne's story on the *Trilogy*, see also Swope, 1998: 211–14, 219–21, 224–7.
2 Aliki Varvogli also cites Emerson as an influential presence in the stories (Varvogli, 2001: 33–5).
3 Auster often presents loss through the death of a family member. The particularly poignant loss of a child here is likely to be influenced by Stéphane Mallarmé's *A Tomb for Anatole*, which Auster translated (1983), and which records Mallarmé's thoughts as his son dies of rheumatism and an enlarged heart. Auster's preface is reprinted as 'Mallarmé's Son' in (Auster 1997a: 238–49). Auster also recounts the story of his own two-year-old son's life-threatening pneumonia (Auster, 1982: 106–8).
4 On the isolated poet, see also Zilcosky, 1998: 201.

5 For a discussion of Quinn's attempt 'to construct a map/text of the walker's path' employing de Certeau's terms, see also Swope, 2002: para. 20.

6 In 'The Hunger Artist', Kafka tells the story of how the moment passes for a previously celebrated performer who starves himself for forty days at a time. Ultimately, he becomes a side attraction at a circus, where he fulfils his desire to extend his fast to the extremes of his endurance, but he dies in the attempt – ignored by both the staff of the circus and the public (Kafka, 2000: 210–19).

7 On the similarities between Quinn's and Bartleby's fasts see also Little, 1997: 158–61.

8 For the relationship between this episode and Reznikoff's poetry, see also Rowen, 1991: 231–2.

9 First published in *Granta*, 44 (Summer 1993): 232–53. For a thorough publishing history for Auster, see also Drenttel, 1994.

10 It is generally accepted that Poe inaugurated the detective form with his Parisian tales of the Chevalier Monsieur C. Auguste Dupin ('The Murders in the Rue Morgue', 'The Mystery of Marie Rogêt' and 'The Purloined Letter'). The formula of the amateur sleuth and his faithful companion-recorder was taken up in England by Arthur Conan Doyle with the creation of Sherlock Holmes and Dr Watson. In the twentieth century, the Los Angeles based writers of *The Black Mask* magazine, amongst them Raymond Chandler and Dashiell Hammett, developed the influential outsider detective (the private investigator) who does the dirty work of a corrupt society (Chandler and Hammett created Philip Marlowe and Sam Spade). See Chandler's essay 'The Simple Art of Murder' (amongst other helpful essays) in Haycraft, 1946: 222–37. For a concise history of the detective form, see also Priestman, 1998: 5–33.

11 For a fuller exploration of the layering of characters, narrators and authors in 'City of Glass' see also Lavender, 1993: 217–40. Lavender uses an author-reader model of narrative structure (proposed by Seymour Chatman) to peel away the layers of single characters with multiple names (Daniel Quinn) and multiple characters with a single name (Paul Auster).

12 See also Malgrem, 2001: 129.

13 Cervantes' famous seventeenth-century novel, *Don Quixote de la Mancha*, is the story of a poor and delusional knight who, having read too many romantic tales of knights-errant, sets off on a quest to perform heroic and chivalric acts, accompanied by his servant, Sancho Pança. Auster has described *Don Quixote* as 'a great source for me', and the complexities of its narrative structure, as well as the delusional central character, emerge in a number of the fictions (Auster, 1997: 275).

14 For more detailed investigations of the relationship between the 'City of Glass' and *Don Quixote*, see also Malgrem, 2001: 124; Russell, 1990: 74; and Lavender, 1993: 221, 224.

15 An early version of 'Ghosts' describes the story as 'Film Noir'. This
    subgenre draws heavily on the narrative conventions of 1930s and 1940s
    detective fiction most associated with Chandler and Cain, and indicates
    the narrative style that Auster wanted to impose on the story. Auster,
    undated c.
16 That the three stories are interchangeable is emphasised by the way that
    Auster has interchanged the titles. During the process of writing these
    stories 'City of Glass' was called 'New York Spleen' and 'New York
    Confidential: experiments with color'. 'Ghosts' was also called 'A Little
    Book of Colors' and 'Black Outs', the name it bore as a one-act play. 'The
    Locked Room' had been called 'Ghosts', and included a description of
    Fanshawe mounting a Quinnesque observation of Sophie's apartment to
    watch her, the Narrator and the child. This episode obviously became
    Quinn's stakeout (Auster, undated c, d, e).
17 For a brief account of Barthes, Foucault, Auster and authorship, see also
    Zilcosky, 1998: 198.
18 For a structuralist survey of the conventional elements of detective fiction
    see also Tzvetan Todorov's 'The Typology of Detective Fiction', reproduced
    in Lodge, 1988: 157–65. On the use of the detective form in *The New York
    Trilogy* see also Russell, 1990, Rowen, 1991, Lewis, 1994 and Swope, 1998.
    See also Holzapfel, 1996, where the author carefully compares each of the
    structural elements of conventional detective fiction with the way they are
    employed in the *Trilogy*.
19 On the motif of the sealed room, see also Russell, 1990: 79.
20 *The Center of the World* is a title adopted for a film developed from a story
    idea by Auster and his wife, the novelist Siri Hustvedt, directed by Wayne
    Wang (2001), who had previously directed Auster-scripted films (see
    Chapter 6).

3

Downtown

[H]ow deeply and passionately most of us live within ourselves. Our attachments are ferocious. Our loves overwhelm us, define us, obliterate the boundaries between ourselves and others (Auster, *True Tales of American Life*, 2001: xvii)

For Auster's writer-characters, as the preceding chapters have shown, 'the word' is a way of being in the world, and in particular the metropolitan world of New York. *Moon Palace* and *Leviathan*, like *The New York Trilogy*, chart their central character's descent into the abyss of linguistic and social failure. However, unlike the *Trilogy*, the novels then go on to explore how characters can emerge from this void. This chapter, then, will trace Auster's characters through their descent, their rescue and their subsequent recovery. Auster's later novels, *Oracle Night* (2004) and *The Brooklyn Follies* (2005), also deal with the themes of urban redemption, and I will discuss these texts briefly at the end of the chapter.

Auster again adopts the figure of an abyss to represent the absolute solitude (social disconnection) and 'the wordless panic' of an 'aphasic' episode discussed in Chapter 1. In contrast, though, the novels which form the focus of this chapter, *Moon Palace* and *Leviathan*, represent a more optimistic period of Auster's career. This is because he presents the possibility of a fragile metropolitan stability and coherence. The central characters in these texts experience the chasm of linguistic and social failure before undergoing a kind of metropolitan redemption when rescued by lovers and caring friends. It is my contention in this chapter that these friends emerge from social networks which extend across New York City. These networks inhabit very particular spaces – bars, restaurants, dinner parties and art galleries. Ray Oldenburg calls these the 'great good places' (in the book of that name): 'informal public gathering places' that become a part 'of the citizen's daily life' (Oldenburg, 1989: xxviii). The pivotal 'rescuers' emerging from these networks and places are women artists. As artists versed in spatial and visual media (dance and photography) rather than writers, these women mediate their metropolitan environment through non-verbal sign systems rather than language. Through the resulting spatial and linguistic competence, the urban rescuers are able to contribute to the recovery of the condition of a fully social being for the 'fallen' characters, which is demonstrated by an effective relationship with language, and is subsequently manifested in writing. The relative coherence of each character's language function becomes a measure of her or his place in that process. This chapter traces the path for the central figures of each novel, examining the specific social and environmental conditions that first shape their descent, the chance encounters which then make possible their rescue, and their subsequent slow recovery. In doing so, it explores how Auster presents social networks of friends and lovers able to support a relatively stable sense of identity, which, however, remains temporary and fragile.

As with Auster's earlier work, linguistic instability prefigures mental and social breakdown. In *Moon Palace*, Marco Stanley (M. S.) Fogg inherits his Uncle Victor's book collection, and he sets out to read it all. However, his personal life is in crisis and his language function has deteriorated to the point where the written word is indecipherable, each symbol becoming indistinguishable from others. 'I could feel my eyes making contact with the words on the page', he records:

> but no meanings rose up to me anymore, no sounds echoed in my head. The black marks seemed wholly bewildering, an arbitrary collection of lines and curves that divulged nothing but their own muteness [but] . . . [i]f I couldn't see the words, at least I wanted to touch them. Things had become so bad for me by then, this actually seemed to make sense. (Auster, 1992a: 30–1)

Much later, after experiencing the very bottom of the chasm separating the material world from language, and then ascending from it, Fogg is required to describe everyday metropolitan objects to his blind employer, Effing. Initially he struggles, 'piling too many words on top of each other' such that the object is not revealed, but is buried 'under an avalanche of subtleties and geometric abstractions' (Auster, 1992a: 123). Fogg labours to bring the word to the world so that, like the flower that 'blooms in a stranger's mouth' in the poem 'Scribe', it can be shared between language users. 'The world enters us through our eyes', Fogg writes, echoing Auster's 1967 'manifesto':

> but we cannot make sense of it until it descends to our mouths. . . . In actual terms, it was no more than two or three inches, but considering how many accidents and losses could occur along the way, it might just as well have been a journey from the earth to the moon. (Auster, 1992a: 122)

In time, however, Fogg comes to realise that he needs to help Effing 'see things for himself', because '[i]n the end, the words didn't matter' (Auster, 1992a: 122). The task of words, he tells us:

> was to enable him to apprehend the objects as quickly as possible, and in order to do that, I had to make them [the words] disappear the moment they were pronounced. . . . I took to practising when I was alone . . . going around the objects in the room. . . . I don't think there was any question that I improved, but that does not mean I was ever entirely satisfied with my efforts. The demands of words are too great for that; one meets with failure too often to exult in the occasional success. (Auster, 1992a: 123)

In this episode, the inadequacy of language to the complexities of the New York environment is apparent, but the relationship between word and object is much more stable than in the earlier passage. Fogg is able to will ontological stability into the world by naming the objects in his room, but unlike Blue in 'Ghosts', Fogg is also able to take this linguistic coherence out into the streets with him.

The story of *Leviathan* is the story of Benjamin Sachs's destruction as he falls unchecked into the abyss, and the struggle of his friend, Paul Aaron, to tell that story.[1] As the narrative progresses it is apparent that Aaron comes to occupy a similar coherent social and linguistic space as that previously occupied by his friend. Aaron's relationship with language, like Fogg's, is troublesome, but through the course of the narrative it achieves some degree of stability and coherence. However, he too is unable to achieve the full accommodation with language that Auster associates with the motif of Edenic innocence, which he employs here once again.

Aaron tells us that for Sachs 'the words always seemed to be there for him, as if he had found a secret passageway that ran straight from his head to the tips of his fingers. . . . Words and things matched up for him . . . , and because Sachs himself was hardly even aware of it, he seemed to live in a state of perfect innocence' (Auster, 1993: 49–50).

Sachs seems to have a prelapsarian relationship with language, but for Aaron the opposite is true. He describes his own relationship with language in this way:

> The smallest word is surrounded by acres of silence for me, and even after I manage to get that word down on the page, it seems to sit there like a mirage, a speck of doubt glimmering in the sand. Language has never been accessible to me in the way that it was for Sachs. I'm shut off from my own thoughts, trapped in a no-man's-land between feeling and articulation. . . . [F]or me [words] are constantly breaking apart, flying off in a hundred different directions. (Auster, 1993: 49)

The figurative notion of language fragmenting and physically disintegrating resonates both with Jameson's description of the failure of the 'signifying chain' and Sachs's ultimate fate. In the first sentence of the book we are told that Sachs has been literally blown apart by his own bomb at the side of a lonely highway in northern Wisconsin (Auster, 1993: 1). On his journey from linguistic innocence to disintegration Sachs loses his power of speech, destroys his marriage and abandons his facility with the written word.

These episodes are triggered by a fall from a fourth-floor fire escape during the Statue of Liberty centennial celebrations, which takes on the linguistic characteristics of the fall of Adam. Sachs miraculously survives, but is thrust into the same postlapsarian state to which Adam and mankind are condemned after the banishment from Eden and the destruction of the Tower of Babel. After the fall, '[t]he garrulous, irrepressible Sachs had fallen silent, and it seemed logical to assume that he had lost the power of speech, that the jolt to his head had caused grave internal damage' (Auster, 1993: 109). He tells Aaron that every time he attempted to write he 'would break out in a cold sweat', his 'head would spin' and he would feel like he was falling again from the fire escape – experiencing 'the same panic, the same feeling of helplessness, the same rush toward oblivion' (Auster, 1993: 226). Later, Aaron employs similar language of social disconnection and a drive to self-destruction to describe Sachs's who has become 'a solitary speck in the American night, hurtling towards his destruction in a stolen car' (Auster, 1993: 237). In contrast, Aaron's relationship with language has become more coherent as he achieves stability and harmony in his own life, which Auster figures once again as a kind of innocence. As we shall see shortly, Aaron's innocence stands in opposition to Sachs's literal temptation and fall, and his consequent postlapsarian state. This innocence places Aaron in a similar linguistic position to the one Sachs had previously occupied, prompting Sachs to entrust his story to Aaron. Sachs writes a note to Aaron, telling him, 'you'll know how to tell it to others. . . . Your books prove that, and when everything is said and done, you're the only person I can count on. You've gone so much farther than I ever did. . . . I admire you for your innocence' (Auster, 1993: 236). How Aaron achieves this innocent linguistic state is, in part, influenced by his metropolitan experiences and the social spaces that he inhabits. The common thread in the New York experiences of Fogg, Sachs and Aaron is their inclusion in artistic social groups – of dancers, writers and photographers. The outcome of each character's narrative depends on the development of their relationships with individuals from these groups. Also, both of these novels are intensely metropolitan texts, and New York is central to the experiences of the protagonists. New York in these novels represents a place to live, socialise, make art of, get destroyed by and get put back together in.

In *Moon Palace* and *Leviathan*, Auster's representation of the alienating properties of the metropolis has developed to encompass the possible recuperation of some form of urban equilibrium. Even in the early and most nihilistic phase of his writing, Auster had suggested a glimmer of hope in locating a coherent sense of self for the Narrator through the character of Sophie. As we have seen, the Narrator finds his 'true place in the world' between himself and Sophie. In 'The Locked Room', Auster was only able to suggest how the isolated individual might emerge from his solitude. Through his ferocious attachment to Sophie, the Narrator begins to obliterate the boundary between himself and the world. These later texts, though, demonstrate that it is possible to uncover small-scale and personal connections in the metropolis. That is, each character apprehends the metropolis through a sensual contact with the physical places that constitute their personal New York, and their contact with people in an immediate (and here artistic) social circle. However, these characters do not venture beyond their immediate environment, and so remain unaware of the vast array of urban possibilities which stretch beyond. As a consequence, the stability they do find is contingent on the material conditions of the moment, and is quickly threatened when those conditions change. That is to say, because of the multitudinous nature of the contemporary metropolis, personal and social conditions are constantly in flux, and so the relationships Fogg, Sachs and Aaron form remain provisional and often fleeting.

Fogg, Sachs and Aaron's everyday experience of the city produces an opaque, chaotic and often contradictory vision of contemporary metropolitan life. In the introduction to the recent collection of true stories edited by Auster, *True Tales of American Life*, he said 'the more we understand of the world, the more elusive and confounding the world becomes' (Auster, 2001: xviii). In these stories, the central characters do establish temporary and provisional stability, but a coherent understanding of their own lives and their place in the fluxes and flows of the vast metropolis proves elusive.

Descent

M. S. Fogg summarises and encapsulates his own life in an exceptional opening paragraph to *Moon Palace*. Here Auster relates the essence of everything that is to happen to his central character. He describes Fogg's impoverishment and dereliction; his chance rescue by Kitty Wu; his subsequent employment by Effing; the discovery of his paternity; and his desert walk from Utah to California (Auster, 1992a: 1). By doing so he signals the central themes of language, identity, dereliction and paternity, and the way that each is influenced by place.

Fogg's descent is set in motion by the death of his mother, Emily Fogg, and he is pushed into freefall by the sudden death of his surrogate parent, Uncle Victor. Emily dies when M. S. is eleven, and he is brought up in Chicago by Uncle Victor, whose death (like Sam Auster's) from an unexpected heart attack occurs soon after Fogg has departed for Columbia University. Fogg receives a small compensation for his mother's death, and inherits Uncle Victor's library, his collection of baseball cards and his suit (Auster, 1992a: 13). Victor's death causes a traumatic change in Fogg's life, and marks the point at which he 'began to vanish into another world' (Auster, 1992a: 3). As Victor is Fogg's sole social coordinate, the 'one link to something larger than myself', and his last remaining connection with the world beyond himself, the loss inevitably produces instability (Auster, 1992a: 3). 'In the end, the problem was not grief', Fogg records:

> Grief was the first cause, perhaps, but it soon gave way to something else – something more tangible, more calculable in its effects, more violent in the damage it produced. A whole chain of forces had been set in motion, and at a certain point I began to wobble, to fly in greater and greater circles around myself, until at last I spun out of orbit. (Auster, 1992a: 19)

Fogg's descent is much like Quinn's in the *Trilogy*. However, Auster shows how Fogg's fragile connections to society are enough to prevent him falling to the same depths of physical and textual erasure. Fogg begins to measure the extent he has vanished 'into another world' by the depletion of his financial and literary inheritances. Uncle Victor's literary bequest consists of 1492 books, which also represents the year that Columbus discovered America (Auster, 1992a: 13). Fogg converts the boxes of books into makeshift furniture for his apartment. By reading and selling each book, Fogg measures the disappearance of his connection to the social world – he is also, of course, dismantling his apartment. Fogg has 'become a gathering zero' and the room in which he lives is 'a machine that measured my condition: how much of me remained, how much of me was no longer there. . . . Piece by piece, I could watch myself disappear' (Auster, 1992a: 24). In this way, the depletion of his money, the disappearance of his uncle's legacy, and the dismantling of his furniture all measure the disintegration of Fogg's interior sense of self and his relationship with his environment. In an earlier version of the book, Auster describes this 'quest for zero' as 'marked by a triple injunction: to want nothing, to have nothing, to be nothing' (Auster, undated g: n.p.) – so Fogg's presence diminishes along with his few material possessions.

Fogg has embarked on a paradoxical strategy of virtual starvation as a means to survive poverty. As he becomes progressively weaker through hunger, he is less able to halt his downward spiral. Fogg's predicament is unlike Quinn's, however, as he is responding to an emotional and financial crisis with a deliberate strategy. His 'militant refusal to take any action at all' (Auster, 1992a: 20–1) is designed to separate his interior sense of self from his physical body (Auster, 1992a: 29). 'I would turn my life into a work of art', he asserts:

> sacrificing myself to such exquisite paradoxes that every breath I took would teach me how to savor my own doom. The signs pointed to a total eclipse, . . . the image of that darkness gradually lured me in, seduced me with the simplicity of its design. . . . The moon would block the sun, and at that point I would vanish. (Auster, 1992a: 21)

Fogg is following the same strategy as Hamsun's hunger artist. It is, he tells us, 'nihilism raised to the level of an aesthetic proposition' (Auster, 1992a: 21). In 'The Art of Hunger' Auster describes the 'narrator-hero' of Hamsun's *Hunger* as 'a monster of intellectual arrogance' (Auster, 1997: 11). Through Fogg's experiences of contemporary

New York, Auster tests Hamsun's model of aesthetic obstinacy to its limits. Both characters embark on an experiment with 'no controls, no stable points of reference – only variables' (Auster, 1997: 12). For both Hamsun's nameless hero and Fogg, the outcome of their fast is inevitably destructive; Auster notes that hunger 'opens the void' but 'does not have the power to seal it up' (Auster, 1997: 13). Hamsun's and Auster's characters play out their predicaments on the streets of the metropolis; one in late nineteenth-century Oslo, the other in late twentieth-century New York. Despite the temporal and geographical distance, there are comparisons to be drawn. Auster describes Oslo in 1890 as 'a labyrinth', in which Hamsun's hero suffers and 'nearly goes mad. He is never more than one step from collapse' (Auster, 1997: 9). Fogg too experiences New York as a labyrinth of streets and social conventions he is unable to navigate because of his total social disconnection. Fogg's plunge towards confusion is assisted by his inability to deploy what Fredric Jameson calls the appropriate 'perceptual equipment' (Jameson, 1991: 38). If he were in possession of the right ontological tools, able to 'map' the metropolis in a coherent way, Fogg would be able to 'disalienate' (Jameson, 1991: 51) his metropolitan environment and form a more effective correspondence with the complexities of his physical and social realm.

Like Quinn, Fogg colonises his vacated sense of self with the stereotype of the urban bum. Occupying the social margins, he confronts the everyday conventions of the streets and the need for physical and behavioural conformity. Fogg's failure to comprehend the norms of the crowd, that most ubiquitous of metropolitan symbols, exemplifies how his descent into the abyss dislocates him from his social world. For example, Walter Benjamin describes how the crowd is the natural environment of the *flâneur* and how this figure emerges from the crowd to observe and record it. However, Fogg does not possess the metropolitan knowledge and composure that the *flâneur* deploys to survive the 'series of shocks and collisions' of the crowd (Benjamin, 1997: 132). Through the work of Poe and Baudelaire, who have both influenced Auster's work, Benjamin examines the conventions of behaviour that the streets require. Fogg's responses owe more to Poe's 'Man of the Crowd' than to the *flâneur*. Like Poe's character, Fogg soon loses his self-control to 'manic behaviour' (Benjamin, 1997: 128) on the crowded streets, and disorientation forces him to retreat to the relative calm of Central Park. Initially, the homeless Fogg wanders mid-town Manhattan indiscriminately. But soon he finds the streets to be an unforgiving environment. The rigid codes of metropolitan behaviour dictate 'the way you act inside your clothes' and preclude any 'spontaneous or involuntary behaviour' (Auster, 1992a: 56–7). 'In the streets', Fogg discovers that:

> everything is bodies and commotion, . . . you cannot enter them without adhering to a rigid protocol of behavior. To walk among the crowd means never going faster than anyone else, never lagging behind your neighbor, never doing anything to disrupt the flow of human traffic. If you play by the rules of the game, people tend to ignore you. (Auster, 1992a: 56)

Where Auster presented Quinn's streets as devoid of life in 'City of Glass', always empty and lonely, he shows Fogg's streets to be tumultuous, so admitting into his literature a sense of the interrelation of myriad lives intersecting in the metropolis. A metropolitan environment teeming with life, even if it is hostile to Fogg's predicament, is more able and likely to offer the possibility of rescue for him. However, the streets become a place that he dreads precisely because they emphasise his status as 'a speck, a vagabond, a pox' (Auster, 1992a: 57).

Central Park is 'a sanctuary, a refuge of inwardness against the grinding demands of the streets'. The park offers a retreat from the gridwork of 'the massive streets and towers', where the self is easily separated from the world (Auster, 1992a: 56). The more democratic space of the park (where difference is more acceptable than on the streets) enables Fogg to contemplate his inner life. The boundary of the park marks the edge of a space that promotes interior reflection, while the streets beyond demand the examination of the individual's relationship to a wider social realm through external projection. The park alone is unable to physically sustain Fogg, however, and he needs to venture onto the streets to buy food when the scraps left by picnickers are insufficient. Fogg's experiences both in the park and on the streets demonstrate to him that 'you cannot live without establishing an equilibrium between inner and outer' (Auster, 1992a: 58). At this point in his narrative, Fogg identifies that his inner terrain of selfhood does not correspond with the outer terrain of New York City. While he is able to find respite from metropolitan confusion by retreating to the park, he is unable to create a balance between the two realms. As a result of this episode in his life, Fogg comes to understand his place in 'the monstrous / sum of particulars', and the need to break the cycle of his isolation. But at the time, these confusing events represent the lowest point in Fogg's life.

Where *The New York Trilogy* figured an incoherent relationship
with the metropolitan environment and with language as a physical
erasure or disappearance, *Leviathan* associates these things with
physical, literal and bodily disintegration. When Aaron describes 'my
poor friend bursting into pieces when the bomb went off, my poor
friend's body scattering in the wind' (Auster, 1993: 242), he is
describing the final event in Sachs's long and eventful descent into the
abyss. 'In fifteen years', Aaron tells us, 'Sachs travelled from one end
of himself to the other, and by the time he came to that last place, I
doubt he even knew who he was anymore' (Auster, 1993: 13). Thus,
Sachs's unstable and incoherent identity drives him towards his own
physical destruction.

When they first meet in the West Village's Nashe's Tavern for a book
reading, Aaron is struck by Sachs's 'generosity and humour and
intelligence' (Auster, 1993: 13). He relates these aspects of Sachs's
identity and personality to his early capacity with language and the way
'he steered himself through the world' with a clear sense of direction
(Auster, 1993: 16). Then Sachs was 'at home in his surroundings', and
his marriage to Fanny is a picture of domestic happiness of the same
order as that of the 'Austers' in 'City of Glass' (Auster, 1993: 17). Sachs's
accomplished writing and storytelling is indicative of his personal
stability, and Auster shows that he has located himself securely in the
world. Sachs's writing is 'marked by great precision and economy, a
genuine gift for the apt phrase' (Auster, 1993: 17). He also apprehends
the world with a literary sensibility; he is able to 'read' the world 'as
though it were a work of imagination, turning documented events into
literary symbols, tropes that pointed to some dark, complex pattern
embedded in the real' (Auster, 1993: 24). By adding an imaginary
dimension to the world he inhabits, Sachs is able to disalienate and re-
enchant his metropolitan environment, and thereby insert himself into
its physical and social structures with a greater degree of flexibility than
Aaron.

In the early passages of the narrative, Auster shows how the
availability of language for Sachs is in part related to his ability to freely
explore the sensations and impressions of the city. Instead of the rigid
social conventions of many New Yorkers, for Sachs:

> impromptu meetings were the norm. He worked when the spirit moved
> him (most often late at night), and the rest of the time he roamed free,
> prowling the streets of the city like some nineteenth-century *flâneur*,

following his nose wherever it happened to take him. . . . He wasn't
beholden to the clock in the way other people are. (Auster, 1993: 40–1)

Auster's representation of an urban wanderer here reaffirms
Benjamin's description of the *flâneur* 'botanizing on the asphalt'
(Benjamin, 1997: 36). The *flâneur*'s experience is formed through
walking in the metropolis. His impression of the city is shaped at street
level, through the confusion and immediacy of the sensual and local
experience of urban phenomena such as the crowd. Through the
immediate experience of the city he gains as a *flâneur*, Sachs is able
to respond to his metropolitan environment intuitively. And by
employing his time to 'peruse' the metropolis, his experience of it
reveals what Benjamin refers to as the 'phantasmagorical' (Benjamin,
1997: 39) and lyrical qualities of metropolitan life that are to be found
in galleries, museums and books. Auster relates the fugitive and
clandestine activity of Sachs's *flâneurie* to his facility with language.
Sachs's ability to orient himself in his Manhattan milieu, and relate
comfortably with the social realm of artists and writers, suggests that
at this point in his career Auster become more comfortable with
incorporating the metropolis into his work as a potential location for
a stable sense of self.

Sachs's unstructured routines result in a stream of essays and a
novel, *The New Colossus*. The novel is named for Emma Lazarus's
poem engraved into plinth of the Statue of Liberty. Lazarus appears as
a character in Sachs's postmodern novel, which incorporates real and
fictional characters in events from across history and literature.[2] *The
New Colossus*, in a similar way to Stillman's fictional thesis in the
Trilogy, explores the national cultural myth of America as the new
Eden, and how that vision has become corrupted by a new 'fall' and the
consequent postlapsarian failure of language. In Sachs's novel, Emma
Lazarus is given Thoreau's pocket compass as a gift. Aaron interprets
this act as America losing its way: 'Thoreau was the one man who could
read the compass for us, and now that he has gone, we have no hope
of finding ourselves again' (Auster, 1993: 38–9). In *Leviathan* this
compass becomes symbolic of Sachs's attempts to locate himself in
the world, and to re-establish his stability.

Sachs's instability is a direct result of his catastrophic fall. At a party
given by Aaron's literary agent in Brooklyn to witness the centennial
celebrations of the Statue of Liberty, he suffers a personal and literal
version of the 'fall' of mankind. Like Adam, Sachs faces the temptation

of a woman (Maria Turner, who will be discussed in depth shortly), and in succumbing to her he topples from the fire escape and is only saved by a clothesline.[3] After his fall, Sachs at first refuses to speak, later claiming this to be a turn inwards to focus on a profound and 'extraordinary' event (Auster, 1993: 119). Auster presents Sachs's fall as a pivotal point in the narrative, marking the point at which his grasp on language begins to fail, and his mental and physical disintegration commence:

> His body mended, but he was never the same after that. In those few seconds before he hit the ground, it was as if Sachs lost everything. His entire life flew apart in midair, and from that moment until his death four years later, he never put it back together. (Auster, 1993: 107)

At this point, the trajectories of the three writer-characters (Fogg, Sachs, Aaron) diverge. Sachs leaves his domestic stability with Fanny to continue his descent into the language void. He becomes lost and confronts death in a parodic American wilderness (Vermont), and he becomes disenchanted with America's political direction, which will lead him ultimately to a bizarre campaign of benign terrorism. Along this route, he attempts to reimpose some stability on his life by participating in Maria Turner's art and inserting himself into a family, but as I will show, the conditions under which this stability are sought is fundamental to its failure. Fogg and Aaron, on the other hand, go on to discover their metropolitan redemptions.

Rescue

Meanwhile, in *Moon Palace*, Fogg's emotional rescue comes through Kitty Wu, a dancer, while the photographer and conceptual artist, Maria Turner, rescues Aaron from his linguistic and social dysfunction. Both Kitty and Maria bear some resemblances to the character Sophie in 'The Locked Room'. Sophie's sensuality and watchfulness come, in part, from her involvement with the arts – she is a music teacher (Auster, 1988: 204). The connection between Sophie's view of the world 'from the heart of a deep inner vigilance' and her music is echoed in the relationship Kitty has with the physical world through her artistic practices. It is with the support of these women that the Narrator and Fogg find their 'true place in the world', and for both of them that place is beyond themselves. Semiotic art forms are exclusively feminine in these texts, but as Effing in *Moon Palace* and Auggie in Auster's films such as *Smoke* and *Blue in the Face* (1995) demonstrate, painting and photographic art forms are not exclusively gendered feminine in his work.

An absolutely central aspect of Kitty and Maria's relationships to the world, and to Auster's literary aesthetic, is chance. For both of them, but for Maria in particular, chance is a primal force that drives their lives and their aesthetic practices. Chance operates in Auster's fiction in one of two contradictory ways. More often than not a key narrative moment is motivated by a purely chance encounter. Sometimes, though, particularly for Fogg in *Moon Palace*, events are ascribed to chance purely because the character is unable to imagine the myriad of possible intersections and relationships the metropolis has to offer. In *Moon Palace* and *Leviathan* chance meetings within artistic and creative social groups provide affirmative connections that enable 'fallen' characters to begin emerging from the abyss.

In an environment as complex and multitudinous as the city, rule and chance can operate to bring some kind of order to chaotic urban artistic forms, such as Maria's photography. Auster uses pure chance to challenge the orderly processes of rule, and rule and chance operate as important aspects of his literary aesthetic. Rule is an ordering discourse, setting limits and providing structures such as conventions of representation, subject matter, composition and interpretation. Chance operates within these structures when the individual, such as the artist Maria, allows aleatorical processes to bring together unexpected elements, images and practices.[4] Auster, then, comes to understand chance too as an organising principle in art and life.

Rule and chance operate in Auster's work on two aesthetic bases. On the one hand, chance paradoxically provides causality in a seemingly chaotic environment, which is nonetheless constrained by highly regulated structures which set limits. On the other hand, the rule and chance encountered in Maria's aleatorical artistic production, like the structures and play of language or the grid and possibilities of the streets, provide Auster with a prime metaphor for urban social relationships. In an interview Auster said:

> In the strictest sense of the word, I consider myself a realist. Chance is a part of reality: we are continually shaped by the forces of coincidence, the unexpected occurs with almost numbing regularity in all our lives. . . . What I am after, I suppose, is to write fiction as strange as the world I live in. . . . [W]hat I am talking about is the presence of the unpredictable, the utterly bewildering nature of human experience. From one moment to

the next, anything can happen. . . . In philosophical terms, I'm talking about the powers of contingency. (Auster, 1997: 287–9)

Precisely this philosophy of the contingent is invoked by Fogg as a motivating force in his life in the opening passage of *Moon Palace*. Of his chance meeting with Kitty, he says: 'I came to see that chance as a form of readiness, a way of saving myself through the minds of others' (Auster, 1992a: 1). Much later, Fogg's paternity is restored by chance when he unknowingly works for his grandfather and subsequently meets his father. However, the conventions of genealogy are constantly undermined here. Genealogy is usurped by coincidence, paternity is discovered by accident, and the privileges that it conventionally confers, such as inheritance, are lost as soon as they are acquired.[5] As such, chance emerges as an aesthetic strategy in Auster's work at this point in his career, and contingency becomes an organising principle in his representation of the chaotic environment of New York. Consequently, we should not see chance in Auster's work as complete randomness, or as a deterministic process. Instead, it is both a denial of statistical reality and an expression of the author's own seemingly bizarre experiences.[6]

Because of the different qualities of the chance events shaping their narratives, Fogg's and Sachs's fates contrast fundamentally. The outcome of Fogg's nihilistic project depends on the combination of random factors intersecting around him at the critical moment – some of his making, some the making of others. Hamsun's model of the 'hunger artist' suggests that in the nineteenth-century metropolis the artist will 'arrive at nothing' because his fate is existentially fixed by his own actions (Auster, 1997: 20). However, in Fogg's contemporary New York, Auster proposes a more optimistic outcome. The artist's fate remains undetermined as a consequence of the complex interrelation of lives in the contemporary metropolis, and Fogg's openness to chance 'through the minds of others'.

The contingent interconnection that emerges from Fogg's 'form of readiness' arrives in the person of Kitty Wu. In his unbalanced life, she represents a balance between control and chance. In contrast to Fogg, Kitty is able to hold herself in physical and mental readiness for the random events with which the metropolis confronts her. Fogg becomes aware of the influence that such a coincidence of powers in one person could hold over his perilous condition, and is immediately drawn to her combination of spirituality and physical grace. Dancing provides Kitty with her physical ease but also, as a non-verbal spatial system of language, it offers an accomplished capacity of expression, which Fogg lacks. It is through his sympathetic relationship with Kitty that Fogg recovers some degree of language facility.

Kitty and Fogg's initial meeting occurs by chance. In a period of desolation just prior to eviction from his apartment, Fogg attempts to contact David Zimmer, his freshman roommate. However, Zimmer's apartment has been taken over by a group of students from Juilliard who are 'musicians, dancers, singers' and who have gathered for a communal breakfast. Kitty is amongst them (Auster, 1992a: 35). Fogg is attracted by the ease of her physical relationship with the space she occupies. She, in turn, is fascinated by the learning and intensity that he displays in an extended and rambling monologue on literature and space travel.

Contingency haunts Fogg and Kitty's early encounters. Their initial meeting and their reunion in the park are the consequence of the intersection of countless possibilities. Michel de Certeau has described how the life of the unsuspecting individual is influenced by the intersection of myriad powers circulating around them, such that 'each individual is a locus in which an incoherent (and often contradictory) plurality of . . . relational determinations interact' (de Certeau, 1984: xi). In *Moon Palace*, Uncle Victor describes the same process in a more lyrical way. 'Everything works out in the end, . . . everything connects', he tells Fogg. 'The nine circles. The nine planets. The nine innings. Our nine lives. . . . The correspondences are infinite' (Auster, 1992a: 14). After his rescue from the park, Fogg attends an army medical to assess his suitability for service in Vietnam. He explains the causal motivations for his current condition in terms that echo his uncle's. 'Our lives are determined by manifold contingencies', he tells the military doctor, 'and every day we struggle against these shocks and accidents in order to keep our balance'. By abandoning himself to the forces of contingency Fogg hopes to 'reveal some secret harmony', a pattern that would give meaning to the world (Auster, 1992a: 80). That he fails to find a coherent pattern confirms Fogg's belief that the world has become entirely random, and that he must seek an ordering principle elsewhere.

One such contingent event, and interaction of incoherent determinants, is the pivotal moment when Kitty and Zimmer discover the delirious Fogg in Central Park. Given the multitudes who inhabit New York, the chances of finding a lost individual are slight. That, against all the probabilities, Kitty and Fogg are reunited, both exemplifies Auster's philosophy of the contingent and prefigures the bizarre coincidences which go on unfolding throughout the novel. The emotional dimension of Fogg's rescue echoes the experiences of the Narrator in the *Trilogy*. Both of these characters suddenly discover that the love of another has redemptive powers. Discovering what his friends did for him prompts Fogg to reassess the reality of his experiences. In a striking passage, Fogg describes how Kitty and Zimmer drop everything to search for him. 'That was how I finally came to be rescued: because the two of them went out and looked for me', he writes:

> To be loved like that makes all the difference. It does not lessen the terror of the fall, but it gives a new perspective on what that terror means. I had jumped off the edge, and then, at the very last moment, something reached out and caught me in midair. That something is what I define as love. It is the one thing that can stop a man from falling, the one thing powerful enough to negate the laws of gravity. (Auster, 1992a: 50)

Fogg's descent is arrested, first through the chance encounters with Kitty, and then through the love of his friends. Once rescued, Fogg realises that his nihilistic experiment has not demonstrated courage, but has displayed instead his 'contempt for the world' (Auster, 1992a: 73). With this realisation, and with the help of his friends, Fogg begins his recovery. Zimmer insists that Fogg recuperate at his apartment; and soon they venture out each night to a nearby West Village bar to drink beer and watch baseball. This time marks 'an exquisitely tranquil period' in their lives: 'a brief moment of standing still before moving on again' (Auster, 1992a: 82). Zimmer – 'room' in German, of course – once again represents a sanctuary from the tumultuous processes of the metropolis.

Fogg moves on from the safety of this pleasant and static existence when he and Kitty become lovers. Physical and emotional love with Kitty alters Fogg. 'I am not just talking about sex or the permutations of desire', he insists, 'but the crumbling of inner walls, an earthquake in the heart of my solitude' (Auster, 1992a: 94). Fogg's inner state is profoundly altered, and to mark the beginning of this new social phase of his life, he shares a meal with his friends at the Moon Palace Chinese restaurant close to his old apartment in Columbia Heights. Fogg had eaten here alone at a particularly desperate time in his experiment. Then he forced the food down his own throat – the lonely and traumatic event conjuring an image of himself in pieces (Auster, 1992a: 43). In contrast, the meal with Kitty and Zimmer represents 'a moment of astonishing joy and equilibrium, as though my friends had gathered there to celebrate my return to the land of the living' (Auster, 1992a: 96). This social space, a 'great, good place' for gathering and sharing, represents Fogg's rehabilitation into a social being.

Auster introduces a further element of ease between the individual and her environment with Kitty's choice of a physical art form: dance. In control of her own bodily space, Kitty is able to exert far greater control over the spatial realm she inhabits. Fogg's discomfort in his own clothes is in stark contrast to Kitty's ease with her own beauty and corporeality. Fogg relates that she is able to dominate the space around her by combining her physical and cerebral powers. 'I found her beautiful', he writes:

> but more than that I liked the way she held herself, the way she did not seem to be paralyzed by her beauty as so many beautiful girls did. Perhaps it was the freedom of her gestures, the blunt, down-to-earth quality I heard in her voice. This was . . . someone who knew her way around, who had managed to learn things for herself. (Auster, 1992a: 37)

Kittys's control over and in space is inherently connected to her dancing, because she is not afraid of her own self: 'she lived inside her body without embarrassment or second thoughts. . . . Because she took pleasure in her body, it was possible for her to dance' (Auster, 1992a: 94). It is, in part, Kitty's control over space which leads her to Fogg in the park. The implication is, of course, that her role in his rescue is not entirely dependent on chance, but is the result of her superior relationship with the metropolis.

Although Fogg finds a new accommodation with language through Kitty, certain linguistic sign systems continue to evade his powers of interpretation. Both the non-linguistic spatial expression of dancing and Chinese symbols remain a mystery to him. Ten years before *Moon Palace* was published, in 'White Spaces', Auster wrote of the relationship between the movement of a body and speech:

> To think of motion not merely as a function of the body but as an extension of the mind. In the same way, to think of speech not as an extension of the mind but as a function of the body. . . . [S]ounds are no less a gesture than a hand is when outstretched in the air toward another hand. (Auster, 1991: 82)

Each move, each gesture of dance, carries meaning that is interpreted between the dancer and the audience. But for Fogg, despite following 'her body around the stage with a kind of delirious concentration', Kitty's dancing remains 'utterly foreign . . . a thing that stood beyond the grasp of words' (Auster, 1992a: 96).

When Fogg and Kitty rent an apartment in New York's Chinatown, Fogg encounters a similar quality of 'dislocation and confusion' promoted by the impenetrability of the Chinese language. Here because of the language barrier and the unfamiliar system of signs, Fogg is unable to 'penetrate the meanings' of his surroundings, and so he is limited to 'the mute surfaces of things' (Auster, 1992a: 230). Ultimately, Fogg's failure to 'read' Kitty, in just the same way he failed to 'read' his metropolitan predicament, results in his losing her.

In *Leviathan*, Aaron's 'rescue' is less dramatic than Fogg's but, given Sachs's ultimate fate, no less timely. Since the breakup of his marriage Aaron has been living, like A. in *Solitude*, in a sublet on Varrick Street that has become his 'sanctuary of inwardness' (Auster, 1993: 57). Through Sachs and Fanny's social network of artistic and creative people, Aaron is drawn out of his solitude. He meets Maria Turner at a dinner party at their Brooklyn apartment that exemplifies their New York social world. It is here that 'half of New York' seems to assemble to eat, drink and talk (Auster, 1993: 58). The parties are made up of '[a]rtists, writers, professors, critics, editors, gallery owners', and it is from this crowd of people that Maria emerges to rescue Aaron from his loneliness. Maria displays many of the same qualities as Kitty in her physical presence. Maria is also a self-possessed woman in control of her body, a power she extends to her physical and social environment. An important aspect of her physicality, like Kitty's, is her eroticism. Aaron describes the graceful 'way she carried herself in her clothes . . . that would unmask itself in little flashes of erotic forgetfulness' (Auster, 1993: 59). It is this sexual charge to Maria's presence that will later tempt Sachs to his fall.

Maria understands the interplay of structure and chaos, rule and chance in contemporary metropolitan life, and she is able to draw many of the seemingly uncontrollable elements of the metropolis into a strategy to contain their disorder. Aaron describes Maria as 'a good bourgeois girl who had mastered the rules of social behavior, but at the same time it was as if she no longer believed in them' (Auster, 1993: 59). Because Maria has such a mastery of the rules of urban living, she is able to place herself into metropolitan settings and experience them as the subject matter of her art. Maria's life is lived as a 'set of bizarre, private rituals', in which experiences are systematised within their own risks and limitations (Auster, 1993: 60). In other words, Maria's life is contained by the limits of rule, but within those structures, chance and contingency are allowed free rein to produce one of any number of outcomes. Because of her influence on people's lives and her mode of artistic production, Aaron calls Maria 'the reigning spirit of chance, . . . the goddess of the unpredictable' (Auster, 1993: 102). The streets of New York City provide an ideal environment for this interplay of rule and chance. Maria has created two particularly metropolitan 'pieces' on the streets. For the first one, she leaves her loft on Duane Street and follows a randomly chosen individual around the streets for the day, photographing them and constructing fictional biographies. For the other, she makes herself the subject of the piece by employing a private detective to follow her and file a report on her movements (Auster, 1993: 62). Maria's purpose as a *flâneuse* is to watch and be watched, to expose the 'fraught meanings of microscopic actions', and to reconstitute the essence of things from a fragment (Auster, 1993: 63). Maria's art focuses on the human scale of metropolitan activity, recording the 'practices of everyday life' (to borrow de Certeau's term) and the visceral and the sensual aspects of the streets. Her attempt to trace and read the movements of individuals around New York is a reaffirmation of de Certeau's 'urban poems' as her pieces attempt to diagnose individuals' metropolitan psychoses from the fragments of observable symptoms. Like Sachs earlier in the novel, she experiences the city in close-up, dense with detail and compelling urban impressions.

Maria's metropolitan stability provides Aaron with a social and personal foundation from which to explore his own social contingencies. A brief affair with Fanny (a curator of American landscape painting at the Brooklyn Museum) provides him with an 'enigmatic point of stillness' (Auster, 1993: 84) amid the turmoil of his life. Then, under the influence of Maria's 'spirit of chance', Aaron meets Iris, and all is motion again. They meet at a gallery on Wooster Street, on the night of the opening of Maria's second exhibition. Iris is drawn into Aaron's social orbit through the network of creative types that has Sachs and Fanny at its centre. It is only through a series of partial and contingent connections that Iris and Aaron come to meet. Aaron acknowledges that '[d]ecades would have passed before we found ourselves standing in the same room again' (Auster, 1993: 101). She becomes his 'happy ending, the miracle that had fallen down on me when I was least expecting it. We took each other by storm and nothing has ever been the same for me since' (Auster, 1993: 103).

The character of Iris remains very much in the background of this story, but provides the stability for Aaron to continue building his secure sense of self and to locate his place in the world. Iris does not conform to the model of the non-verbal artist negotiating an exceptional spatial environment set by Kitty and Maria. Iris is a literary character, a graduate student in English at Columbia. Her name, too, is resonant of Auster's poetic concerns, and those of the Objectivists, as they sought to occupy the 'realm of the naked eye'. Iris's symbolic ocularity also stands in contrast to Fanny's (symbolic and actual) corporeality, and Maria's physical and erotic presence. These qualities put Iris in the poetic order that Oppen and Reznikoff occupy. This suggests that, for Auster in these texts, corporeal characters, such as Fanny and Maria, are essential to 'fallen' writer-characters' recovery of the relationship between the word and the world. However, once the writer-characters have achieved a stable relationship with the world, they need to form new relationships in order to maintain that stability. Finally, Iris spelled backwards is Siri, the name of Auster's second wife, with whom there are a number of biographical correspondences.[7]

Aaron's story acts as a counternarrative or counterweight to Sachs's; as one ascends, the other descends. After his fall, Sachs renegotiates the terms of his relationship with the physical and social metropolis. Aaron sees little of him until he encounters him on the street in Downtown Manhattan. Sachs is on an aimless urban wander similar to his earlier *flâneurie*. However, his engagement with the urban environment has deteriorated; he appears to apprehend objects in a partial and fleeting way, merely acknowledging their surface. In the two hours that Aaron follows him through the 'canyons of New York', 'Sachs wandered around the streets like a lost soul, roaming haphazardly between Times Square and Greenwich Village at the same slow and contemplative pace, . . . never seeming to care where he was' (Auster, 1993: 125). But Aaron himself is going on 'partial evidence' (Auster, 1993: 126). Sachs has become one of Maria's pieces, and she is following him around Manhattan photographing him for a project called 'Thursdays with Ben', a 'combination of documentary and play, the objectification of inner states' (Auster, 1993: 127). Maria tries to capture Sachs's inner state with her camera as he wanders the streets of New York. Similarly, Auster employs the city itself as the measure of Sachs's turmoil, and his partial connections with it indicate the imbalance between his interior and exterior selves. Maria plays the part of the detective (reversing again the roles of her earlier piece) who attempts to reveal some truthful or authentic sense of Sachs from the evidence because 'he was no longer able to see himself' (Auster, 1993: 129). Ultimately, the project fails because Sachs is no longer able to recover the social connections that had formed the basis for his earlier self, and he is unable to retake his place in metropolitan society. These failures, of Sachs as a *flâneur* and of Maria's project, suggest that the metropolis as Sachs experiences it here is illegible, and that in contemporary New York *flâneurie* is an inappropriate tool for engaging with the city.

Sachs withdraws from New York society completely when, at Aaron's prompting, he is offered the chance to publish a collection of his essays. He leaves Fanny and goes to the family farmhouse in the Vermont countryside to work. However, when Sachs attempts to explore the Vermont woods, just as Thoreau explored the Massachusetts countryside, he soon becomes lost. He becomes disorientated and is unable to establish coordinates that will either reveal his location or allow him to navigate his way out of this new predicament. Sachs is literally unable to locate himself in the world. The disorientation he experiences and the environment in which he finds himself recall the key theme of Thoreau's compass explored in *The New Colossus*; without it, Sachs has no hope of finding himself again. Beaten by the impenetrability of the woods, he sleeps on the ground, and the next morning flags down a truck on the first highway he comes to. The young driver, Dwight, takes a country road back towards the farmhouse. It is on this journey that violence and terrorism enter Sachs's life.

They encounter a car on the lonely road and Dwight stops to offer assistance. When the driver of the car shoots Dwight dead, Sachs, in both anger and self-defence, bludgeons the killer to death. He then flees the scene in panic, taking the assailant's car. Later, when he stops, he discovers in the trunk bomb-making equipment, around one hundred and sixty-five thousand dollars in cash, and a passport in the name of Reed Dimaggio. Sachs's experiences demonstrate that even in rural Vermont the innocent spaces of the American Eden have been swept away by the 'fallen' society of modern America. Like the metropolis, the Vermont countryside is a corrupt space containing the potential for disorientation and acts of random, anonymous violence. The chance encounter with the gunman also serves Auster as a causal narrative event that provides a link between Sachs's 'fall' and his eventual destruction. Coincidence can clearly be the bearer of misfortune as well as rescue.

In *Moon Palace*, Uncle Victor identified the infinite coincidences that can occur in life. It is one of these 'confluences' that hauls Fogg from the void into the light of the social realm and back to sanity. In *Leviathan*, Aaron asserts that '[e]verything is connected to everything else, every story overlaps with every other story' (Auster, 1993: 51). He also believes that '*[a]nything can happen*. And one way or another, it always does' (Auster, 1993: 160, original emphasis). For Sachs, the powers of contingency act not to rescue him, but to accelerate his descent into the abyss. Maria Turner knows Reed Dimmagio as the husband of a friend, Lillian Stern, demonstrating, in Auster's fiction, the almost infinite interconnectedness of lives and the power of the metropolis to bring them together. The rapidly disintegrating Sachs grasps the opportunity of this 'nightmare coincidence' (Auster, 1993: 167) to redress the balance of his actions. He would embrace this uncanny event and 'breathe it into himself as a sustaining event' (Auster, 1993: 167). He travels to Berkeley in California to hand the money over to Lillian.

Auster once again exploits the uncanny results of coincidence when Maria decides to use a diary she has found in the street as the basis for a project, and it is through this re-establishes her friendship with Lillian. Maria anticipates a 'portrait *in absentia*' of the man the diary belonged to, 'an outline drawn around an empty space' that she could fill in by exploring his social world and interviewing the individuals who constitute it (Auster, 1993: 67, original emphasis). Lillian is an actress paying her way through drama school by prostitution, and the owner of the diary has been a client. This combination of actress and prostitute, of imitation and eroticism, reveals itself in a series of photographs that Maria takes of Lillian. Lillian, Maria tells Aaron, has 'a quality that is always coming to the surface. . . . She's completely relaxed in her own skin' (Auster, 1993: 71). At this stage in their lives, Lillian and Maria seem similarly visceral; like Kitty, they are corporeal and sensuous, spontaneous and open to chance.

In California, Lillian and her daughter, Maria, come to represent for Sachs the opportunity for redemption and domestic stability that Aaron has achieved with Iris. Sachs takes the place of the man he has killed: as husband to Dimaggio's wife, and father to his daughter. However, the prevailing conditions are unpromising. Auster shows that, unlike

Kitty, instead of representing a series of connections to a wider society, Lillian represents a withdrawal from it. She is not in New York, where Sachs's social circle operates, and he has severed his connections with Maria and Fanny. As a result, rather than finding stability with Lillian, Sachs is put 'permanently off balance' because Maria only reveals to him her surface beauty: 'she refused to reveal herself . . ., which meant that she never became more than an object, never more than the sum of her physical self' (Auster, 1993: 198). Consequently, Lillian does not have the depth of personality or the necessary relationship with the world to become a stable point of reference in Sachs's life, the foundation on which to establish a coherent sense of self, and the catalyst to launch the progressively disconnected Sachs back into the social realm where he was once so effective.

For less than two weeks Sachs and Lillian do manage to create a kind of domestic stability, following a night of passion during which Lillian 'emptied him out' and 'dismantled him' (Auster, 1993: 211), but she fails to release him from the solitude consuming him. Later Sachs describes Lillian as 'wild', 'incandescent' and 'out of control' (Auster, 1993: 228). It is this absence of boundaries in Lillian that sets her apart from Maria or Iris in the life of Aaron, or Kitty in the life of Fogg. These other women understand the limits that structures – artistic, social or physical – inscribe in their everyday lives. Sachs's attempt to locate himself in the world with Lillian as the point of reference founders because she is as unstable and disoriented as he is.

Finally, the end of the relationship with Lillian strips Sachs of his last vestige of social contact, and he embarks on his nihilistic campaign. Under the pseudonym 'The Phantom of Liberty', he tapes explosives to the crown of scale models of the Statue of Liberty in America's small towns (Auster, 1993: 215–16). Dimaggio's emergent campaign against environmental targets for The Children of the Planet provides the inspiration, while the money finances the four-year bombing spree. After completing his thesis on the anarchist Alexander Berkman, Dimaggio abandoned academia and writing for direct political action. Sachs adds his personal dimension to the crusade by incorporating the Statue of Liberty, which is central to both his personal fall and *The New Colossus*, and channels his creative energies into concocting false identities and cover stories for his activities. 'The Phantom of Liberty' attempts to rearticulate the fallen America with its founding principles by offering a version of Thoreau's compass by which to map a political and moral path, and 'to look after itself and mend its ways' (Auster,

1993: 217). The extent to which America has fallen, however, is measured by the way the 'Phantom' is commodified, even to the extent of inspiring a stripping act in which the 'Phantom' seduces and disrobes the Statue of Liberty (Auster, 1993: 234).[8]

Leviathan is dedicated to Auster's friend Don DeLillo, and is contemporaneous with *Mao II*, a book that is also about terrorism. Both these novels question the power of literature in a complex world where the transparently violent acts of terrorists are more influential than books and poems. Aliki Varvogli notes that *Leviathan* may be 'fruitfully read as a response to, or in dialogue with *Mao II*, rather than a capitulation of similar thematic concerns' (Varvogli, 2001: 144). This is because DeLillo is concerned with 'postmodernist consumerist concerns', while 'Auster negotiates his writer's position in the world by invoking . . . the spirit and rhetoric of nineteenth-century American writing' (Varvogli, 2001: 144–5). That Sachs's terrorism fails, and he entrusts his story to Aaron, strongly suggests that Auster retains his belief in the power of art and that he personally, as an artist, feels more attuned to the experience of Aaron (with whom, of course, he shares initials) than that of Sachs. Interestingly, while DeLillo was writing and publishing his epic *Underworld* (1998), encompassing most of America's postwar history, Auster was producing his slight, introverted and autobiographical *Hand to Mouth*, which once more records his early years of struggle. This divergence of artistic paths suggests that Auster perceives fiction more as a way of examining the personal than of confronting the political, an emphasis suggested too by the peripheral role that major historical events, such as the depression, wars and the moon landings, play in his work.

Sachs's political project is not just his own, however, since his choice of direct intervention is driven by the work started by the man he killed, Reed Dimaggio (Auster, 1993: 228). Accompanying his abandonment of social contacts (first Fanny, then Maria and finally Lillian) is a sense that Sachs is emptying himself out, vacating his interiority for the man he has killed – 'a gradual surrender to Dimaggio', Aaron calls it (Auster, 1993: 223). By abandoning the personality of his disintegrating self, Sachs finds new purpose and coherence. 'It was a marvellous confluence', Sachs tells Aaron:

> a startling conjunction of motives and ambitions. I had found the unifying principle, and this one idea would bring all the broken pieces of myself together. For the first time in my life, I would be whole. (Auster, 1993: 228)

This statement is prescient, given the information that the reader is armed with from the opening passage of the book. Clearly Sachs's 'unifying principle' is unable to prevent his 'body burst[ing] into dozens of small pieces' (Auster, 1993: 1).

In many ways, the symptoms of Sachs's breakdown parallel Fredric Jameson's descriptive model of cultural and linguistic schizophrenia. When the relationship between a word and what it means disintegrates, 'the links of the signifying chain snap'. Jameson continues:

> If we are unable to unify the past, present, and future of the sentence, then we are similarly unable to unify the past, present, and future of our own biographical experience or psychic life. With the breakdown of the signifying chain, therefore, the schizophrenic is reduced to an experience of pure material signifiers, or, in other words, a series of pure and unrelated presents in time. (Jameson, 1991: 26–7)

Sachs too struggles to stabilise his language, his temporal experience and his 'psychic' internal life. Because Sachs has surrendered his internal terrain to his perception of Dimaggio's motives, as well as suffering a loss of his linguistic faculty, Sachs is embarking on a schizophrenic episode in his life. Along with the rubble of his language and his life, Auster represents Sachs's interior disunity as a literal disintegration into thousands of bodily fragments.[9] Sachs is unable to differentiate his past from his future and create for himself a stable present. Like his novel, episodes from across his life, such as a childhood anecdote about the Statue of Liberty, his fall from the fire escape and his violent encounter with Dimaggio in the woods, fail to form a coherent and linear 'unifying principle' able to justify his actions and his ultimate fate.

Recovery

At this point in the story, the counternarratives of Sachs and Aaron intersect in Vermont on their different trajectories. Sachs entrusts his story to Aaron, and the mantle of linguistic and literary achievement passes to him as Sachs concedes that he is no longer able to connect with the earlier self who had such a close relationship with the word. Soon Sachs is dead, and the book of his story, Leviathan, stands as a testament to Aaron's recovery.[10]

Fogg comes to occupy a similar position to Aaron. He too produces the book to testify to his recovery from his 'aphasic' episode. The story of Fogg's salvation, from the time of the indecipherable squiggles of Uncle Victor's books to the accomplished first-person narrative of *Moon Palace* effortlessly straddling the twentieth-century, is also the story of artistic lives – including his own. Fogg's text supports another of Uncle Victor's philosophical observations. Referring to the initials, M.S., Victor tells Fogg that '[e]very man is the author of his own life. . . . The book you are writing is not finished yet. Therefore, it's a manuscript' (Auster, 1992a: 7). More than twenty years later, Fogg attains the linguistic ability to tackle the subject of his own life; to give it shape and form and rescue it from the symbolic indistinctness that his name implies. By doing so he relates the experiences that shape him as a person to the larger social and political processes of the time – the moon landings, Vietnam, campus revolts and Woodstock – without admitting them into the narrative as causal agents. Auster describes this process in the introduction to *True Tales of American Life*, where he observes that we 'all have inner lives. We all feel that we are part of the world and yet exiled from it. We all burn with the fires of our own existence. Words are needed to express what is in us' (Auster, 2001: xvii).

Artists help Fogg to form points of reference upon which to construct his progressively resocialised self. Kitty provides Fogg with a particular focus as he emerges from his personal abyss. Effing's life too supplies an example of an artist attempting to a find way of being in the world. His story of isolation and representation in the Nevada desert exemplifies the artistic struggle for expression. Here Effing learns that art is not only about beautiful objects, but also 'a method of understanding, a way of penetrating the world and finding one's place in it, and whatever aesthetic qualities an individual canvas might have were almost an incidental by-product of the effort to engage oneself in this struggle, to enter into the thick of things' (Auster, 1992a: 171). The work of the marginal American landscape artist Ralph Alfred Blakelock also has an instructive role in Fogg's understanding of how representational art can help the observer to understand the world (Auster, 1992a: 133–9). Effing directs Fogg to study Blakelock's painting, *Moonlight*, in the Brooklyn Museum.[11] The painting is 'a deeply contemplative work, a landscape of inwardness and calm' (Auster, 1992a: 137). Blakelock's paintings are dominated by moons, which become 'holes in the canvas, apertures of whiteness looking into another world' (Auster, 1992a: 141). *Moonlight* is no exception; here the moon represents an aperture able to connect the interior self to the exterior world. William Dow notes that 'Auster's moon allusions not only impose form on Marco's "fears" and "desires" but are examples of how knowledge in *Moon Palace*, as in all Auster's novels, is derived from consciously perceived glimmers [and] intuitions' (Dow, 1996: 197). As so often in Auster's literature, the figure of circles and pinpricks in the fabric of life and reality represents the channel between inner consciousness and an outer social world, 'a tiny hole between self and not-self' (Auster, 1988: 232).[12] This picture, like *The New Colossus*, also represents the America that lost its innocence to the advance of the white man (Auster, 1992a: 139).

Fogg's encounter with Blakelock's picture helps him to find a fuller accommodation with language so that he is able to take Effing's words and record them as a documentary representation of that man's life. Effing 'authors' the 'text' of his own life through Fogg, and so Fogg needs to accurately represent what he is told. The journeys around the streets of New York prove to be a training for this central task. The accidents and losses that occur there cannot be tolerated in a biography: where words come to be the representation of the man, his whole life is at stake. This is borne out by the brief appearance of the character Orlando. He is a 'linguistic alchemist' in the tradition of the Narrator and Stillman Sr. who gifts Effing the skeleton of an umbrella that is now like 'some huge and improbable steel flower' (Auster, 1992a: 209). When Effing deliberately uses this 'magic' umbrella in a storm he catches pneumonia and dies. Effing's deliberate misapprehension of a linguistic sign therefore leads directly to his death.

On the death of Effing, Fogg discovers his paternity, but with the death of Sol, his life starts to disintegrate again. Fogg's own chance at fatherhood is denied when Kitty has an abortion, and the happiness they found together proves to be temporary and fragile. Despite the insights gained from his experience, Fogg is too inflexible to reconcile his internal feelings and emotions to Kitty's needs. With the loss of Kitty, Fogg's life, like Sachs's, 'flew apart' and his 'Chinatown paradise' (Auster, 1992a: 278, 273) comes to an end.

When his inheritance is stolen, along with his car, Fogg's narrative begins to draw to a close, but not a conclusion. He walks west from Nevada, and three months later reaches the Pacific Ocean at Laguna Beach. Fogg has traversed the continental United States in what appears to be a traditional quest narrative.[13] However, despite reaching journey's end, he has not found his place in the world. In a novel saturated with word plays (Fogg connoting indistinctness, Effing suggesting vulgarity and Sol reflecting the character's filial relationship to Effing and associating him with a large orb) the use of the word laguna at the end of the novel raises questions of resolution similar to those raised in *The New York Trilogy*. Lagune is a French word, the Latin root of which is lacuna, meaning hiatus or gap. Consequently,the resolution of this novel suggests the ending is an empty space, into which nothing should be read. This interpretation is supported by the definition of lacuna as a missing page from a manuscript. Thus, the manuscript of this portion of Fogg's life remains incomplete. Instead of an ending, Auster offers us a potential beginning, where the rest of Fogg's life starts (Auster, 1992a: 306). His attempts to place himself in his vast and incomprehensible world of New York and America find their symbolic expression in the path of the moon into the Western sky:

> Then the moon came up from behind the hills. It was a full moon, as round and yellow as a burning stone. I kept my eyes on it as it rose into the night sky, not turning away until it had found its place in the darkness. (Auster, 1992a: 307)

Auster's two most recent novels, *Oracle Night* and *The Brooklyn Follies*, return to the themes of friendship and family in a metropolitan setting. Both books are set predominantly in Brooklyn. As will be discussed in Chapter 6, Brooklyn is the borough in which Auster lives. It is a place which affords him a personal sense of well-being and belonging, and it is also a source for his work.

Like *Leviathan*, *Oracle Night* is the story of two authors. The primary focus is the young but sickly Sidney Orr, and alongside him is the older and established writer, John Trause (an anagram of Auster). The novel takes place over nine days in September 1982, and is recounted from 'more than twenty years after the fact' (Auster, 2004: 222). The stories of the two men are complexly interwoven with the fictional narratives they write. While Sidney's story is slight in comparison with the detailed narratives of Auster's earlier texts, the way in which the various fictions ebb and flow in this work is a testament to his literary craftsmanship.

To a large extent the novel explores the creative process, trying to locate the moment at which an idea becomes a story, becomes a novel. It is also a meditation, as is much of Auster's work, on the magical powers of storytelling and writing. Auster traces the development of a 'premise' for a novel gifted to Sidney by Trause. Sidney adapts 'the

Flitcraft episode in . . . *The Maltese Falcon*, the curious parable . . .
about the man who walks away from his life and disappears' (Auster,
2004: 13). Clearly this echoes Hawthorne's 'Wakefield', but the story
is reworked here for the twentieth century by both Hammett and
Auster. In the unnamed novel Sidney is writing, part of a building falls
eleven floors, just missing his central character, Nick Bowen. Bowen
realises that 'a new life has been given to him – that his old life is
finished' (Auster, 2004: 26). Sidney's central character is a literary
editor, and he has just come into possession of the manuscript of a
missing novel by a renowned 1920s woman writer. It is from this
text that *Oracle Night* takes its title. The layering of narratives in
this way is symptomatic of the recursive structures Brian McHale
identifies as 'mise-en-abyme' – effectively, narrative worlds falling
into and, crucially, resembling each other (McHale, 1987: 124). As
McHale notes, '[s]trategies involving recursive structures – nesting or
embedding, as in a set of Chinese boxes. . . . [–] have the effect of
interrupting and complicating the ontological "horizon" of the fiction,
multiplying its worlds, and laying bear the process of world-
construction' (McHale, 1987: 112). Because Auster is exploring the
nature of literary creativity in *Oracle Night*, by embedding a novel
within a novel within a novel, he is also necessarily exposing the ways
in which authors create fictional worlds. Auster continually draws
attention to the practice of writing by punctuating the narrative with
footnotes, which shift backwards and forwards from the book's present,
and between Sidney's 'real' world, created by Auster, and the fictional
worlds which Sidney, as a writer, is creating.

The magical power stories can possess is demonstrated through both
place and practice. The place is the stationery store, Paper Palace, which
Sidney discovers. The store is a place of stillness where Sidney's story
really begins, and where 'the sound of [a] pencil was the only sound in
the world' (Auster, 2004: 5). The story begins at the store because this
is where Sidney buys a new notebook to begin writing again after a
long illness. The practice is the habit of writing in notebooks which
Auster has discussed in 'The Red Notebook'. Sidney's notebook has
strange properties, powers of which Trause has already warned. 'The
first time I used the notebook', Sidney tells Trause, 'I wasn't there
anymore . . . I disappeared' (Auster, 2004: 165). When Sidney's wife
Grace tries to find him, it is as though he has crossed what McHale calls
'the ontological threshold to a different narrative level', or fallen into
his own story world (McHale, 1987: 125). Towards the end of the novel,

Sidney records an observation which, one suspects, is Auster's understanding of his own aesthetic practice. Sidney has become, he insists, 'a transparent, porous membrane through which all the invisible forces of the world could pass – a nexus . . . of the thoughts and feelings of others' (Auster, 2004: 223). This assertion reflects Auster's own stated beliefs about writing and authorship, expounded in any number of interviews in various media, that he is a simple storyteller at the whim of creativity.[14] However, a text which employs footnotes, and other novels which employ literary devices in such knowing ways, suggest that Auster is far more aware of his practice than his public pronouncements indicate.

Sidney's narrative explores the destructive power of families, but also the redemptive power of friendship. Trause's son Jacob, whose behaviour is modelled in part on problems Auster's own son Daniel had with drugs and the law, is an agent of destruction.[15] He robs Sidney's apartment and then attacks Grace, ending her pregnancy. However, Sidney's friendship with Trause is one of genuine kindness and mutual benefit, and though Trause dies before the end, the warmth between the two author-characters is a palpable presence throughout the book.

The Brooklyn Follies explores two places, one real and one imaginary. First there is the neighbourhood in Brooklyn where the book's narrator, Nathan Glass, has settled to await his own death; 'I was looking for a quiet place to die' is the arresting first line (Auster, 2005: 1). Here, because of the nature of cities and the myriad potential interconnections, he re-establishes contact with his favourite nephew, Tom. Together they form a firm bond, and gather a group of unconventional Brooklynite friends around them. Secondly there is the imaginary and abstract Hotel Existence, a 'place where a man goes to when life in the real world is no longer possible' (Auster, 2005: 100). Earlier in the novel, this exact phrase has been used to describe some of the works of Poe and Thoreau (Auster, 2005: 14). The implication is, of course, that literature and society can create spaces of 'community' and 'utopia' (Auster, 2005: 106). We will return to these ideas of utopia, community and Brooklyn in later chapters.

Notes

1   Although Aaron is a writer and shares Auster's initials, his character has more basis in the figure of a New York painter whom Auster knew. In 'The

Red Notebook' he records B.'s story of fatherhood, divorce, lovers (of which Aaron has a number), eviction, dinner parties and finally true love (Auster, 1997: 354–7).

2 This is a type of fiction which Linda Hutcheon has termed 'historiographic metafiction' (Hutcheon, 1988: 106). The novels of E. L. Doctorow are notable examples, particularly *Ragtime* (1976), in which Freud and Jung visit Coney Island together.

3 This event is a reinterpretation of a fall Auster's father had from the roof of a tenement. His fall was broken by a clothesline, and he escaped virtually unhurt (Auster, 1997: 374).

4 Maria is based on the French artist Sophie Calle. An inscription in this book reads: 'The author extends special thanks to Sophie Calle for permission to mingle fact with fiction' (Auster, 1993: n.p.). For more about Maria's 'pieces' and their origins in the artistic career of Sophie Calle, see Calle, 1999, in which Parts I and II explore the 'rituals' that Auster borrows from Calle, and reinterpret two of these using the additional rules supplied by Auster in *Leviathan*. Calle also collaborated with Auster on a piece called 'Gotham Handbook', included in *Double Game* (see Chapter 6).

5 On the conventional use of genealogy in the *Moon Palace* see also Weisenburger, 1995: 130–4.

6 'The Red Notebook' is an extended meditation on a number of seemingly contingent events which have happened directly or indirectly to Auster (Auster, 1997: 341–80).

7 Iris is not just a representation of Siri in Auster's work; she also represents one of his intertextual borrowings. In an interview, Siri Hustvedt has described how Iris is a character in her own book *Blindfold* (1994), and how Auster asked if her character could marry his in *Leviathan* (*Front Row*, 2003).

8 As Joseph S. Walker notes, the reabsorption of the Phantom's acts of resistance into commercial culture merely demonstrates 'the grinding wheels of popular consumption' (Walker, 2004: 342–3).

9 On Jameson, language and the fragmentary nature of Sachs's experiences, see also Fleck, 1998: 262–3.

10 Aaron takes the name *Leviathan* from the unfinished manuscript of Sachs's last novel. The term, once again, refers to Auster's concern with living numerously. Mark Osteen considers the parallels between Hobbes's and Auster's *Leviathan*, and he compares the state to an artificial man, 'a multitude unified in one person' (Osteen, 1994: 87).

11 This section of the novel was first published as a critical essay, 'Moonlight in the Brooklyn Museum', in *Art News* (Auster, 1987).

12 See also Weisenburger, 1995: 140–1.

13 On Auster's use of the traditional conventions of the quest form, see also Shilo, 2002a.

14 See, for example, an interview which accompanied the publication
    of *Oracle Night*. Here Auster insists of his literary method: 'I don't
    understand it either. See, so much of what I do is simply unconscious; I
    don't know where the ideas come from. I don't know how to explain the
    work I do' (O'Hagan, 2004: n.p.).
15 Auster's wife, Siri Hustvedt, draws on the same autobiographical material
    in her acclaimed third novel, *What I Loved* (2003). Here, Daniel is renamed
    Mark, respectively the son and stepson of Bill and Violet. Their friends in
    a New York artistic milieu (similar to Sachs's in *Leviathan*) are Leo and
    Erica. These friends support each other through a series of crises, while
    Bill's art and their various writings chart the emotions of their lives.

4

Out of town

The epigraph to Auster's 2002 novel, *The Book of Illusions*, reads:
'Man has not one and the same life. He has many lives, placed end to
end, and that is the cause of his misery' (Auster, 2002a: n.p.). The
quotation derives from François-René de Chateaubriand (1768–1848),
whose autobiography, *Mémoires d'outre-tombe* (*Memories from
Beyond the Grave*), is also the biography of his age. Chateaubriand's
tortuous life-history represents a significant key to understanding
Auster's novel, and also reflects back over the novels that immediately
precede it. By invoking Chateaubriand's sentiment, Auster suggests
to the reader that the characters narrated here live a number of lives
within the one life, and that we should be sensitive to the various phases
these lives encompass.

Auster said in 1987 that by writing 'The Book of Memory' in the
third person he had fulfilled Rimbaud's dictum of 'Je est un autre' ('I
am another'). At the same time, he suggested that this capacity to
become somebody else writing about himself revealed something
about the solitude of the writer. Being alone in his room, which is at
the same time inhabited by someone else ('un autre'), is 'the moment
when you are not alone anymore, when you start to feel your
connection with others' (Auster, 1997: 277). However, the notion of the
many lives in the one life adds a subtle new dimension to looking into
yourself and finding 'the world' (Auster, 1997: 315–16). While for
Auster the world inside him is a place to write from, the central
characters in *Illusions* find a number of selves out in the world, each
influenced by the material conditions of place. These characters
journey in search of a 'harmony' between their inner terrain and the
external terrain, constantly searching for an inner peace.

Auster's earlier novels, as the preceding chapters demonstrate, explore a particular phase in each of the central characters' lives. In *Moon Palace*, for example, Fogg describes how the story he has to tell marks the beginning of his life. The later novels considered in this chapter seek a broader view which acknowledges Uncle Victor's observation in *Moon Palace* that a man's life is a 'manuscript', incomplete until his death. These texts describe phases in the lives of the characters which accumulate to form a fuller appreciation of a life than Auster has represented in his earlier works. As a consequence, his temporal and geographical focus has expanded to encompass a greater range in a single text than before. For the characters in these novels, each phase of their lives is associated with a place and gives rise to an identity associated with and, to an extent, shaped by that place. The time to move on marks the end of that identity and the emergence of a new one.

An indication that the focus of Auster's work might expand to encompass a character's whole life – told, as it were, from beyond the grave at a point where it can be viewed as complete – can be found in the following quotation from an abandoned narrative frame for 'City of Glass' (then called *New York Spleen*). The unnamed narrator, in describing the mysterious Quinn, writes:

> No man is ever just one thing. To some, he will be one man, to others another, and to himself a third, or perhaps even many, all of these various men constantly appearing and receding, given the various situations in which he variously finds himself. Any number of human contradictions can exist in a single body. That has never presented a problem for the faithful observer of mankind. (Auster, undated c: n.p.)

Here, then, Auster is proposing the individual, and her or his sense of self, to be what Michel de Certeau would describe as 'a locus in which an incoherent (and often contradictory) plurality of . . . relational determinants interact' (de Certeau, 1984: xi). We can see that identity, for Auster and de Certeau, depends to a significant extent on the intersecting and competing currents of the social and physical environment, and is as a result multifaceted. Crucially for us here, Auster is the 'faithful observer of mankind', recording how different manifestations of self advance and recede according to the various circumstances of place in his novels. Mobility and movement inevitably mean the abandonment of New York City, for Auster a constant presence in his earlier novels, and the introduction of a multitude of geographical locations across Europe and the American continent.

The places beyond New York City which Auster's work visits, from his own experiences described in *The Invention of Solitude* through to the events described by the narrator of *Illusions*, embrace the capital cities of Western Europe (London, Paris, Amsterdam, Dublin), the cities and prairie-lands of America's mid-west (Chicago, Kansas), the cities and countryside of the north east (Boston, Baltimore, Vermont), and the western deserts of New Mexico. Each of the places has an effect on the sense of self experienced by the characters. This chapter will focus on the lives of characters who move around the north east of the United States, and then trace the journeys of those going west. By moving from place to place, we see how constructions of self shift in the later novels.

As earlier chapters show, Auster's characters rarely fare well outside their metropolitan and predominantly New York environment. The Narrator in 'The Locked Room' suffers a complete social and linguistic breakdown in Paris. Sachs's attempt to balance the scales of justice in *Leviathan* by going to Berkeley proves misjudged, and his lonely campaign around America's small towns ends in tragedy in Wisconsin. In *Moon Palace*, Fogg begins his life in Chicago with his Uncle Victor, but Victor's quest to realise his musical talent ends in a lonely and untimely death in Bois, Indiana. The unfortunate Fogg then ventures to Los Angeles, only to find that irresolution and uncertainty reign there too.

In this chapter, the spaces explored range from the mid-west and Chicago of *Mister Vertigo*, to the north-eastern states of America in *Timbuktu*. Rural Vermont figures as the scene of arbitrary violence and crime – a predominantly urban concern – in *The Book of Illusions*, in much the same way as it did for Sachs. The central character, Zimmer, then seeks solace in the deserts of New Mexico. First, though, we shall explore the fabular spaces of *The Music of Chance*, in which a mansion in rural Pennsylvania is the site of a bizarre and ritualistic poker game that robs the nomadic protagonists of their freedom.

There is a temptation to think that an extension of geographical scale, moving from the metropolitan to the regional or continental, might represent a further opening of the fist to which Auster alludes in describing his move from poetry to prose. Chapter I described how the fist 'opens' as his focus expands from the individual to the metropolitan. As we move from the metropolitan to the regional, can we then expect a new form of expression which can accommodate social relationships on this new scale? Quite simply, we do not get a further opening of the fist. The reason for this is that disconnection and emptiness are the defining experiences of these new places. Foreign and distant cities lack the extended social circles that characters such as Sachs need to feed their gregarious natures. Equally, the reality of non-metropolitan spaces is that they can be literally empty, and the opportunities for locating references for self-formation and the social relationships for maintaining coherence are few.

The experience of place in these texts is also necessarily partial. Here, place, unlike the density of New York, is an underdetermined quantity in relatively empty spaces. Unlike the novels considered in preceding chapters, these places in Europe, the mid-west and the north east are 'un-engaging', not because they might be complex and overwhelming like a city, but because they are empty, sterile or socially limiting.

The Auster novel that best exemplifies mobility is *The Music of Chance*. This book presents the different phases in the life of Jim Nashe as he passes from family man, to wanderer, to gambler, and then to the prisoner of unseen powers of control and oppression in a mysterious meadow. Here our concern will be with the effect of travelling across the United States in a car, while the period of enforced labour in the dystopic world of the meadow will be dealt with in Chapter 5. Auster told Sinda Gregory that the origins of his central character's desire to wander lie in the closing pages of *Moon Palace*:

> I realized that I wanted to get back inside that car, to give myself a chance to go on driving around America. So there was that very immediate and visceral impulse, which is how *The Music of Chance* begins – with Nashe sitting behind the wheel of a car. (Auster, 1997: 325)

So Nashe (figuratively) gets back into Fogg's car and sets off across the continent on his own quest for identity. Like Fogg, Nashe has been stripped of his family; his wife has left him and his daughter has gone to live with his sister in Minnesota (Auster, 1992b: 2).[1] However, unlike Fogg's, Nashe's fate is signposted by Auster with an obscure literary hint. In his introduction to *The Random House Book of Twentieth Century French Poetry* (1982),[2] Auster mentions Thomas Nashe, the author of the 1594 prose narrative *The Unfortunate Traveler*, 'generally considered to be the first novel written in the English language' (Auster, 1997: 200–1). Nashe's literary antecedence clearly marks him out as a character with an uncertain future.

Supported by an unexpected inheritance of nearly two hundred thousand dollars from a father he has never known, the unfortunate traveller sets off around the United States guided by instinct and chance. In this way, Auster again examines two of his favourite themes: the role of contingency, and the inheritance that he received on the death of his own father.[3] Auster weaves these together to explore the nature of freedom through Nashe's unfettered ability to go anywhere, and his subsequent incarceration in Pennsylvania.[4]

Chance intervenes in Nashe's adventure early, and marks the transition from one life to another – from Boston fireman and family man to wanderer. Instead of returning to Massachusetts after visiting his daughter, Nashe

> soon found himself traveling in the opposite direction. That was because he missed the ramp to the freeway – a common enough mistake – but instead of driving the extra twenty miles that would have put him back on course, he impulsively went up the next ramp. . . . [I]n the brief time that elapsed between the two ramps, Nashe understood that there was no difference, that both ramps were finally the same. . . . It was a dizzying prospect – to imagine all that freedom, to understand how little it mattered what choice he made. He could go anywhere he wanted.
> (Auster, 1992b: 6)

Everything that follows is the result of this single chance event, and it releases Nashe from the fixity of his previous life in Boston.

Chance intervenes again a year later. With Nashe's financial resources rapidly disappearing (like the pages in Quinn's notebook), he is driving along a back road when he encounters the beaten and penniless Jack Pozzi, whose friends (ironically?) call him 'Jackpot' (Auster, 1992b: 23). As the narrative progresses, the reader can't help but think that Pozzi neither has friends, nor enough luck to deserve his sobriquet. As a consequence of their intersection, Nashe enters a new phase as a gambler and bankroller. He comes to understand meeting Pozzi as a completely arbitrary happening, 'one of those random, accidental encounters that seem to materialize out of thin air' (Auster, 1992b: 1).

The title encapsulates the operation of chance in this novel. It also captures the way coincidence and contingency provide the accompanying 'music of chance' to the lives of Auster's characters. Here, specifically, the phrase refers to François Couperin's 'Les Barricades mistérieuses', which Nashe plays in the novel.[5] In a passage subsequently abandoned, Auster describes the piece of music as 'a strange, paradoxical little work . . . its meaning eluded him. It was as though the piece represented everything all at once . . . a resolution that never came' (Auster, undated h: 23). This description could easily be applied to this novel, as well as to much of Auster's other work. For Auster, the mysterious barricades refer to the transitions in the composition: its pauses, suspensions and repetitions. 'The music started and stopped', he writes, 'then started again, then stopped again, and yet through it all the piece continued to advance, pushing on toward a resolution that never came' (Auster, 1992b: 181). These crescendos and lulls, without satisfactory musical closure, display the same unresolved harmonies as Auster's fiction, and offer yet another literary-artistic clue to Nashe's fate.

The early part of the novel traces a geography of the country's backwoods. As a principle Nashe avoids cities, sticking instead to the back roads of upstate New York, New England, the prairies of the midwest and the western deserts – before heading south for the winter (Auster, 1992b: 12). In the car he becomes both totally free and totally solitary, barely speaking to another person, 'except for the odd sentence . . . when buying gas or ordering food' (Auster, 1992b: 7).

Similarly, in *America*, Jean Baudrillard recognises the power of the car and speed, and the effects of driving large distances alone. 'Speed creates pure objects', he writes. 'It is itself a pure object, since it cancels out the ground and territorial reference-points. . . . Speed is the triumph of effect over cause' (Baudrillard, 1988: 6). 'Driving', he goes on, 'is a spectacular form of amnesia' (Baudrillard, 1988: 9). For Nashe, the solitude he experiences in his car promotes a solipsism that, combined with speed, makes him feel as if he is 'a fixed point in a whirl of changes, a body poised in utter stillness as the world rushed through him and disappeared' (Auster, 1992b: 11–12). As a result of this motion and solitude he becomes lost in the vast spaces of America, reduced to a point of fixity in a landscape which rapidly moves past him, rather than the other way around. In time, the car becomes 'a sanctum of invulnerability, a refuge' in which he felt 'that he was coming loose from his body, that once he put his foot down on the gas and started driving, the music would carry him into a realm of weightlessness' (Auster, 1992b: 12). The effect on Nashe of his speed and his solitude is to strip him of the geographic and social points of reference which might have given his life meaning and provided the basis for selfhood. Instead, the freedom he has to follow his instincts, and to give himself up entirely to chance, has the effect of emptying out his identity, leaving a void to be filled and creating a desire for fixity and certainty.

Travel and mobility act to both release Auster's characters from their corporeal reality, and to convey them from one phase of their lives to another – from one sense of self to the next. However, we should remember Sachs, a speck racing across America, and measure Auster's characters in terms of their disconnection or dis-harmony when anticipating what fate they hurtle towards.

European cities, in both Auster's early autobiographical writings and his fiction, promote disorientation and confusion (as previously discussed). This is because they are not New York. In 'The Locked Room', the Narrator compares Paris to New York:

> I felt as though I had been turned upside-down. This was an old-world city, and it had nothing to do with New York – with its slow skies and chaotic streets, its bland clouds and aggressive buildings. I had been displaced, and it made me suddenly unsure of myself. I felt my grip loosening. (Auster, 1988: 287)

This Old-World chaos is to be found too in Amsterdam. When he visited the Anne Frank House and the Van Gogh Museum, Auster spent three days wandering around the city. In *The Invention of Solitude*, he describes how disorientation forced his third-person self further and further inwards:

> Cut off from everything that was familiar to him, unable to discover even a single point of reference, he saw that his steps, by taking him nowhere, were taking him nowhere but into himself. He was wondering inside himself, and he was lost. (Auster, 1982: 86–7)

A. is lost because Amsterdam does not follow the rational street pattern of New York's grid. Although Amsterdam is a small city in comparison to New York, it is easy to get lost because 'you cannot simply "follow" a street as you can in other cities' (Auster, 1982: 86). Because his urban expectations have been shaped by the grid system of American cities, A. possesses no 'cognitive map' to navigate a city which is based on a circular pattern with intersecting roads, canals and bridges, and as a result he often finds that he has been within feet of his destination before turning away in the wrong direction. Eventually he feels 'that the city had been designed as a model of the underworld, based on some classical representation of the place. . . . And if Amsterdam was hell, . . . then he realized there was some point to him being lost' (Auster, 1982: 86).

The 'point' is, of course, that these events in Old-World European cities are a part of the self-formation process for A. and the Narrator.

They are unable to establish the geographical and social coordinates to begin a coherent Parisian or Dutch episode in their lives, so they leave, heading back to New York and the familiar spaces and networks upon which they can potentially build a coherent sense of self. However, as we shall see, this sort of confusion is not restricted to irrational European cities, but is as much a result of straying from New York as it is the failure of a perceptual model.

The mid-west

Auster's sixth novel, *Mr. Vertigo*, leaves New York behind to explore both the urban and the rural mid-west, and at the same time to explore the many selves that eventually form the life of Walter Clairborne Rawley. The novel describes the five major and discernible stages of his life, and plots each onto a map of the urban centres of St Louis, Chicago and Wichita, as well as the plains of Kansas and the backwoods towns of the mid-west.

The various incarnations are not given equal weight by Auster. Walt's early years occupy more than two-thirds of the book, which chronicles his childhood, sexual awakening (which marks the emergence of his ability to levitate) and his maturity into manhood. But by pursuing a life to its conclusion – however briefly – Auster is bringing the manuscript to a close and ensuring that it is complete. This frame, looking back on and recording events from the end of a life, gives the narrative a particular quality of authenticity. Also, Walt's first-person narrative recalls his life as a series of scenes, and his dialogue is reminiscent of a gangster B-movie (for example, 'I was a boogie-toed prankster, a midget scatman with a quick tongue and a hundred angles' (Auster, 1995a: 14)). These stylistic aspects of the novel prefigure Walt's desire to turn his fame as a levitator into a movie career in Hollywood, his slide into Chicago's criminal gangs at the end of prohibition, and Auster's own film projects that were taking shape around this time.

The novel's themes encompass selfhood, family, the idea of a record of a life and illusion, told against the indistinct background of central twentieth-century events: the Wall Street Crash, the Depression and the Second World War. The element of illusion is explored through Walt's ability to levitate. Family is explored through the father–son relationship that develops between Walt and the master, and the experience of love and support from the small group of misfits Walt encounters during his initiation as a levitator.

Walt's first incarnation is as a nine-year-old, begging for change on the streets of St Louis in the late 1920s. As an orphan he has no family other than Aunt Peg and the evil Uncle Slim. Master Yehudi takes Walt away from this, promising to teach him to fly by the time he is twelve (Auster, 1995a: 3). The master takes Walt on a journey to begin the next phase of his life, as a disciple and pupil. They travel by train to Kansas (the home of Dorothy in *The Wizard of Oz*) and on to the claustrophobic city of Wichita, 'a town built so low to the ground that your elbow knocked against the sky' (Auster, 1995a: 28). From there they travel to nearby Cibola and the master's farm. The property consists of 'thirty-seven acres of dirt, a two-story farmhouse, a chicken coop, a pigpen and a barn'. This is no place for 'a city boy . . . with jazz in his blood, a street kid with his eye on the main chance', used to 'the hurly-burly of the crowds, the screech of trolley cars and the throb of neon' (Auster, 1995a: 14). The comparison between the two could not be more marked. '[A] flatter, more desolate place you've never seen in your life', the master tells Walt, and there is 'nothing to tell you where you are. No mountains, no trees, no bumps in the road' (Auster, 1995a: 10). Thus Auster's ever-present theme of locating oneself in the world finds its expression in a geography that is literally without features or landmarks. Location is then further problematised by Auster's fictionalising of certain places. Walt notes the association of Kansas with the mythical Oz, and compares Cibola to it. As a result, the farm has an unreal or dreamlike quality, reinforced by the tricks of weather and geography that hamper Walt's early attempts to escape.

The farm is the scene of Walt's thirty-three-step 'initiation' (Auster, 1995a: 38). These tests include being buried alive, flogged, thrown from a horse, lashed to a barn roof, swarmed by insects, struck by lightning, with each test 'more terrible than the one before it' (Auster, 1995a: 41–2). Walt's toughest test is to cut a joint from his little finger, physically losing a part of himself (Auster, 1995a: 42). Walt is driven into himself to look for points of reference there, and forced to examine his most deeply buried inner self. To fly, he must ultimately disconnect his interior self from his body and (literally) let it float free. Part of this process is Walt's severance from his worldly or corporeal past, and the disembodied pinky joint is symbolic of this. Auster relates the missing digit to Walt's St Louis boyhood, which by now has become mere words that 'summoned forth no pictures, took [him] on no journeys' (Auster, 1995a: 46–7). Walt's fabular Cibola self is taking over from his previous real and grounded St Louis one. Eventually he is able to approach 'places of such inwardness that I no longer knew who I was' (Auster, 1995a: 49). These events are voyages of discovery – self-discovery – and like Marco Stanley Fogg, Auster gives Walt the name of a great explorer, the 'adventurer and hero' Sir Walter Ralegh (Auster, 1995a: 43). The magical quality of Walt's existence is further emphasised by his middle name, which can be read as Cl / airborne to reinforce the ungrounded episode in his story.

During this time, the other inhabitants of the house, along with Walt and Master Yehudi, are forming themselves into an unconventional family – the family that Walt has never known. Along with the father–son relationship, Walt finds a brother in a crippled black boy, Aesop, and a mother in an elderly Native American woman, Mother Sioux. These characters, particularly Aesop, reinforce the dreamlike quality of Cibola, and emphasise the fabular quality with which Auster invests these novels. *Mr. Vertigo* adopts what Dennis Barone calls a 'sufficient realism' that is supported by the narrative frame containing Walt's story (Barone, 1995: 6). Here fable allows Auster to investigate places that do not appear on maps, but in myths, dreams and the imagination, particularly in childhood or in association with children's stories.

Walt's dreams and imagination are a way of escaping the harsh realities of a childhood spent on the streets. As an escape from the rigours of the master's training Walt retreats into the experience of family he has never had. The 'family' at Cibola is unconventionally constituted from the margins of American society – 'a Jew, a black man, and an Indian', as Aesop points out to Walt (Auster, 1995a: 22). In Walt, the household gains a representative of the white urban underclass. Aesop lends moral support during Walt's mental battles with the master and they form a strong fraternal bond. In a landscape without points of reference, Aesop provides coordinates to Walt's emerging sense of self. 'He marked me in ways that altered who I was', Walt records, 'that changed the course and substance of my life. . . . Aesop became my comrade, my anchor in a sea of undifferentiated sky' (Auster, 1995a: 36–7). Mother Sioux plays a similar role in supporting Walt through his torments. From her he receives the love of a mother which he retains as only a distant memory. It is she who gives him his first kiss since his mother's death, leaving a 'warm and welcoming glow' (Auster, 1995a: 33). During his initiation Aesop and Mother Sioux stick with Walt like 'flesh and blood', making him 'the darling of their hearts' (Auster, 1995a: 43).

Despite the torments inflicted upon Walt by the master, the relationship between the two develops into a strong paternal bond, frequently a principal force in Auster's work. *The Invention of Solitude*, for example, includes a long meditation on the relationship between Auster and his son Daniel, in which he recalls lying in the dark telling his son Collodi's story of Pinocchio. Pinocchio is 'made' from wood by his father, Gepetto, emerging from the magical block in the same way that he also emerges from the author's pen. Auster connects the practice of storytelling to his son's developing imagination and personality (Auster, 1982: 154, 162–5). In *Mr. Vertigo*, Auster again explores the extent to which the son is influenced by the father-figure's presence, and how the stories the child is told will help to shape his adult imagination. When Walt becomes dangerously ill, the master comes to understand that he needs Walt as more than just a spectacle; he needs him on an emotional level too. The master sits stroking Walt's hand and sobbing, unconsciously adopting the pose of the concerned father at his son's bedside (Auster, 1995a: 34). Two parallel concerns are explored here. On the one hand, there is the bond between fathers and sons. On the other, there is the creative process of creating or authoring a character.

The strength of the paternal bond is exemplified by the events leading up to Walt's first levitation. The master disappears, and Walt learns that 'everything I was flowed directly from him. He had made me in his own image' (Auster, 1995a: 53). Like Pinocchio, Walt has been fashioned or 'authored' by the master. When Walt thinks he has been abandoned by his creator he experiences a fit of panic, rage and grief. His emotional response is so extreme that he enters a state of disconnection able to separate his inner self from his physical one, and he rises from the ground. 'I was weightless inside my own body', Walt writes, 'floating on a placid wave of nothingness, utterly detached and indifferent to the world around me' (Auster, 1995a: 58). As he describes this experience, 'my soul began to rush out of my body and I was no longer conscious of who I was' (Auster, 1995a: 227). The change to Walt's sense of self is so profound that he likens it to waking up with a new face (Auster, 1995a: 62). In fact, Auster is relating Walt's newfound powers of levitation to his sexual awakening. This feeling is reinforced by the symbolic presence of Mrs Witherspoon, the master's lover and a woman who appears at every turn of Walt's life. She features in this episode as an apparition charged with erotic imagery. She is standing in the doorway, 'wearing a crimson overcoat and a black fur

hat, . . . and her cheeks were still flush from the winter cold' (Auster,
1995a: 60). This figurative description of Mrs Witherspoon as female
genitalia invests her with a sexual potential that marks Walt's
awakening and recurs from time to time throughout his lives.
Walt soon hones his levitation skills, while Aesop and the master
explore colleges in the east. This period in the lives of the characters
marks a point of transition in the novel. For Walt this is 'the end of an
era, and we were all looking ahead to the future now, anticipating the
new lives that waited for us beyond the boundaries of the farm' (Auster,
1995a: 81). Aesop is to depart for Yale, and Walt and the master are to
embark on a tour of small towns promoting the levitation act. But
tragedy intervenes when the local Ku Klux Klan burn down the farm
and lynch Mother Sioux and Aesop (Auster, 1995a: 90). Walt is robbed
of his surrogate mother and brother. Once again, one of Auster's
central characters suffers the loss of the emotional connections from
which they are constructing their identity, and in relation to which they
are locating themselves in the world. The tragedy marks a time to move
on, and a new identity.
Walt's new incarnation is as 'Walt the Wonder Boy', levitator. The
animosity of the local population in Cibola drives the master and Walt
away and they embark on the next phase of their lives, as travelling
entertainers. Starting at the Pawnee county show in Larned, Kansas
(Auster, 1995a: 110), the pair begin a tour of the southern state's county
fairs. '[M]oving around from one backwater to another', they cover
Oklahoma, 'Texas, Arkansas, Louisiana' (Auster, 1995a: 122). Eventually the act becomes bigtime, moving into the theatres of the eastern
cities. In the theatre the act requires a different dimension to the
outdoor shows of the county fairs. The master dubs Walt an 'aerial
artist' (Auster, 1995a: 162). To achieve a sense of narrative progression
the act requires '[s]tructure, rhythm, and surprise' (Auster, 1995a: 165),
which Walt injects with the visual and corporeal language of slapstick.
Walt's career as 'Walt the Wonder Boy' comes to an end in the
northern city of Scranton, Pennsylvania, with the onset of puberty and
what the master explains as 'bodily changes that turn a boy into a man'
(Auster, 1995a: 190). These changes also cause debilitating headaches
whenever Walt leaves the ground, and thus inaugurate the next phase
of his life. He and the master attempt to drive to Los Angeles, where
Walt is to use his slapstick skills to break into the movies. But they are
robbed on a lonely and empty highway, and the master is killed, finally
depriving Walt of the last vestige of his Cibola family.

This next, lonely phase of Walter's life, at the age of fourteen, turns him back into a vagrant, and the beggar he 'was born to be' (Auster, 1995a: 215). He hunts down his Uncle Slim, who carried out the holdup. Once Slim is dead, Walt takes his place in the Chicago underworld and opens his ironically named nightclub, Mr. Vertigo's (Auster, 1995a: 239–41). When he is forced out of Chicago he begins a phase in his life as an ordinary guy. He has an undistinguished war, before taking a job in construction, helping to form the postwar suburban landscape of 'ranch houses and tidy lawns' (Auster, 1995a: 264). Finally, he meets and marries Molly, who, in an echo of Auster's earlier novels, puts him back together again (Auster, 1995a: 265).

Molly dies young, and Walt finds his way back to Wichita. The city is much changed as a result of the same forces of suburbanisation that he served earlier in his life. Discovering that Mrs Witherspoon is still alive, Walt joins her in business and, despite her great age, becomes her lover. After her death, and with his own mortality in the forefront of his mind, Walt decides to write the record of his life for posthumous publication, like Chateaubriand.

In closing, Walt writes of the secret of levitation. It reads like an instruction manual on how to perform the transition from one self to another, reflecting how he has moved around the country, in each place leaving his old self behind and inventing a new one. Levitation and transformation can be achieved, he says, by learning 'to stop being yourself. . . . [y]ou . . . let yourself evaporate' (Auster, 1995a: 278). Like Nashe, through travel and the experience of disconnection from the physical world, Walt fully understands the process that can cleave the self loose from the physical body, so that it enters a 'realm of weightlessness'.

Walt's 'lives', then, oscillate between the city and the country, from notoriety to anonymity, and from contentment to tragedy. The spaces and environments which have been the crucible for his ascendancies and reversals help to shape both a sense of self for Walt, and the outcomes of each narrative episode. Where else, for example, could Walt be a gangster but in 1930s Chicago? However, Auster adopts more subtlety in evoking the wide-open and undifferentiated spaces of the mid-west. Kansas inspires Walt into a move, not to the west, as is traditional in the American novel (in Auster too, as in *Moon Palace*), but upwards, into a dreamlike realm, disconnected from the realities and certainties of firm ground.

Beyond the fabular quality of this novel, Auster adopts the form of the fragment to layer a number of stories into the one narrative, and so present a number of lives within the one life. The fragment as a form of literary practice has interested Auster since he translated Mallarmé's *A Tomb for Anatole*.[6] *Mr. Vertigo*, in the manner of its sudden transitions brought about by catastrophic events, suggests a lack of continuity between the selves which constitute Walt's life and the stories composing his narrative. Auster's next novel, *Timbuktu*, suggests that an underlying metaphysical or 'original' harmonious selfhood is unattainable or is in fact an illusion. In the later *The Book of Illusions*, Auster treats this same predicament not as a loss, but as a necessarily unresolved or unharmonious part of identity – where identity is simultaneously maintained and deferred through the artifices of acting and naming.

The north east

When the master and Walt are at the height of their fame, and their relationship is at its closest, they take a holiday on Cape Cod. Here they pose as a father and son, Tim Buck and Tim Buck the Second, or Tim Buck One and Tim Buck Two (Auster, 1995a: 160). Timbuktu functions here, and in Auster's 1999 novel of that name, as a place of mythical and dreamlike happiness, where two people who find their identities defined by the presence of the other can achieve equilibrium and contentment.

Timbuktu is a novel haunted by mythical and magical places that inhabit the imaginations of the two central characters. The beatific tramp, Willie G. Christmas (a.k.a. William Guerevitch), and his scruffy mongrel, Mr Bones, pursue their Nirvanas through myth, dream, history and literature. Mr Bones has four lives in the course of the novel. At first he finds happiness as Willie's disciple on the road. After Willie's death, he seeks contentment first as the canine friend of a lonely Chinese-American boy in Baltimore, then in the suburban tracts of Virginia, in an American nuclear family, which, as one critic points out, Auster shows to be 'wanting' (Brooker, 2002: 130). Having found suburban life to be a compromise between comfort and monotony, he sets off again to find Willy in Timbuktu. Both master and dog direct their search for fulfilment towards 'other' spaces, beyond the limits of the material and knowable world.

Willie and Mr Bones embark on a road trip from New York to Baltimore to secure the future of Willie's manuscripts with Mrs Swanson, his old high-school teacher (Auster, 1999: 9). Their life together ends with Willie's death outside Edgar Allan Poe's house in Baltimore, which Willie christens Poe-land in an echo of both his family's origins in Eastern Europe, and his literary debt to Poe (Auster, 1999: 46–7). Willie is the archetype of a tramp; he is on the margins of society, alone in the world with only his dog, racked by mental illness and alcoholism, but harbouring a literary talent. He is a 'troubled soul' (Auster, 1999: 9), the death of whose father when he is twelve marks him 'as a tragic figure, disqualified . . . from the rat race of vain hopes and sentimental illusions, bestowed . . . [with] an aura of legitimate suffering' (Auster, 1999: 14–15). By the time he arrives as freshman at Columbia, Willie is a 'malcontent, . . . rebel, . . . outlaw poet prowling the gutters of a ruined world' (Auster, 1999: 16). Willie's descent into vagrancy is prompted and accelerated first by drugs, then by mental illness, alcoholism and eventually his mother's death.

As with many elements of Auster's novels, there is an auto-biographical basis for Willie. In *Moon Palace* Fogg writes of how his method is drawn from Montaigne, adopting personal experience as a scaffolding for writing, and so constructing a 'subterranean version' of his own life (Auster, 1992a: 233). Indeed, it is possible to delineate episodes in the autobiographical texts (*Solitude* and *Hand to Mouth*) which also occur in the lives of characters. By being first a traveller, then a struggling and penniless poet, receiving an unforeseen inheritance, remarrying and finally achieving a successful literary career, Auster himself has a number of 'subterranean selves' within the one. Willie is a prime example of the autobiographical emerging in the fictional. He is based on the 'the legendary, forgotten novelist, H. L. Humes', who became an unwelcome house-guest in Auster's senior year at Columbia (Auster, 1998a: 38). Humes was a founding member of the *Paris Review* and played chess with Tristan Tzara (Auster, 1998a: 44).[7] Like Willie, Humes was a 'logomaniac' (Auster, 1999: 6) and 'a living example of failed promise and blighted literary fortune' (Auster, 1998a: 37). And like the Jimmy Rose character from 'Ghosts', Humes 'had endured a long run of reversals and miseries' – 'a ruined marriage, several stays in mental hospitals' – all of which leave him unable to write (Auster, 1998a: 38–9).

Mr Bones is prepared for Willie's death with stories of the afterlife, when he will enter a land called Timbuktu. Auster relates how

Mr Bones has come to understand Timbuktu through Willie's ramblings:

> That was where people went after they died. Once your soul had been separated from your body, your body was buried in the ground and your soul lit out for the next world. Willy had been harping on this subject for the past several weeks, and by now there was no doubt in the dog's mind that the next world was a real place. It was called Timbuktu. (Auster, 1999: 48)

Timbuktu is not the 'real' desert city in Mali, but the place designated by popular use as so distant and exotic as to be unimaginable. Willie tells Mr Bones that it is 'an oasis of spirits', begining '[w]here the map of this world ends' (Auster, 1999: 49). The other-worldly quality of Timbuktu is emphasised after Willie's death by his appearance in dreams. Willie appears to Mr Bones to issue warnings, to encourage him with stories of Timbuktu and to admonish him for selling out to the materialist comforts of the suburbs. *Timbuktu*, through the illusion of dreams, demonstrates the power of imagination in the pursuit of happiness, love and stability. The theme of unreal places as a refuge from the turmoil of everyday life occurs in previous novels, but as we shall see in Chapter 5, this becomes a dominant idea in later works.

Once Willy is dead, Mr Bones has to fend for himself. He has been with Willie since a puppy and feels that the world is 'saturated with Willie's presence' (Auster, 1999: 4). A world without Willie would be one of 'ontological terror'; it is possible even 'that the world itself would cease to exist' (Auster, 1999: 4). Of course, Mr Bones's worst fears are not realised, and the world goes on. However, he is unable to bring the right ontological tools to bear on his environment, and constantly finds himself under attack. In the city he is kicked and threatened by a gang of boys, and in the country he is considered a pest and shot at. Now, alone without Willie, Mr Bones is turning into a homeless and friendless dog travelling 'around in circles, lost in the limbo between one nowhere and the next' (Auster, 1999: 92). Like Willie, Mr Bones becomes a vagrant as his 'cognitive map' proves not to match up to the reality of his experience.

Mr Bones is rescued from the violent attentions of the boys by one of their classmates, Henry Chow. Henry, like Willie and his dog, is at the margins of his society. As a Chinese-American he is not accepted by his (white) classmates, and as the only child of hard-working immigrant parents, he is lonely. The relationship he forms with Mr Bones is symbiotic. 'Thus begun an exemplary friendship between dog and boy', Auster writes:

Each wound up giving to the other something he had never had before. For Mr Bones, Henry proved that love was not a quantifiable substance. ... For Henry, ... whose parents ... had steadfastly refused to allow a pet in the apartment, Mr Bones was the answer to his prayers. (Auster, 1999: 103)

Mr Bones connects to the wider world, beyond himself, through this fraternal bond, rather than the paternal relationship between master and dog that preceded it. When their friendship is broken up by Mr Chow, Mr Bones seeks sanctuary from the perils of metropolitan Baltimore in rural Virginia. But here too he faces dangers. In a dream he tells Willy how he is nearly shot and run over taking a shortcut through a field (Auster, 1999: 121). The countryside, it seems, is as dangerous as the city.

Finally Mr Bones stumbles upon a vision of the happy American family embedded in an idealised landscape. He wanders into a place of 'lawn mowers, sprinklers and birds', where 'on an invisible highway ... a dull bee-swarm of traffic pulsed under the suburban landscape' (Auster, 1999: 124). This is the environment that Walt helped to form. The postwar spread of suburbia pushed city limits further and further from the old urban population centres, creating residential nodes to serve the major metropoli, which themselves in time became significant cityscapes. Edward Soja calls these emerging population nodes 'Edge Cities', or 'Exopolis' (Soja, 1996: 238). He describes these new centres and the mode of living they promote:

Ex-centrically perched beyond the vortex of the old agglomerative nodes, the Exopolis spins new whorls of its own, turning the city inside-out and outside-in at the same time, unravelling in its paths the memories of more familiar urban fabrics, even where such older fabrics never existed in the first place. (Soja, 1996: 239)

David Harvey identifies a 'recursive and serial monotony' associated with urban growth of this kind (Harvey, 1990: 295), that promotes a repeatable aesthetic though the creation of reproducible spaces. Auster recognises this same monotony and represents a landscape of shopping malls and identical housing developments, connected to each other and the distant metropolitan hub by a network of super-highways. In *Timbuktu* this suburban landscape is reimagined as a series of ordered economic and gender power relationships, played out through the conventional suburban family. However, the capacity of the individual to experience extended and stimulating networks of people becomes severely limited when existence is embedded in the serial monotony of recursive spaces strung out along super-highways. The inevitable result is disconnection and loneliness.

Auster describes this suburbia as 'the America of two-car garages, home-improvement loans, and neo-Renaissance shopping malls' (Auster, 1999: 162). Here, in contrast to Mr Bones's time on the road with Willie, time does not flow 'without interruption' (Auster, 1999: 164). Instead, he finds that the calendar is broken down into the structures of work and rest, national holidays and so forth. The structured nature of the physical and temporal environment of the suburbs is emphasised by the promise of a trip to Disney World (Auster, 1999: 165–6). Here time is dictated by the routine of the park entertainment. Culture is presented in a palimpsest of pastiche where partial representations of American history are simultaneously available in a perpetual and repeated present, which Jameson considers to be endemic to contemporary American culture (Jameson, 1991: 20, 26–7). In *Timbuktu*, suburbia is presented as the domestic expression of a cultural process encapsulated by Disney, and translated to the contemporary landscape as the 'serial monotony' of the mall, the ranch house and the lawn. Despite the material benefits Mr Bones experiences, he soon sees the rigid structures of this life as carceral and oppressive.

Mr Bones emerges from the Virginia woods onto the manicured lawn of the Jones family. The two perfect children persuade their beautiful mother to keep the dog, and once the almost impossibly masculine father (an airline pilot) gives his assent, Mr Bones has a new home and has become a new dog (with, of course, a new and diminutive name: Sparky). This arrangement appears to be perfect; he is cleaned and clipped, well fed and has his own house in the garden. Mr Bones is 'no longer a bum, no longer an embarrassment', but a 'dandified, . . . bourgeois dog-about-town' (Auster, 1999: 146). However, Auster knowingly critiques this presentation of the suburban myth, and undermines its reality with the imagery of Disney when a deer (Bambi?) walks across the Jones's perfectly manicured garden (Auster, 1999: 154). The doghouse and a trip to the vet begin to expose the price to be paid for the comforts of Mr Bones's new domestic arrangement, and to reveal a destructive undercurrent in suburban family life.

The spatial formations of suburbia express the economic and social relations that support the conventional view of family life. Mr Bones finds himself trapped by a symbolic expression of how power is deployed in an environment like this. During the day Mr Bones is restrained by a mechanical lead that allows him a degree of movement, but only as far as the lead will stretch:

> They had turned him into a prisoner. They had chained him to this infernal bouncing wire, this metallic torture device . . . to remind him that he was no longer free, that he had sold his birthright for a mess of porridge and an ugly, ready-made house. (Auster, 1999: 144)

The father, Richard, imposes these outward signs of control on Mr Bones. He also instigates a less obvious expression of the unnatural sterility of suburbia by insisting on the dog being neutered. Mr Bones remains unaware that a constituent part of his physical and psychological self has been removed. Auster thus echoes the insidious actions of power, control and homogenisation in suburbia, which are able to manipulate and co-opt the subject without their knowledge. Richard embodies the anti-imaginative sterility of the suburban environment, which he enforces on his family and the dog. Richard's will oppresses the hopes and wishes of his beautiful but miserable and lonely wife, Polly. Below the surface of the 'perfect' family seethes resentment and 'the plots and counterplots of dying love' (Auster, 1999: 162). Through Mr Bones's experiences, Auster critiques the newly centred and homogenising 'post-suburbia'. The geographical dispersal of formerly urban populations into these domestic prisons makes community (reduced to the conformity of domestic architecture and lawn care) an unlikely process, and forces Polly to rely on the dog as her friend and her distant sister as her only human confidante.

The chance to escape from the artifice and contestations of the Joneses' life presents itself when Mr Bones is sent to a boarding kennels while the family vacations in Florida. Once free, he finds his 'salvation' in the same 'dazzling' six-lane highway that 'pulsed' across the landscape (Auster, 1999: 184–5). Mr Bones employs this driving force and symbol of suburbanisation to join his master in Timbuktu.

Ultimately, the many lives of Mr Bones demonstrate the provisional nature of stability and selfhood in Auster's later work. With Willie he discovers that disappointment and failure can lead to premature death, and with this loss comes disconnection and loneliness. Friendship proves to be no more robust with Henry Chow. Mr Bones also finds the family to be undermined by the illusory nature of the suburban dream. In this story, the 'places' that harbour the potential for true companionship for Mr Bones are restricted to the illusory and imagined worlds of Poe-land and Timbuktu. The fabular rendering of Mr Bones's story can only propose a better place that is literally out of this world.

The west

The west functions in Auster's work as just the sort of site of revelation and discovery you would expect in the quest form that the novels at times adopt. However, the westward journeys of Effing, Fogg and Sachs reveal only further layers of disconnection, loneliness, confusion and irresolution.

The Book of Illusions also traces the westward journey of Professor David Zimmer in pursuit of the 1920s silent film actor Hector Mann, who himself embarked upon an epic journey of self-discovery in the western United States. Auster presents the constant movement of these two men, and the construction of a strange family in the desert of New Mexico, as attempts to achieve some kind of inner peace. Illusions also meditates on the relative values inherent in the practices of the film maker and the writer. The novel here stands as a testament to the power of the word in comparison with that of moving images. This novel was published after two highly acclaimed films, Smoke and Blue in the Face (1995), and Auster's declaration of belief in the communal power of the film-making process (see Chapter 6). However, Auster's subsequent venture into film, Lulu on the Bridge (1998), has been a critical disaster and remains virtually unseen.[8] Consequently, the representation of film making in Illusions, as potentially ephemeral, critiques the capacity of film to continue to speak to a film-going public, while the novel stands as a testament to both the power of storytelling and the primacy of the form.[9]

The Book of Illusions returns to the themes of many lives contained in the one, and how the 'manuscript' of that life is brought to completion by death. Like Mr. Vertigo (and Timbuktu to a degree), Illusions considers how the story of a life can be told, and adopts the model of a posthumous address to reinforce the completion of the narrative cycle. This novel also returns to the persistent insecurities of being singular in a plural world. The torment and loneliness of singularity is explored through bereavement and an unconventionally composed family, this time hidden away in the New Mexico desert, which again proves to be fragile and provisional. Auster also examines, as he did through the many lives of Walt Rawley, how movement from place to place reconstitutes the sense of self, and how different environments, constituted through different historical and social processes, influence those identities.

Early on, Auster insisted that '[a]ll of my work is of a piece' (Auster, 1997: 275). Professor David Zimmer, the central character and first-person narrator of *The Book of Illusions*, reinforces the notion of continuity in the Auster canon, as he is Fogg's friend from *Moon Palace* and the addressee of the narrative of *In The Country of Last Things*. Moreover, the name Zimmer is closely associated with the solitude of the writer's room in Auster's early writing. Zimmer's experiences in this novel serve to explore the implications of not just leaving the room, but leaving the city and the country, and entering a wholly alien environment. In terms of theme also, Hector is the slapstick star Walt never became in *Mr Vertigo*. This is not to suggest that Auster's work rehearses the same concerns over and over. Rather, his fiction and films explore recurrent themes in different and testing environments and conditions for the characters. Thus, each of Auster's works reimagines familiar narrative tropes, setting these in motion in new and extreme – often fantastical – scenarios.

The concept of the many lives, or stories, within the one is explored through the narratives of Zimmer and Hector Mann, a film actor from the slapstick heyday of silent film who mysteriously disappeared in 1929. Through their narratives, interwoven into a delicate balance of differentiated presents, many similarities emerge. Both men suffer tragedy and loss and both contemplate suicide as a result, before finding companionship and some contentment.

The episodes of Zimmer's life recorded here encompass life as an academic committed to the study of literature and the word, the despair he experiences at the loss of his family, his spell as a translator, and his conversion to the power of the image as he writes a treatise on Hector's films as a way of dealing with his sorrow. Hector's life, like Walt's, oscillates between fame and anonymity, notoriety and obscurity. His lives encompass his origins as Chaim Mandelbaum, a Dutch-Jewish refugee, his film career in Hollywood as Hector Mann, his travels around America as an itinerant worker under the pseudonym Herman Loesser, and his final incarnation as Hector Spelling in New Mexico. But it is as Hector – significantly employing the artifices of acting – that he achieves his most secure and persistent self. At the very end of

Hector's life, he and Zimmer meet, allowing their narratives to overlap and creating the conditions for their stories to be told.

Until his wife and two young sons are killed in an air disaster, Zimmer enjoys a happy and complete family and professional life in Vermont (Auster, 2002a: 5–6). Like Quinn in 'The City of Glass', the loneliness that this causes disconnects Zimmer from the world. He withdraws from his academic life and plunges into 'a blur of alcoholic grief and self pity' (Auster, 2002a: 7). The depth of Zimmer's loneliness is emphasised by his desperate attempts to hold on to his memories of his family. He plays with his children's toys, and touches his wife's clothes and smells her perfume 'to bring her back more vividly, to evoke her presence for longer periods of time' (Auster, 2002a: 7–8).

The writing of a book, *The Silent World of Hector Mann*, becomes Zimmer's escape from his grief (Auster, 2002a: 5). The research gives a purpose to his life, requiring him to travel to see the copies of Hector's films kept in six different film archives in Europe and America. Once the research is complete, Zimmer retreats to New York to write the book because it is the city 'least likely to wear on my nerves' (Auster, 2002a: 27). But for once, New York does not have a significant impact on this novel. Zimmer does not return to the Greenwich Village where he and Fogg had spent the period of tranquillity recounted in *Moon Palace*. Instead he buries himself in an apartment in Pierrepont Street, Brooklyn Heights, within sight of the Brooklyn Bridge. This place becomes a sanctuary for Zimmer, where he can hide in his own thoughts and the book, but of all the manifold possibilities available to him, it is the one best suited to his circumstances. 'I wasn't really in Brooklyn', he writes:

> I was in the book, and the book was in my head, and as long as I stayed inside my head, I could go on writing the book. It was like living in a padded cell, but of all the lives I could have lived at that moment, it was the only one that made sense to me. I wasn't capable of being in the world, and I knew that if I tried to go back into it before I was ready, I would be crushed. (Auster, 2002a: 55)

Zimmer recognises that he is only 'half human' without the family that has constituted so much of his identity, and until he has established who he is and what he wants he cannot begin to construct a new self (Auster, 2002a: 56). So far, this story echoes that of the disconnected characters in the earlier novels, particularly Quinn and Fogg. However,

Zimmer's cultural connection to Hector opens up a whole new world to him.

The book reveals a previously unexplored lexicon for Zimmer. His earlier academic work explored 'books, language, the written word' (Auster, 2002a: 13). Now he has become an expert on silent film and cinema as a 'visual language' (Auster, 2002a: 14). Hector's medium is slapstick and he is a 'talented gag-man with exceptional body control' (Auster, 2002a: 12). He has adopted two forms of physical expression – his body and his mustache. The physical comedians of this time are more compelling for Zimmer, who writes of these actors: 'they had understood the language they were speaking', and 'had invented a syntax of the eye, a grammar of pure kinesis. . . . It was thought translated into action, human will expressing itself through the human body' (Auster, 2002a: 15). There are parallels between this physical comedy and dance; each is a form of expression that adopts a spatial vocabulary. Slapstick and music also have structural similarities. Auster's description in *The Music of Chance* of Couperin's 'Les Barricades mistérieuses' as a series of 'unresolved harmonies' invites a comparison of all three forms as modes of artistic expression. Both music and dance rely on the resolution or irresolution of refrains in the creation of their effects. The appeal of slapstick lies in the unexpected resolution of its passages to provide comic effect, and Hector is an accomplished practitioner of this art form.

To emphasise the emotional power of the physical language of slapstick, silent films adopt many facial close-ups. In an attempt to analyse the semiotic powers of Hector's face, Zimmer embarks upon a long discourse on the communicative powers of his moustache. Hector's facial adornment is 'the link to his inner self, a metonym of urges, cogitations and mental storms' (Auster, 2002a: 31). In other words, the moustache is a 'seismograph' of Hector's 'inner states'. In Hector's films, his moustache is a 'twitching filament of anxieties, a metaphysical jump rope, a dancing thread of discombobulation, . . . it tells what Hector is thinking, . . . allows you into the machinery of his thoughts' (Auster, 2002a: 29). As a result of these new insights, Zimmer, like Auster in 'White Spaces' and Fogg speaking of Kitty's dancing, is introduced to a new form of non-verbal communication that opens the possibility of reading previously unencountered cultural forms.

Once the book is finished, Zimmer moves out of the family home and into a new house in Vermont, and begins a new phase of his life.

He takes on the task of translating Chateaubriand's two-volume, two-thousand-page memoirs, the title of which Zimmer prosaically interprets as '*Memoirs of a Dead Man*' (Auster, 2002a: 62). By placing this text at the centre of his own story Auster is revealing the mechanics of *Illusions*, and illustrating the way in which the lives of both the narrator and his subject are posthumously presented.

François-René Chateaubriand was a remarkable man who stood

> astride . . . two epochs, Chateaubriand saw three revolutions; he was by turn soldier, teacher, traveller, ambassador, plenipotentiary, minister and journalist; he concluded a peace . . . and made a war . . .; he directed the election of a pope and . . . [built] one of the most voluminous and important literary edifices of modern times. (Roger, 1926: 5–6)

Like Couperin, then, Chateaubriand's posthumous autobiography, and his many lives, inhabit Auster's novel to provide clues as to its literary method. The many lives of Chateaubriand are projected forward to become the many lives of Hector Mann, and then again to those of David Zimmer – each spoken in the voice of a dead man.

It is the voice of a dead man which propels Zimmer into the new phase of his life which results from his book on Hector. Despite having disappeared in 1929, and becoming a mere footnote in film history, a letter arrives claiming that Hector is still alive. As a result, Zimmer is forced out of his solitude and into a dreamlike and mythical community in New Mexico. 'Everyone thought he was dead', Zimmer begins his narrative, because in January 1929, Hector Mann:

> without saying good-bye to any of his friends or associates, without leaving behind a letter or informing anyone of his plans, . . . walked out of his rented house on North Orange Drive and was never seen again. . . . [I]t was as if Hector Mann had vanished from the face of the earth. (Auster, 2002a: 1)

What happened to Hector Mann, and how he disappeared so effectively, become apparent when an emissary is sent to Vermont to take Zimmer to New Mexico. A woman named Alma arrives with a gun to persuade him to go with her to the Blue Stone ranch in Tierra del Sueño, where Hector now lives. Alma means soul in Spanish, and Tierra del Sueño means land of dreams (as D. T. Max reminds us in his review of the novel (Max, 2002: 6)). After a violent confrontation, in which Zimmer blatantly courts his own death, Alma persuades him to accompany her to the ranch where he is to bear witness to the genius of Hector's secret films, which will be destroyed, at his own insistence, within twenty-four hours of his death. In Alma, Zimmer finds a lover and an escape from his intense solitude. He records that '[a] series of accidents had stolen my life from me and then given it back, and in the interval, in the tiny gap between those two moments, my life had become a different life' (Auster, 2002a: 112). Zimmer, like the Narrator and Fogg before him, experiences 'microscopic holes in the universe' through which he has been able to pass and begin to build a new sense of self (Auster, 2002a: 115). Fogg encountered the circles and holes of Blakelock's *Moonlight* painting, while the Narrator found in 'the tiny hole between self and not self' the power of his relationship with Sophie to reconnect him with the world. Zimmer puts himself uncomfortably close to death, and now, through Alma, he views the world from a new perspective. However, Zimmer, like Hector, lives a number of lives before he is able to fully comprehend the implications of Alma's role here, and only then is he able to find adequate words and commit them to paper.

Hector also moves from one life-changing event to another, gradually accumulating them into the life that Zimmer relates in *Illusions*. Auster employs a complex narrative structure to set out Hector's life between 1929 and the novel's present (1988). Auster narrates Zimmer, narrating Alma, recounting Hector's life in both his own words (from her memory, related to us through Zimmer) and from his journal. She is collecting this information for her own biography of Hector, to be published after his death. Despite the complexity of the narrative structure, this extended passage (seventy-two pages) provides the most compelling section of the book.

Hector's first narrated reincarnation occurs when his pregnant former lover, Bridgette O'Fallon, is accidentally killed by his fiancée, Dolores St John. Hector buries the body out in the hills beyond Los Angeles that will later become suburban Malibu. Believing his movie career to be at an end, Hector flees to Seattle and takes on a new identity. First he shaves off his trademark moustache, and then adds a workman's hat found in a public bathroom. To complete the transformation, he adopts the name inside the comfortably fitting cap: Herman Loesser. This name satisfies both Auster's sense of word play and Hector's need to retain some small part of his previous self, while also acknowledging his remorse for his part in Bridgette's death – an act of penance which is to haunt each of his subsequent incarnations. While he remains Herr Mann, he is also '*Lesser*' or '*Loser*', and 'Hector figured that he had found the name he deserved' (Auster, 2002a: 144, original italics).

However, because he has not been connected with Bridgette's disappearance, he is not pursued for his part in it. Instead he administers his own punishment, squirming 'under the stringencies imposed on himself, to make himself as uncomfortable as possible' (Auster, 2002a: 146). The next phase of his life begins when he embarks on the most tortuous and painful test: to live in the same city as Bridgette's family, Spokane.

In Spokane, Hector ends up working in the O'Fallon family business, where he is necessarily required to deny his own identity at every turn. Bridgette's younger sister, Nora, coaches Hector in elocution to disguise his accent. She talks to him about her sister, and asks if he knows of Hector Mann. He is compelled to deny his own existence, and destroy another part of that self still residing within him (Auster, 2002a: 163–4).

When it becomes clear that Nora has fallen in love with him, Hector flees again – this time to Chicago. Here he discovers a way to 'go on killing himself without having to finish the job . . . to drink his own blood . . . devouring his own heart' (Auster, 2002a: 176–7). Hector becomes the male half of a sex act with a prostitute called Sylvia Meers, giving live performances for the wealthy of Chicago. Again Hector is forced to deny himself, maintaining his anonymity by wearing a mask during the act. Hector literally empties himself out during this episode, unable to look into himself and record his thoughts in his journal.

When Sylvia becomes aware of Hector's identity and attempts to turn it to her own financial advantage, Hector flees once again. He is reaching his lowest ebb, and his sense of identity is becoming so unstable that he barely has any coherent residue of selfhood at all. The transition from one life to another, from one sense of self to the next, evacuates Hector's humanity. In a crucial passage, Auster projects the emptiness of Hector's soul onto the Depression era industrial landscape of Sandusky, Ohio. Hector 'found himself looking at a dreary expanse of broken-down factories and empty warehouses', Auster writes:

> Cold gray weather, a threat of snow in the air, and a mangy three-legged dog the only living creature within a hundred yards. . . . he was gripped by a feeling of nullity. . . . He couldn't remember his name. Bricks and cobblestones, his breath gusting into the air in front of it, and the three-legged dog limping around the corner and vanishing from sight. It was

the picture of his own death, . . . the portrait of a soul in ruins, and long
after he . . . had moved on, a part of him was still there, standing on that
empty street in Sandusky, Ohio, gasping for breath as his existence
dribbled out of him. (Auster, 2002a: 192)

Despite this nihilistic and despairing experience, Sandusky provides
Hector with his salvation. Here he meets a young and headstrong
banking heiress, Frieda Spelling, who is to become his wife and who,
much later, will write to David Zimmer. They move to New Mexico,
where they can live anonymously in a 'blank and savage' landscape.
Demonstrating that the natural environment can harbour dangers at
least as savage as the urban one, their three-year-old son dies when
stung by a bee. Hector and Frieda take up film making as a way to
displace their grief. This episode marks Hector's last environment, his
last new self and his last change of name. After Chaim Mandelbaum,
Hector Mann and Herman Loesser, 'Hector became Hector again'
(Auster, 2002a: 202). This time, and in a play on the arbitrary nature
of names and naming which has characterised so much of his work,
Auster christens his central character Hector Spelling.

Hector has vowed to never make films again as part of his life-long
penance. Now, he seeks a way to justify breaking his own promise. 'He
would make movies that would never be shown to audiences', Alma
tells Zimmer. 'It was an act of breathtaking nihilism' (Auster, 2002a:
207). So Hector and Frieda gather together a group of film makers,
including Alma's father, from his Hollywood days, and they set about
building a film studio in the desert.

Like Auster's own films, which are made with independent pro-
ducers, Hector's films are out of 'the commercial loop' of Hollywood.
They are both able 'to work without constraints' such as conventional
style and subject matter (Auster, 2002a: 209). And like all of Auster's
work, Hector's fourteen desert films have a 'fantastical element
running through them, a weird kind of poetry', which breaks with
narrative conventions (Auster, 2002a: 208–9). Hector and Frieda
achieve this by creating a small community of film makers on the
ranch, 'a self-contained universe, a private compound for making films'
(Auster, 2002a: 209). Movie making becomes the fabric of the ranch,
a communal process where '[n]o one did just one thing. They were all
involved' (Auster, 2002a: 211). With the arrival of Alma the community
becomes a family.

Hector dies and Zimmer returns to Vermont after having seen only
one of the films. Frieda is determined to destroy all traces of Hector's

life after 1929, and sets about systematically destroying his work, his journals and Alma's biography. In a tussle with Alma, Frieda falls and is killed (Auster, 2002a: 302–5). Alma is unable to bear another tragic loss; with the deaths of Hector and Frieda she has lost the last two remaining coordinates in her life. She commits suicide using the tranquillisers meant to sedate Zimmer on the flight to New Mexico. Zimmer is left alone once again. The remainder of the book sketches in brief details of the rest of Zimmer's life, before informing the reader that he speaks from beyond the grave. Like the 'unresolved harmonies' of slapstick, this is not the ending the reader expects. However, like the unresolved endings of Auster's metaphysical detective fiction, this ending draws attention to the conventions of writing. As we shall see, it also draws attention to the ways in which Auster layers fictional worlds within each other, and how the connection between 'our' world and the world of the book is broken by the death of the first-person narrator.

The journeys Hector and Zimmer embark upon are, ultimately, a search for some form of inner peace from which to build a stable sense of identity. The family as a form of community, for the characters of this book at least, provides just such a point of equilibrium, with the potential to remain constant under certain conditions. However, once those conditions are disrupted and the points of reference start slipping away, the capacity of the family to provide a site of self-formation is eroded. The family – as experienced by Zimmer, Hector and Alma – is shown to be fragile and provisional. Zimmer's sense of self suffers catastrophic deterioration with the loss of his family. Similarly, the location and conditions of the desert experiment in film making demonstrate that without the network of social connections radiating out from a central relationship of self and other (here variously represented as Zimmer and his wife, Hector and Frieda, and Zimmer and Alma), the arrangement remains fragile and prone to disintegration. Importantly, though, prior to her death Alma begins to heal Zimmer's psychosis, allowing him to emerge into the world without being crushed. In time, this new vision allows him the clarity to set down his own story, along with that of Hector.

The Book of Illusions, then, is a meditation on the nature of love and the family. It is also a statement of the power of the word over the image. If we examine the novel through the lens of the one film of Hector's that Zimmer was able to see at the ranch, we can also read it as an exploration of the power of stories and storytelling. *The Inner*

Life of Martin Frost is a text-within-a-text in which the eponymous author creates and falls in love with a beautiful female character. But as the pages of the story he is writing begin to run out, he realises that to keep her alive in his imagination he needs to destroy the manuscript, as once the text is finished she will fully become a fiction – a character and nothing more. If we take this as another example of 'mise-en-abyme', and look for structural resonances between the recursive structures of these embedded narrative worlds, then Claire is a character created by Martin Frost, Alma becomes the imaginative creation of the author-character, David Zimmer, and Zimmer is the creation of the Paul Auster whose name appears on the cover of the book.

Interpreting the film within the novel in this way suggests that Auster is setting up a comparison between filmic and novelistic forms. His return to the novel, after the failure of *Lulu on the Bridge* and in contrast to the smoky fate of Hector's canon, suggests that Auster believes the word to be more enduring than the image, while – most importantly – storytelling is held in common.

Ultimately we can read the novels considered in this chapter as road novels which take their central characters to places that do not exist. As well as the real and physical locations of these books, characters go to the place of imagination and dreams, which Mr Bones knows as Timbuktu. Mr Bones clings to the promise of Timbuktu as the place where unity will be achieved, where he will be with his master and will be whole again. Walt achieves a unity of spirit when in his fabular, airborne state, but once this is lost he becomes a confused and wandering soul whose incarnations are collected as a series of random stories. Hector's lives, in contrast, have an underlying 'unresolved harmony' based not in any fundamental origin or identity, but in his most vigorous incarnation: that of Hector Mann, actor. Chaim Mandelbaum is a character born in transition (on an immigrant boat from Holland), but he gains a conditional stability as Hector. When each disaster strikes, Hector moves on to a new self, each time retaining the persona of actor. In Spokane he is a salesman using the sporting goods as props (Auster, 2002a: 168), in Chicago he becomes a sexual spectacle, and in the desert he becomes the consummate film maker. But film and acting are artifice and illusion. Ultimately, where harmonies do connect the phases of Hector's life and hold his identity together, they have no metaphysical basis, and are founded instead on illusion, just as levitation and dreams are. In Auster's art, this work of reimagining a life as story is the work of identity.

Notes

1   As a result of divesting himself of his emotional responsibilities, Mark
    Irwin describes Nashe's life as being without 'centre' (Irwin, 1994: 80).

2   Edited and translated by Auster. The introduction is reprinted in Auster,
    1997.

3   Auster also borrows heavily from the true story, told in 'The Red Notebook',
    of his friend C.'s inheritance from a virtually unknown father (Auster,
    1997: 363–8).

4   Tim Woods describes an 'interrelated matrix of agency, freedom and
    power' at work in this novel that constantly undermines the central figures'
    ontological status (Woods, 1995a: 145).

5   *The Mysterious Barricades* was also to be the title of the novel. Auster gives
    the book its published title in a marginal note at the point where Nashe and
    Pozzi are set to work on the wall (Auster, undated h: n.p.).

6   *Moon Palace*, *Leviathan* and *The Brooklyn Follies* also exhibit a
    fragmentary form, with abrupt transitions in the lives of the characters
    prompted by critical events.

7   Tzara was instrumental in spreading 'the corrosive exuberance' of Dada to
    America (Auster, 1997: 209). Auster notes that America has its own
    natural Dada, and quotes Man Ray in response to Tzara: 'Cher Tzara –
    Dada cannot live in New York. All New York is Dada, and will not tolerate
    a rival' (Auster, 1997: 210).

8   The film received poor reviews when screened at Cannes in 1998, and it
    failed to receive either a cinema or video release. It was eventually released
    on DVD in 2006. In 2001 Auster told the author that the distributors had
    blocked the release. Auster has since told novelist Jonathan Lethem in an
    interview that one of the mistakes he made with *Lulu* was to write it too
    much as a novel, which means that it has to be seen a number of times
    'before you can really penetrate what's going on' (Vida, 2005: 38).

9   Auster himself has insisted that this is not the case. He told Lethem that
    Hector 'predated' his 'foray into filmmaking' (Vida, 2005: 30).

5

No place

Chapter 4 demonstrated the way in which movement and travel can be constitutive of a series of relational and situated selves. Walt, Mr Bones and Hector search for inner peace and find it ultimately, not in a real place, but in the space of imagination and illusion: in flying, dreams and films. These places, like the mythical idea of 'Timbuktu' itself, are beyond the rational capacities of cartography. Flight, dreams and film are, then, no-places – unreal, unlocatable and unmappable. They are, in short, utopian places.

Auster's fiction incorporates many unreal or unearthly places. In each, there is an important contrast in the experience of social relations, time and space with that experienced elsewhere. The farm at Cibola in *Mr. Vertigo* and the Blue Stone Ranch in *The Book of Illusions* are prime examples of this, and Fogg's Central Park experiences in *Moon Palace* also display qualities at odds with the tumultuous streets in which they and the park are embedded. It is because these places are subject to different social forces to those shaping the more conventional spaces of St Louis, Vermont and New York that they generate such a different experience of space. They are also, to an extent, spaces of imagination themselves, intended by their creators to act as a refuge from the cruel practices of the world beyond their boundaries. Places constructed entirely within the realm of the imagination, or occupied by the imaginary and the symbolic, are, according to Henri Lefebvre, 'utopian' (Lefebvre, 1991: 366). Auster has explored the fine line between utopias and dystopias in his work since Quinn discovered Stillman Sr's apocryphal story of Henry Dark in *The New York Trilogy*, and his attempts to establish a new innocent language and Eden in America.[1] 'Unlike the other writers on the subject', Auster records:

Dark did not assume paradise to be a place that could be discovered. There were no maps that could lead a man to its shores. Rather, its existence was immanent within man himself: the idea of a beyond he might one day create in the here and now. For utopia was nowhere – even, as Dark explained, in its 'wordhood.' (Auster, 1988: 46–7)

This chapter will examine how in two novels in particular, Auster represents spaces which, like the unimaginable 'Timbuktu' or Eden, cannot be found on the map. The places represented in *The Music of Chance* and *In the Country of Last Things* are born entirely of imagination, and contain unreal and unknowable forces. These places do however exhibit characteristics that have their origin in real locations. The 'fictional' places which result allow Auster to explore the extremes of human experience, and to show how ontological stability is constantly undermined by spatial instability. *The Music of Chance* explores the results of translating a political and aesthetic conception of utopia, as encoded in a model of 'The City of the World', into spatial experience. *In the Country of Last Things* presents a dystopic vision of urban possibilities and explores the capacities and strategies of the human spirit to survive even the most extreme brutalities of the metropolis. This chapter explores how utopian thinking creates models of spatial organisation, and how these are translated in actual spaces. It shows that the outcomes of spatial (dis-) organisation can be dystopic, and investigates how characters in these novels seek out sanctuary. For some characters, as we saw in the case of Mr Bones and Walt in Chapter 4, these spaces can be in the realm of illusion.

In these novels, and those discussed in Chapter 4, it is apparent that illusion, in the forms of magic and dreams, is important to Auster's representations of place. Illusory practices contribute to how his characters subsequently construct their sense of self. For the central characters in *Mr. Vertigo*, *Timbuktu* and *Illusions* fantasy provides a refuge from their corporeal and emotional reality. In the much earlier *Last Things*, Auster demonstrates that language and storytelling also have the power to create an illusion which is able to obscure the reality of a cruel, incomprehensible and intolerable existence. However, storytelling can also supply a refuge from an unstable and complex world, providing shared references which help to make sense of the complexities of urban living. Other equally illusory practices – such as flying, high-wire walking, dreams and film making – are central features of Auster's later texts, and each represents a way for the central character to establish a more secure sense of self than those available in the seemingly unknowable material world. This chapter explores Auster's places of the imagination, and considers the role 'non-places' play in the novels.

The 'City of the World'

In Chapter 4 we left Nashe hurtling towards his fate in a car. His relentless and mobile pursuit of a grounded self in *The Music of Chance* comes to an end in bizarre circumstances. He stakes the last ten thousand dollars of his inheritance on Pozzi's poker game with the two eccentric lottery millionaires, Flower and Stone. Bernd Herzogenrath notes that the card game 'is placed in the exact center of the book and thus can be said to separate the "realm of the road" from the "realm of the wall"'; it is consequently the point about which the novel symmetrically pivots (Herzogenrath, 1999: 193). Poker functions here as another expression of the intersection of rule and chance shaping the lives and narrative outcomes of Auster's novels. Like baseball (as we shall see in Chapter 6), poker comprises a series of uncontrolled, chance events occurring within a highly regulated structure of rules and etiquette. Each chance event (hand) translates into a tangible and measurable outcome, and each game ends with winners and losers.

To participate in this ritual of contingency, Nashe first reduces his life to ten one-thousand-dollar bills. 'There was something clean and abstract about . . . this', Auster writes, 'a sense of mathematical wonder in seeing his world reduced to ten small pieces of paper' (Auster, 1992b: 92). However, this rational simplicity takes on a menacing quality when the game is lost and Nashe's money becomes the property of Flower and Stone. With the loss of the money goes the agency and freedom for Nashe to dictate the course of his own life. When he cuts the cards for his car, and loses, Nashe even forfeits his capacity to leave (Auster, 1992b: 100). Acknowledging that he has not found freedom through wealth and travel, Nashe has reached a nihilistic point in his life, and is ready to risk his liberty. Nashe's incoherent inner state drives him to trust entirely to chance, hoping that from chaos order will emerge. The life on the road, stripped of connections and responsibilities, has not provided a coherent and grounded inner self for Nashe. Thus, when the game turns against Pozzi, he feels that this is a 'crisis that he had been searching for all along' (Auster, 1992b: 98).

Baudrillard identifies a desire for stability behind contemporary society's need for speed and change. 'Speed is simply the rite that initiates us into emptiness', he writes, 'a nostalgic desire for forms to revert to immobility, concealed beneath the very intensification of their mobility' (Baudrillard, 1988: 7). It is exactly this nostalgia for stillness and certainty which motivates Nashe's cavalier attitude to chance and freedom.

As Auster himself observes in an interview, Nashe's position swings rapidly from freedom to confinement during the game (Auster, 1992b: 327–8). Later in the narrative, Nashe comes across a line in William Faulkner's *The Sound and The Fury*: 'until someday in very disgust he risks everything on the single blind turn of a card' (Auster, 1992b: 202). The pivotal moment in the novel is encapsulated in this statement, which Auster settled on (appropriately) by chance while writing *The Music of Chance* (Auster, 1997: 337). Pozzi, on the other hand, relies on a different organising principle to comprehend his world. He trusts to a mystical superstition which Nashe calls 'some hidden purpose . . . God or luck or harmony' (Auster, 1992b: 139). Pozzi blames Nashe for swinging the game away from him by breaking off the model figures of Flower and Stone from the 'City of the World' (Auster, 1992b: 96–7). Pozzi sees this as 'violating a fundamental law' before which they had 'everything in harmony . . . turning into music' (Auster, 1992b: 138). However, Pozzi's strategy for achieving harmony with the world proves no more successful than Nashe's. Ultimately, neither character establishes any degree of ontological certainty because they are unable to locate correspondences between their understanding of reality and their experience of it.

The card game takes place at Flower and Stone's Pennsylvania mansion. The house itself has a quality which distorts both the experience of space and the rational sense of present reality, giving the estate and the novel the characteristics of a dream. This is reflected in the description of Nashe's arrival at the gate:

> An overpowering sense of happiness washed through him. It lasted only an instant, then gave way to a brief, almost imperceptible feeling of dizziness. . . . After that, his head seemed curiously emptied out, and for the first time in many years, he fell into one of those trances that had sometimes afflicted him as a boy: an abrupt and radical shift of his inner bearings, as if the world around him had suddenly lost all its reality.
> (Auster, 1992b: 65)

Like characters in the novels examined in earlier chapters, Nashe is unable to locate himself in the physical realm with any certainty. Also, like *Vertigo*, *Timbuktu* and *The Book of Illusions*, this novel is suffused with what Dennis Barone terms a 'sufficient realism', which represents the characters' experiences as plausible in a recognisable world, but admits telling unreal qualities (Barone, 1995: 6). The interior of the house, for example, and the resemblance of Flower and Stone to Laurel and Hardy, remind Nashe of a movie set, and reinforce the representation of the house as 'an illusion' (Auster, 1992b: 69). This impression is compounded by the mazelike roads leading up to it (Auster, 1992b: 64) and its location in Ockham, Pennsylvania, which, like the town of Cibola in *Mr. Vertigo*, is not on a map. All of these elements combine to emphasise the importance of the cognition of space and the experience of spatiality in Auster's work.

In a room which feels as though it is 'suspended in the middle of the air', these stands an object that is of fundamental importance to how we read *The Music of Chance* (Auster, 1992b: 77–8). Stone's 'City of the World' is a 'miniature scale-model', with 'crazy spires and lifelike buildings, . . . narrow streets and microscopic human figures' (Auster, 1992b: 79). The model has a space reserved for a representation of the house, with a model of the room containing a model of the model, and so on. Nashe sees the futility of this endless cycle of representation, as each model eternally refers to all the others in a nightmare of perpetual and continuous presents. But Flower sees Stone's work differently, describing it as 'an artistic vision of mankind', 'an autobiography' and, crucially, 'a utopia' (Auster, 1992b: 79). Stone himself sees the model as the way the world should look. Flower goes on to describe the institutional forces which first create the spatial formations of the city, and then maintain order in it. He points out the Hall of Justice, the Library, the Bank and the Prison; 'Willie calls them the Four Realms of Togetherness, and each one plays a vital role in maintaining the harmony of the city' (Auster, 1992b: 80). Here then is a social order that seeks to impose harmony on the spatial organisation and lives of its subjects, through the rational power of state institutions. This (modernist) order stands in contrast to the (postmodern) contingent and random composition that Nashe has so far brought to his life, taken to an extreme by the 'single blind turn of a card'.

Stone's vision is presented as a utopian one and, as such, is in a tradition of an ideology of space stretching back to Thomas More's *Utopia*. As Joseph Rykwert notes in *The Seduction of Place* (2000),

More 'founded a new literary genre, since utopias – in which the problems of society may be discussed by reference to some fictional ideal and remote city or country – are inevitably a criticism of current urban practice and a polemic about policy' (Rykwert, 2000: 17). Both the 'City of the World' and its practical spatial application in the meadow, which comprises this second half of the novel, hold up a vision of deterministic social organisation that is destructive to individual consciousness. Tim Woods notes that the model city in *The Music of Chance* expresses an 'architecture of control' (Woods, 1995a: 152) that encodes Flower and Stone's ideological constructions and their relationship to American capital (Woods, 1995a: 150). That is to say, the spaces of 'The City of the World' are 'literally filled with ideologies' (to use the expression Edward Soja borrows from Lefebvre (Soja, 1989: 80)).

The 'City of the World' conforms to a model of a utopian space described by Lefebvre. The 'Four Realms of Togetherness' contain aspects of what Lefebvre terms 'the symbolic' and 'the imaginary', which will be discussed in detail later. The model also confirms Rykwert's observation that utopian visions are a 'rationally conceived social order incorporated into a city plan' as a 'cure for conceptual chaos' (Rykwert, 2000: 57). In the prison, for example, the prisoners appear happy in their rehabilitation through work. For Stone, such aspects of life in his metropolis are positive as they reimpose order and certainty where he sees chaos. Consequently, Stone's vision conforms to Rykwert's contention that utopia can be both a 'no-place' and 'the good place' (Rykwert, 2000: 17). Here, Nashe's chaotic (postmodern) understandings collide with Stone's rational (and modernist) model. The elision of the two in the meadow interrogates both as 'organising principles' for the contemporary environment, and finds both wanting.[2]

Thomas More's *Utopia* is a fictional narrative, but subsequent visions have taken the form of manifestos or blueprints for the future-present city – such as Bentham's 'Panopticon' and Le Corbusier's plans for Paris.[3] The novel has also been a primary form for the communication of utopian thinking, presenting an opportunity to explore spatial and social formations within contexts that do not yet exist. This freedom allows writers to examine an imagined space without the rational and scientific constraints that limit much geographical thinking. The spatial imagination that Auster's novels display is a way of interrogating imaginary spaces to their utmost limits and stepping, by way of fiction, onto the territory of geographers. The geographer David Harvey attempts the inverse of this in *Spaces of Hope* (2000). Exemplifying the emerging correspondences between theories of the metropolis and metropolitan fiction, Harvey's analysis is embellished with an appendix which (unwittingly?) uncovers some of the contradictions between utopian discourse and utopian practice (Harvey, 2000: 257–81). Harvey describes a possible vision of future social relations constructed from the ashes of our present society (the concrete realities of material social practice). Through the frame of a dream, he describes an anarcho-syndicalist world able to use technology and industry in the pursuit of an egalitarian society and universal human rights. The dream format indicates the problematics of representing utopias which remain exclusively vested in the imaginary. It also demonstrates the way in which empirical social sciences (such as cultural geography) are beginning to incorporate imaginary and mythical elements of metropolitan life into their rational discourses. Thus, a compelling dialogue between the discourses of art and science emerges that is helping to shape a debate on contemporary forms of metropolitan living. In imagining this possible future, Harvey employs the practices of fiction to illustrate the spatial possibilities proposed in the rational-empirical geographical text preceding it. He takes the premise of existing material social conditions, and 'reimagines' their potential for a more socially just society.

In *Justice, Nature and the Geography of Difference* and *Spaces of Hope*, Harvey identifies two types of utopian expression – the utopianism of process, and the utopianism of fixed spatial form. The utopianism of process holds the greatest potential for successful realisation in practice as it is a 'dialectical utopianism' which is both flexible and builds upon material social conditions (Harvey, 2000: 173–96). In contrast, the utopianism of fixed spatial form, of which the 'City of the World' is emblematic, represents a dangerous recipe for 'authoritarian oppressions in the name of law, stability and order' (Harvey, 1996: 435). In *The Music of Chance*, the 'Four Realms' represent powerful, unknowable and authoritarian metropolitan forces. They also share aspects of the 'citadel-panopticon' Edward Soja identifies at the heart of Los Angeles. This site incorporates the state and corporate powers of control, surveillance and incarceration.[4] As such, the processes at work in Stone's aesthetic vision contradict and oppress the social and spatial elements that Lefebvre identifies for 'Spaces of Representation', which include the liberating practices of art and language. Instead, the 'City of the World' conforms wholly to Lefebvre's conception of 'Representations of Space' as a 'conceived' space of administrative forces.

Lefebvre's influential 'conceptual triad' constitutes three categories of social space which give rise to particular spatial experiences. Briefly, these are *'spatial practice'*, *'representations of space'* and *'representational spaces'* (Lefebvre, 1991: 33, original emphasis), which Lefebvre abbreviates to 'the perceived, the conceived and the lived' (Lefebvre, 1991: 39). S*patial practice* refers to a material experience of space as it is produced and reproduced by the mode of production. *Representations of space* are institutional, and refer to the 'frontal' relations imposed on space by dominant ideologies, social groups and institutions. Finally, *representational spaces* are the most apparent location of the social spatial imagination and are loaded with personal and social symbolisms capable of subverting social spaces. Art and literature are naturally clandestine constituents of *representational spaces*, as they harbour elements of imagination, symbolism and the potential for subversion of dominant ideologies. I will discuss *representational spaces* again in a different context in the next chapter.

Following the identification of the material, the social and the imagined levels of social space, Lefebvre describes how such spaces can be encountered analytically. S*patial practice* can be revealed through 'deciphering', and can be plotted empirically (Lefebvre, 1991: 38). *Representations of space* are the dominant spaces in a society or mode of production; they benefit the scientific practitioners (planners, architects etc.), and can be accessed through a 'system of verbal (and therefore intellectually worked out) signs' (Lefebvre, 1991: 37–8). *Representational space*, though, is 'directly lived' by 'inhabitants' and 'users', and is understood through a system of non-verbal sign systems as physical space is overlaid with symbolic meaning, assisted by artistic and literary representations (Lefebvre, 1991: 39).

Following Lefebvre, we can see that the 'City of the World' is constructed of purely rational, scientific and controlled spaces that invariably fall under the jurisdiction of the institutions of state control and the rational and deterministic practices of planners, like Stone himself. Consequently, the 'City' offers no possibility for subversive or fugitive activity. Indeed, on closer inspection, Nashe finds the organisation of the 'City' to be oppressive and menacing, rather than cooperative and benign. The model displays a 'voodoo logic', with 'a hint of violence, an atmosphere of cruelty and revenge' (Auster, 1992b:

87). This is confirmed by an execution taking place in the prison yard, and Nashe realises that there is an 'overriding mood . . . of terror, of dark dreams. . . . A threat of punishment seemed to hang in the air' (Auster, 1992b: 96). The 'City of the World' is clearly a society based on surveillance and discipline. The cruel and carceral nature of a society controlled by powers that punish non-conformist acts soon becomes apparent in *The Music of Chance*. Lefebvre calls ideologies with this level of abstraction 'negative utopias' (Lefebvre, 1991: 60). The outcome represented by the model for the inhabitants of the 'City of the World' is one of fear and menace, suggesting that a practical application of Stone's vision would be profoundly dystopic.

The opportunity for Stone to realise his vision comes with the outcome of the game. Without a car, with the last of his inheritance lost, and a further ten thousand dollars in debt, Nashe and Pozzi are 'employed' by Flower and Stone to build a wall '[t]wo thousand feet long and twenty feet high' across a meadow on the estate (Auster, 1992b: 117). The wall will be built from the stones of a fifteenth-century Irish castle and will be 'a memorial to itself' (Auster, 1992b: 86), but it is to be built without foundations (Auster, 1992b: 123). Although not a dominant theme in this novel, stones and walls are consistently associated with words and language in Auster's earlier work. As we saw in Chapter 1, the poetry (particularly in 'Disappearances') employs 'the language of stones / . . . to make a wall' (Auster, 1991: 61).

Crucially for us here, the meadow is a site for the translation of Stone's aesthetic vision of utopian society into spatial practice. Like the house itself, this space has the unreal quality of an enchanted meadow in a fable. It is '[s]urrounded by woods on all four sides', a 'desolate place' with a 'certain forlorn beauty to it, an air of remoteness and calm' (Auster, 1992b: 116). This section of the book has its origins in a play Auster wrote in the 1970s, which was performed only once. Originally called 'Eclipse', the play was a Beckettian story of Schubert and Brahms building a wall that eventually separates them from the audience (Auster, undated j: n.p.). It is reprinted in a revised version as *Laurel and Hardy Go To Heaven* in *Hand to Mouth*, where Auster also describes the only performance of the play (Auster, 1998a: 129–66 and 101–5).

Nashe and Pozzi's new relationship with Flower and Stone as employees is formalised in contract and agreement, with conditions to be fulfilled on both sides (Auster, 1992b: 112). However, the mystical meadow unexpectedly becomes the site of a brutal regime of control and repression. The futile labour of building the wall becomes a corrective measure imposed by Flower and Stone upon Nashe and Pozzi, in a parallel with the prisoners in the model. Cooperation is enforced by a translation of the panoptic forces from the model to the meadow. Woods notes that an 'allegorical and symbolic structure' emerges between the 'City of the World' such that the 'ideologies that are theorized and conceptualized in the model are reproduced practically in the meadow' (Woods, 1995a: 153). Flower and Stone's authority is imposed by a combination of confinement, coercion and fear. Nashe and Pozzi find themselves imprisoned on the estate by a newly erected barbed-wire fence which suggests a sinister degree of forward planning by Flower and Stone. The work is supervised by Calvin Murks, an employee of theirs, who rigidly enforces the terms of the contract. When relationships between the men – between control and labour – become confrontational, Murks demonstrates his power by wearing a gun, the threat of which temporarily gains the cooperation of the rapidly disintegrating Pozzi. The threat of violence also alerts Nashe to the full extent of their predicament (Auster, 1992b: 144–5).

Finally, when Pozzi's battered and nearly lifeless body is dumped in the meadow after an escape attempt, and Nashe is forced at gunpoint to remain in the meadow rather than go to the hospital, his already fragile sense of self-determination begins to disintegrate (Auster, 1992b: 172–4). Like the 'City of the World', the meadow has become disciplinary, repressive and carceral. The powers that control the space in which Nashe's life is enacted are remote, incomprehensible and cruel. The clear expression of the unequal and oppressive power relationships in the meadow, above all the other events that befall Nashe, force him to question his capacity to control his own life, and further undermine his increasingly unstable sense of self.

In a contrast with the meadow's fairytale qualities, then, Auster presents the development of a set of labour relations in a starkly empty landscape. Stripped down to the barest and most extreme expression of a social structure, the differential power relations of labour come to dominate.[5] By establishing a correspondence between the model 'city' and the meadow, Auster emphasises how these same forces produce social relations, which can then be inscribed through the spatial formations of the metropolis. The reading of the meadow sequence of this novel as a meditation on the confining nature of labour relations is reinforced by a poem handwritten by Auster on the back of one of the pages in a draft manuscript. The order of the first lines is unclear, but the poem appears to be called 'Labor is the life of the lost':

Life is a labor of love,
And labor is the life
Of the lost.

But I who live
But to love, am lost
In the labor of life.
What is this strife
That haunts me?
What is this life
That taunts me?

O me O my –
I am alone with the lost
And labor is not love
Love is the labor of the lost

(Auster, undated h: n.p.)

Two issues are foregrounded by these scribbled verses. Clearly there is a play on Shakespeare's *Love's Labour's Lost*, a play in which three French courtiers pledge to live monastic lives of denial and scholarship, only to be thwarted by the arrival of a beautiful princess and her attendants. At the same time, despite our own romantic expectations of love and beauty, which Shakespeare's comedies often address, the reality is a life of hard work, while love merely 'haunts' and 'taunts' us.

Nashe throws himself into the labour of building the wall in an attempt to re-establish the coherent and balanced sense of self lost during his itinerant phase. However, the close of this novel, as with the irresolution of some of the novels already examined, shows that for Auster the difficulty of locating a metaphysical basis for the construction of selfhood and identity is in the same order as the deferral of resolution and the constant deferrals of language. Once Nashe has worked off his debt, he finds himself once more behind the wheel of his car, alongside Murks, who was given it as a reward for 'policing' the work. He speeds along the wrong side of the road towards the 'cyclops' headlight of an oncoming vehicle (Auster, 1992b: 216). The novel finishes with this line: 'And then the light was upon him, and Nashe shut his eyes, unable to look at it anymore' (Auster, 1992b: 217). The ending encapsulates the important philosophical questions about personal freedom which have pursued Nashe through the various stages of his narrative. Warren Oberman, for example, sees the reader's dilemma throughout as deciding whether Nashe 'exemplifies moral heroism or tragic self-deception' (Oberman, 2004: 193). He concludes that: 'In a text filled with ambiguities, perhaps the most important question the reader must face is whether or not, by the end of the novel, Nashe accepts the existential nature of his freedom' (Oberman, 2004: 198). The difficult choice the reader is left with is whether Nashe finds freedom through his inheritance, through the 'turn of a card', in his labour or in his own death.

This novel, then, presents a series of processes that are condemned to endlessly refer to themselves without establishing a metaphysical point of origin. The model of the 'City of the World' depicts Stone in his studio making models of himself; the wall that Nashe and Pozzi build is destabilised by its lack of foundations, and only memorialises its own existence; Nashe's search for a coherent and stable construction of self founders on ontological uncertainty; and the reader's attempt to establish a secure philosophical perspective on Nashe's predicament is undermined by narrative irresolution.

Ultimately, *The Music of Chance* is an exploration of freedom and control in contemporary American society. In the contemporary metropolis, in the 'City of the World', and in the meadow these relations are expressed spatially. By exposing the relative power relations of the labour process, Auster is laying bare the brutality of the carceral and surveillance apparatus that is emerging in metropolitan spatial formations (of which LA's 'citadel-panopticon' is just one example). The consequence for Nashe in the extreme environment of the meadow, with society reduced to a population of just three, is that he is unable to exercise control over his surroundings because uncertainty and exploitation haunt him at every turn, while Pozzi is beaten nearly to death, and even Murks is imprisoned by his role as supervisor.

The city of 'Last Things'

Although sections of *In the Country of Last Things* appeared in the *Columbia Review Magazine* in 1969 as 'Letter from the City', this text was Auster's second published full-length novel. It immediately succeeded *The New York Trilogy*, with which it shares the concerns of language, the influence of the urban environment on individual consciousness, and a form adequate to the complexities of the metropolis. In particular, *Last Things* explores the capacity of the individual to maintain a unified mental self when the physical self is subject to the most extreme urban conditions. The central character, Anna Blume (a homage to *Ulysses*, perhaps), undergoes an urban nightmare in a distant and apocalyptically dystopic city. Turbulent metropolitan spaces, language, places of sanctuary and their effect on identity are the key themes in the novel. Auster presents Anna's experience at the extremes of human suffering and cruelty, and the metropolis at the limits of change, disorientation and alienation. Like the 'City of the World', this is an unreal place, filled with the imaginary and the symbolic. Thus, like the 'City of the World', it displays the characteristics of a 'negative utopia'. However, unlike the model in *The Music of Chance*, the city is a dystopia of process rather than physical form.

Anna has gone to the city to search for her journalist brother. This demonstrates the central position of the unnamed city in this novel. The city is already a story, generating its own narrative, with its own causal paths and outcomes. Anna's personal narrative takes the form of an extended letter detailing her experiences in the city. As with so many of Auster's texts, it is written in a notebook by a central character and subsequently related to the reader through an intermediary narrator, in this case David Zimmer (who reappears in *Moon Palace* and *The Book of Illusions*). The story is told predominantly in Anna's first person, but is interrupted by Zimmer's interventions. This narrative strategy simultaneously draws the reader's attention to the layering and mediation of the narrative, and to the many lapses and losses of memory and language.

Anna's experiences are formed through the constant reinscription of social relations onto the fabric of the metropolis. Frequently shifting social formations lead to a spatial instability, which is destructive to both her sense of self and the language necessary to express shared experiences. Like Nashe in *The Music of Chance*, Anna is subject to multiplying uncertainties in an extreme and rarefied environment. Auster shows that Anna's experience of the city is massively stimulating, complex and disorientating because both the physical and social urban fabric are in a constant process of disintegration. The novel follows Anna's battle for survival, her attempts to stabilise her sense of self, and her search for sanctuary from the city's many hardships.

Through her letter-diary, Auster describes Anna's initial experience of the city:

> Life as we know it has ended, and yet no one is able to grasp what has taken its place. Those of us who were brought up somewhere else, or are

old enough to remember a world different from this one, find it an
enormous struggle just to keep up from one day to the next. . . . The brain
is in a muddle. All around you one change follows another, each day
produces a new upheaval, the old assumptions are so much air and
emptiness. (Auster, 1989: 20)

Tim Woods describes *In the Country of Last Things* as 'a spatial
cartography that explores the manner in which human history is
subject to various structures and forms of power that traverse the body
and the world, break it down, shape it, and rearrange it' (Woods, 1995b:
109). This city demonstrates a number of material attributes that reveal
how Auster has constructed it from the human history of the twentieth
century. As a result, the city is not a recognisably real, locatable and
mappable place, but it does display characteristics that relate it to the
material experience of cities in crisis – or to put it more simply, real
places and events. Among identifiable features of recent history are
the Holocaust, the siege of Leningrad, the New York fiscal crisis of the
1970s and the Cairo garbage system. Thus, this city is both a no-place
and an every-place at the same time. While writing the book Auster
subtitled it 'Anna Blume Walks Through the 20th Century'; she
encounters some of the most horrifying manifestations of historical
events in the city from the outset (Auster, 1997: 284–5).

Anna's intensified and almost simultaneous experience of terrible
urban events echoes Soja's concepts of 'Thirdspace' and the 'Aleph'.
Here, the city contains multiple spaces and times, presenting them in
a dystopia of disturbing presents. Soja identifies how in some spaces
everything can be seen 'as a simultaneously historical-social-spatial
palimpsest . . . in which inextricably intertwined temporal, social, and
spatial relations are being constantly reinscribed, erased, and reinscribed again' (Soja, 1996: 18). It is the same process of social relations
being constantly renewed that proves so disorientating for Anna.

Reinscription of social and power relations is enacted on the material
urban fabric in a graphic way, in what Walker calls a 'dystopic city of
continually shifting landscapes' (Walker, 2002: 406). That is to say, the
tangible manifestation of social change is displayed in new spatial
formations. Anna describes the physical experience of a shifting
landscape at the very beginning of her narrative. 'A house is there one
day, and the next day it is gone', she writes. 'A street you walked down
yesterday is no longer there today' (Auster, 1989: 1). Anna goes on
to describe the mental toll of a constantly altering cityscape on the
individual:

When you live in the city, you learn to take nothing for granted. Close your
eyes for a moment, turn around to look at something else, and the thing
that was before you is suddenly gone. Nothing lasts, you see, not even the
thoughts inside you. And you mustn't waste your time looking for them.
Once a thing is gone, that is the end of it. (Auster, 1989: 1–2)

Anna witnesses a dangerously unpredictable environment at the
confluence of competing social forces, which constantly erase and
reinscribe social relations. The way these forces alter the physical
formations in the city can be accounted for by applying the spatial
thinking of Henri Lefebvre and David Harvey, and is particularly
captured by Soja's term, 'the socio-spatial dialectic' (Soja, 1980: 208).
Lefebvre insists that '(social) space is a (social) product' (Lefebvre, 1991:
26). Consequently, he is able to demonstrate that social relations are
'concrete abstractions' which 'have no real existence in and through
space. *Their underpinning is spatial*' (Lefebvre, 1991: 404, original
emphasis).

Soja, extending Lefebvre's thinking, explains that 'the organization,
use and meaning of space is a product of social translation, transformation and experience' (Soja, 1980: 210), such that 'all social
relations become real and concrete, a part of our lived social existence,
only when they are spatially "inscribed" – that is, *concretely represented*
– in the social production of social space' (Soja, 1996: 46, original
emphasis). Social relations and spatial relations are fundamentally
linked in the work of both Lefebvre and Soja in a two-way process; social
relations form space, but space also influences social relations in a
constant dialectic of production and reproduction. Or, as Soja puts it,
spatiality is 'simultaneously . . . a social product (an outcome) and a
shaping force (a medium)' (Soja, 1989: 7). Thus Anna's experience of
a constantly shifting cityscape is driven by constantly changing social
relations. Equally, because of the dialectical relationship between space
and society, this spatial disruption further destabilises social relations,
creating a dystopic vortex.

These spatial understandings lead us to consider how spatial
formations change under the stress of significant shifts in social
relations. The individual's response to change will vary according to
their knowledge of and control over the forces at work. Not surpris-
ingly, the less control there is, the more confusing these forces are.
Consequently, Anna's lack of power renders the city disorientating.
The geographer Doreen Massey describes the relationship between
the individual and the forces at work in their environment as a

'power-geometry' (Massey, 1993: 234), while Harvey calls it 'situated-ness' (Harvey, 2000: 236). Auster shows repeatedly how Anna's place in the 'power-geometry' of the city is a weak and distant one, and how she is manipulated by forces beyond her control or comprehension. In *The Condition of Postmodernity*, Harvey considers the outcomes from the changes in financial practices and production processes in the most recent phase of capitalism. He describes how a transition in the formation of social relations, in the shift from one mode of production to another, for example, will result in a change in spatial formations and, very importantly, the way that individuals experience space. Thus Harvey asserts that during 'phases of maximal change, the spatial and temporal bases for reproduction of the social order are subject to the severest disruptions' (Harvey, 1990: 239). What accompanies these shifts has been an accentuation of the 'volatility and ephemerality of . . . values and established practices' (Harvey, 1990: 285). In *Last Things* Anna experiences precisely this volatility when neither the things around her nor the thoughts inside her remain stable for long enough for her to establish a sense of where and who she is. Harvey insists that the result of the 'bombardment of stimuli' that assails the individual at these times 'creates problems of sensory overload that makes Simmel's dissection of the problems of modernist living at the turn of the century seem to pale into insignificance by comparison' (Harvey, 1990: 286). The experience of these social changes and the crisis in representation that goes with it are encapsulated in what Harvey terms 'time–space compression', under which continuing and rapid change promotes a feeling of instability (Harvey, 1990: 284). For Harvey, the alteration of the way that time and space are experienced results from the revolutionising of 'the objective qualities of space and time', forcing us to alter 'how we represent the world to ourselves' (Harvey, 1990: 240). For Auster too, Anna's struggle to grasp the changes that occur in the city, and the trans-formations of the cityscape, are caused by the constant rearticulation of social relations under pressure from a new mode of production. Anna therefore finds it necessary to completely overhaul her internal value system, and needs constantly to reassess the 'established practices' that make up her everyday life in order to survive.

A consequence of the constant disintegration of the physical environment is Anna's battle to retain or re-establish control over her understanding of it. The correspondences between her inner terrain, and the external terrain of the physical and social city, are progressively eroded. Fredric Jameson records how the individual attempts to familiarise her- or himself with city space by 'the practical reconquest of a sense of place and the construction or reconstruction of an articulated ensemble which can be retained in memory and which the individual subject can map and remap along the moments of mobile, alternative trajectories' (Jameson, 1991: 51). Auster shows that Anna's attempts to deploy the appropriate 'cognitive map' or 'articulated ensemble' in this city will be constantly undermined by the altering spatial formations, denying her the opportunity to memorise potential alternative trajectories through the city in a conventional and rational cartography. Like Quinn before her and Fogg and Sachs after, Anna does not possess the appropriate navigational tools for her city. Or perhaps more appropriately here, the city no longer coincides with her urban expectations and comprehensions. De Certeau too identifies the streets as presenting a *'forest of gestures'* (de Certeau, 1984: 102, original emphasis) for the individual to interpret as they navigate through the metropolitan environment. In Anna's city, these markers are constantly remade and the individual loses the ability to read the signs, making the urban text illegible. For Anna, this most extreme of urban environments proves to be unmappable, and provides no stable landmarks upon which to establish herself in relation to a physical or social environment, or a way to locate herself in the world. The result is a struggle to retain a hold on identity. Auster shows here how the intensity of the contemporary metropolitan process can be presented in the novel at its most extreme. When the city is portrayed in this way it is shown to be destructive of all manner of personal coordinates and references.

As a consequence of the 'ungraspable' nature of the city and her 'situatedness' in it, Anna's experience of metropolitan processes remains beyond her comprehension. At the same time, a significant example of the constant reinscription of power relations in the city is the obscure nature of governance and policing. Where urban territory has been relinquished by the institutions of the state, new power groups then quickly move in to occupy city spaces. In *Last Things* gangs use fear and intimidation to impose an order based on the extraction of 'tolls', sometimes in the form of money and sometimes in the form of food or sex (Auster, 1989: 6). These 'tollists' block streets with the debris of the disintegrating urban fabric, and are actively engaged in re-forming the cityscape. To overcome the resultant incomprehensibility of the city, Anna attempts to deploy local, sensual and tactile strategies of engagement and negotiation. From time to time this proves successful, but she often finds the urban text illegible, with terrible consequences. Anna endeavours to avoid the possessors of social power, because in this environment such power is predominantly gained and held by force. Her strategy is visceral, makeshift and provisional, relying on intuition rather than rational interpretation to navigate through the streets and away from trouble. Anna is Auster's only female central protagonist, and her mode of urban engagement parallels that of the artist Maria Turner. While these two women seem to be connected by their improvised responses to urban life, so are some of the male characters (particularly Sachs in the early sections of *Leviathan*). Similarly, their status as artists is not peculiarly feminine, as we shall see when considering Auggie Wren in Chapter 6.[6]

Like all of Auster's urban characters, Anna experiences the city in the most immediate of ways, on foot. Her status as a wanderer places her in the category of de Certeau's pedestrian practitioners. What emerges, however, is not the pattern of 'pedestrian speech acts' with a syntax of 'walking rhetorics' we saw in *The New York Trilogy*, but an illegible and constantly shifting text of competing social powers and confusing reinscriptions of social (dis)organisation. Auster records how Anna puts 'one foot in front of the other, and then the other foot in front of the first, and then I hope I can do it again' (Auster, 1989: 2). This is a long way from the relative optimism of 'White Spaces', in which the poet 'put one foot in front of the other. I put one word in front of the other, and for each step I take I add another word'. In *The Invention of Solitude* 'just as one step will inevitably lead to the next step, so it is that one thought inevitably follows from the previous thought'. However, for Anna, walking is not part of a thought or enunciative process, but a battle to survive in which 'the only thing that counts is staying on your feet' (Auster, 1989: 2).[7]

The instability of the environment forces the inhabitants of the city into ever more extreme and bizarre attempts to make sense of their experiences, and Anna describes some of the strategies people adopt to explain or escape the reality of their lives. Quasi-religious sects emerge and invent stories about surviving the city; none of them is simple, and all employ complex and illusory narratives and strategies. Some go as far as removing limbs to reduce the body's physical presence in the world. Each sect attempts to provide a means of comprehending the city's condition, and to relate members' lives in some mystical way to the events that surround them.

The economy of the city has also reached a profound point of decay and disintegration. The primary activity is now 'scavenging' on the streets for refuse. In *Last Things* the collection of waste and salvage has become the dominant mode of production – effectively replacing production with recycling. As we have seen, Lefebvre relates social relations and their spatial expression to the prevailing mode of production, while Harvey notes that transitions between modes of production create the experience of social and spatial crisis. The economic crisis in Auster's imagined city is so deep, and the social consequences so profound, that Anna estimates up to 20 per cent of the population are engaged as either 'garbage collectors' or 'object hunters' (Auster, 1989: 31). Such activities have become necessary as this city has no municipal system of garbage collection. Instead, each census zone has a private garbage broker who owns the rights to collect garbage. He, in turn, sells permits to the individuals who do the collecting, and then takes a cut from their earnings. Auster based this seemingly bizarre system on a *New York Times* article on the 'garbage collectors' of contemporary Cairo (Auster, 1997: 285, 321), which describes the poor migrants who collect the city's refuse and sell it on for recycling.[8] In *Last Things*, all refuse, including bodies, is burned at power plants on the edge of the city. The social structure that emerges from this regressive mode of production – really a mode of gradual destruction (nothing is made, just recycled and eventually destroyed) – is a hierarchy with street collectors at the bottom, rising through inspectors, Resurrection Agents and garbage brokers. While 'garbage collectors' trade in waste to power the city, the 'object hunters' seek out 'broken and discarded things' and salvage them before they reach the state of 'absolute decay' (Auster, 1989: 35–6). As in 'City of Glass', broken objects become symbolic of the broken-down metropolis.

It is clear that Auster is influenced by Baudelaire and is allying Anna with the figure of the ragpicker. She becomes an object hunter, an activity which is recognisably close to that of ragpicker. In his essay on Baudelaire's Paris, for example, Benjamin notes:

> When the new industrial processes had given refuse a certain value, ragpickers appeared in the cities in large numbers. They worked for middlemen and constituted a sort of cottage industry located in the streets. The ragpicker fascinated his epoch. The eyes of the first investigators of pauperism were fixed on him with the mute question as to where the limit of human misery lay. (Benjamin, 1997: 19)

Auster has consistently shown an awareness of the relationship
between the urban observer-recorder and the marginal figures of the
metropolis (Quinn, Fogg and now Anna). He clearly links Anna's
experience of human misery as a ragpicker to her status as an urban
recorder, and through her contemplates the contemporary complexities of urban representation in a way which echoes Baudelaire's
concerns in nineteenth-century Paris. That Auster considered 'New
York Spleen' as a title for 'City of Glass', that he consciously inserts a
ragpicker character into his degraded cityscape, and that he too is
searching for a language adequate to the urban experience, all go to
demonstrate the influence of Baudelaire. However, while the city has
the power to fascinate and compel for the nineteenth-century recorder-
wanderer, Anna's encounters with 'the crowd' are typified instead by
fear and danger.[9]

In *Last Things*, Anna experiences the 'limit of human misery',
and the intensification of urban processes to which she is subject
problematises the nature of her urban record in similar ways to those
in the *Trilogy*. Anna's record is layered and mediated and in places
unknowable in a way that echoes the complexity and unknowability of
the city. She admits that some of her recollections are not linear or
complete, but are instead 'random clusters, isolated images removed
from any context, bursts of light and shadow' (Auster, 1989: 124).
Through Anna, Auster joins Baudelaire and Benjamin in the debate on
the complexities of urban representation for the artist. Anna's anguish
at her inability to conjure the misery of the city in words is a reflection
of Baudelaire's famous appeal for a 'poetic prose', flexible 'enough to
adapt to the lyrical stirrings of the soul, the undulations of dreams, and
the sudden leaps of consciousness' that for him typified 'the experience
of giant cities' and 'the intersecting of their myriad relations', as
discussed in Chapter 1. Anna, though, writes: 'unless I write things
down as they occur to me, I feel I will lose them for good'. She goes on:

> The words come only when I think I won't be able to find them anymore,
> at the moment I despair of ever bringing them out again. Each day brings
> the same struggle, the same blankness, the same desire to forget and
> then not to forget. When it begins, it is never anywhere but here, never
> anywhere but at this limit that the pencil begins to write. The story starts
> and stops, goes forward and loses itself, and between each word, what
> silences, what words escape and vanish, never to be seen again. (Auster,
> 1989: 38)

The intensity of Anna's urban experiences creates a conflict between the word and the world. In a reflection of what she sees in the city, she is unable to find the words to represent the horror of her existence except under the conditions of absolute despair. Her difficulties are a consequence of both the mental instability that results from the constantly changing physical and social environment, and the effect this has on the language of the city.

The capacity of language to represent the intensities and extremities of city life is a central concern of *Last Things*. Early provisional titles convey the importance of language to the construction of the urban environment (as 'City of Words'), and the corrosive effect of an extreme urban condition upon words (as 'Dead Letters' (Auster, undated i)). In this novel language has an illusory quality and the power to obscure, which in turn translates as a misapprehension of the physical environment for Anna. The breakdown between language and the physical realm (word and world) is driven by the constant destruction that defines the cityscape. As Anna writes at the start: '[o]nce a thing is gone, that is the end of it' (Auster, 1989: 2). This is specifically illustrated when Anna seeks a way to escape the city. When she enquires about an airplane she finds that the word has disappeared from the language. She rationalises the erasure of things and then their words from the collective social consciousness in this way:

> It's not just that things vanish – but once they vanish, the memory of them vanishes as well. Dark areas form in the brain, and unless you make a constant effort to summon up the things that are gone, they will quickly be lost to you forever. . . . Memory is not an act of will, after all. It is something that happens in spite of oneself, and when too much is changing all the time, the brain is bound to falter, things are bound to slip through it. (Auster, 1989: 87)

However, it is not only an environmental amnesia that erodes language in collective social use, but also individuals differentially forgetting a degrading physical realm. Because the city is what Soja calls a 'historical-social-spatial palimpsest', people's experiences of its decay are located at different temporal points. When individuals forget different things at different times, their capacity to use language to generate shared meanings is eroded. Tim Woods notes how the 'gradual obsolescence of language and the entropy of reference causes isolation and the collapse of social interaction. The disappearance of the material realm destroys the realm of representation, and this in turn destroys collective understanding and comprehension' (Woods, 1995b: 121). Anna puts it this way: 'In effect, each person is speaking his own private language, and as the instances of shared language under-standing diminish, it becomes increasingly difficult to communicate with anyone' (Auster, 1989: 88–9).

Sanctuary

Anna's narrative is not inhabited entirely by the nihilism and uncertainty of the streets. From time to time Auster shows that a provisional and temporary stability can be found in even the most volatile environment. Anna is able to find and occupy small, almost utopian spaces of stability which offer shelter, refuge and even renewal.[10] These spaces are the apartment of a fellow object hunter, Isabel; the city's library with Samuel Farr, who becomes her lover; and the utopian calm of Woburn House, where Victoria Woburn helps the city's dispossessed. In these spaces of sanctuary Anna finds companionship with Isabel, love with Sam and friendship with Victoria. Through these episodes of relative stillness Auster illustrates how small and local experiences of calm can provide the metropolitan subject with a degree of stability and even the chance to establish some equilibrium with stable points of reference in other people. The time Anna spends in these places gives her a sense of identity that is relational, but not necessarily situated. That is to say, she can identify her sense of self with the social coordinates of others close by, but does not locate herself in the wider world beyond the boundaries of this geographical experience with any degree of fixity. In effect, the writer retreats again to the sanctuary of the room.

For a while Anna shares a room with Isabel and is initiated in the ways of the city. But Isabel dies after an illness that robs her of speech, and Anna returns to the streets.[11] Once she is evicted from the stillness and security of the room, Anna's life once again involves fear, confu-sion and instability. But when she takes shelter in the National Library during a food riot, she finds scholarly and religious communities studying and praying. There, Anna meets Samuel Farr, a journalist sent by the newspaper to find her brother. He lives in a garret room on the ninth floor of the library, collecting material for a book that will explain the city's condition. It is an immense and probably futile task; the 'story is so big . . . it's impossible for any one person to tell it', he acknowledges (Auster, 1989: 102). In other words, the city is so vast and complex that its totality is beyond the experience or understanding of a single point of view, consciousness or intellect. Because this city is beyond the comprehension of any individual it is also beyond any totalising representational capacities of language or narrative. Through the figure of Sam, Auster demonstrates how even in the same environment, alternative metropolitan perspectives are available. Sam's view of the city contrasts with Anna's experience of it, and the unfolding of the narrative illustrates the weaknesses of both. Sam's presence in Anna's narrative not only provides her with a point of stability and love (again by retreating to a room), but also represents an alternative perspective on the city. Where Anna's everyday view of city life is local and immediate (the streets, the decay and the fear), Sam's analytical position is a panoptic one, attempting to gain an overview of the city through its political economy, history and geography. So while Anna's contingent strategies for survival allow her flexibility in dealing with the city at an intuitive level, Sam is steadily consuming his reserves of strength and money in the pursuit of a futile and ultimately impossible project. Sam's relationship to the city is encoded in the physical characteristics of his garret room. Anna describes how an intricate window from which the limits of the city are visible occupies the whole of one wall of the room (Auster, 1989: 101). From this panoptic perspective, Sam is able to view the larger processes at work in the city, such as the constant remaking of the urban fabric. He is not, however, able to apprehend and interpret the micro-processes at work at street level that are implicated in the changes, because of their indistinctness below what de Certeau would call the 'threshold of visibility' (de Certeau, 1984: 93).

However, the happiness and stability Anna finds with Sam prove to be ephemeral, as the horror of the city once again undermines permanence and destroys certainty. Anna's security breeds complacency, and she is soon catastrophically ambushed by the overwhelming incomprehensibility of the city. Auster told Joseph Malia that 'the pivotal scene in which Anna is lured into a human slaughterhouse is based on . . . the siege of Leningrad. . . . [I]n many cases, reality is far more terrible than anything we can imagine' (Auster, 1997: 285). The scene Anna witnesses undermines her ontological stability, and her physical well-being is destroyed in her escape. She describes 'three or four human bodies hanging naked from meat-hooks, and another man with a hatchet leaning over a table and lopping off the limbs of another corpse' (Auster, 1989: 125). Anna only escapes by crashing through the window and falling several storeys to street level.

Anna survives and is taken to Woburn House, a 'positive utopia' embedded in the 'negative utopia' of the city, and a sanctuary from the turmoil of the streets. Here she is cared for, and, in turn, becomes a carer for the city's indigents who are given temporary refuge. Woburn House proves to be an otherworldly place. The people who work there form a bizarre but supportive family. The house, in contrast to the decay and disintegration of the city, is an elegant mansion in a private park that Anna calls 'a haven, an idyllic refuge from the misery and squalor around it' (Auster, 1989: 139). Woburn House produces a very particular sense of place at odds with the dystopic city precisely because of its utopian, unreal qualities. Anna experiences time, for example, differently to the way that she experienced it on the streets. This is because the social relationships inside the house contrast starkly with those outside. When this is the case it is likely, as David Harvey observes, that subjective experiences of time and of space will differ. The city outside undergoes rapid and overwhelming change, constantly destabilising Anna's sense of space and time, and eroding language through differential experiences. At the same time Woburn House represents a stability that grounds and stabilises the permanent inhabitants. In early drafts of the novel Auster signalled this more directly by naming it 'The House of Calm' (Auster, undated i: n.p.).

Victoria's charitable actions have correspondences with those of Rose Hawthorne, the daughter of Nathaniel, and we can speculate that Victoria is based on Rose.[12] According to *The Dictionary of American Biography*, Rose founded a religious sisterhood known as the Servants for Relief of Incurable Cancer, then thought to be a communicable disease. As Mother Alphonsa she opened on the banks of the East River in Manhattan a home called St Roses (sic), dedicated to helping victims of cancer who were without friends or resources (Johnson, 1928: 226). In time, Anna's intimacy with Victoria and the stability she finds in the house form her social and physical surroundings into referential points of stillness. Upon these foundations she begins to rebuild her shattered physical and inner self. She and Victoria share a 'bond' that expresses itself as an obligation to each other. Consequently, Victoria becomes a 'permanent place' for Anna to 'anchor [her] feelings' (Auster, 1989: 158).

The calm of Woburn House is eventually destroyed when the nightmare of the streets penetrates the utopian space, and the values that support it are undermined. Once the trivial rules and corruption of institutional control, in the shape of the police, trespass on the ideals of the utopian project, the 'illusion' of Woburn House becomes apparent and its 'foundation of clouds' is revealed (Auster, 1989: 187). Once again, we see how in Auster's fiction sanctuary from the turmoil of the urban process is necessarily fragile and contingent. Walker too notes how each of the institutions of stability that Anna seeks out (daughter, lover, nurse) is vulnerable from attack both from within and without (Walker, 2002: 409). Under less extreme social conditions these institutions would be able to provide certainty and discipline. But once the forces of chaos and contingency have disrupted the delicately balanced order of these environments, their ability to persist is catastrophically undermined.

The Woburn House utopian project echoes the ungrounded and constantly deferred meanings of words and identity that Auster represents in many of his novels. For socially exchangeable meanings to emerge from language it is necessary for users to call a halt to the endless process of deferral, and to adopt an 'adequate' and provisional sense for words. Equally, Auster's characters stumble upon places where a similarly provisional and temporary halt is possible in the constant deferral of self and identity. Here they find that for a time their inner terrain engages with their outer physical and social environment more fully. When this happens they are able to establish a fragile and fleeting stability. Anna's brief spells of happiness with Isabel, Sam and at Woburn House all exemplify this process. In other novels, in 'The Locked Room', for example, the Narrator begins to find a similar stability with Sophie. Of the greatest importance to Anna, though, is that Woburn House represents a halt in the processes of deferral in a relatively stable, familiar and comprehensible place. In this place she finds the stability to tell her story and the language to convey her experiences. The problem with spaces of utopian process, when they are embedded in environments of antithetical or antagonistic processes, is that they will always be at risk of attack, erosion or degradation by the forces that surround them. In *Last Things*, Auster shows how the occupants of places such as Woburn House need to be sensitive to these shifts in the environment and flexible enough in their routines to accommodate them.

Ultimately, Auster demonstrates that life in the city can be survived by employing Anna's restricted strategy of an infinitely flexible and sensitive approach to the rhythms of the street. But Sam's model of panoptic observation proves insensitive to the nature of the processes at work in the city, and he comes close to being destroyed. Sam lives according to the destructive triple injunction (like Fogg), to 'want nothing, . . . to have nothing, to be nothing' (Auster, 1989: 163), leaving him 'drifting inside himself, . . . utterly lost' (Auster, 1989: 161). In short, this city does not permit any strategies of reading to interpret the metropolitan text. Its volatility and complexity consistently resist description and recording.

Instead of comprehending the city, the inhabitants of Woburn House choose to escape it. They form a magic show to tour the countryside beyond the city. In early drafts this forms a further episode to Anna's adventures (Auster, undated i), but it receives only a brief treatment in the published version.[13] The tricks they perform will be an ironic comment on the illusory nature of life in the city, not least the cults which emerge from such a damaged society. In the 'grande finale' Anna, as the glamorous assistant, will be sawn in half: '[a] long delirious pause will follow, and then, at the precise moment when all hope has been lost, I will emerge from the box with my limbs intact' (Auster, 1989: 187). However, these illusions are also a diversion from the alienation of everyday life in this dystopic city. Here, as in the texts considered in Chapter 4, illusory devices – magic and storytelling – operate to take the characters out of themselves, to separate their consciousness from their bodies, and to provide respite from the extreme condition of modern living.

Illusion

Walt escapes from the reality of his adolescent body through levitation, Mr Bones speaks to the dead Willy through dreams, and David Zimmer and Hector escape the trauma of loss through watching and making films (respectively). These dreamlike states have about them the characteristics of a utopian place – and characters are able to will themselves there, to escape the reality of here. These 'places' have the quality of an illusion that separates an event into its corporeal experience and its impression on the imagination, and emphasises the imaginary element. By bringing the imaginary content of life to the fore, the individual is able to distort reality by wishing, dreaming and speaking of a better life. The inhabitants of the city attempt to escape their lives by using the opacity of language as a veil to conceal their misery. Anna refers to this use of language to alter material reality as entering 'the arena of the sustaining nimbus' (Auster, 1989: 10). City inhabitants use this linguistic space in order to conquer their feelings of hunger when they do not have enough food. When a group gathers they describe to each other in intricate detail the sensations of a meal, bound by a rigid structure and protocol. 'For best results', Anna insists:

> you must allow your mind to leap into the words coming from the mouths of others. If the words can consume you, you will be able to forget your present hunger and enter what people call the 'arena of the sustaining nimbus.' There are even those who say there is nutritional value in these food talks – given the proper concentration and an equal desire to believe in the words among those who take part. (Auster, 1989: 9–10)

The inhabitants indulge in storytelling to alleviate the symptoms of their suffering – specifically hunger. As earlier chapters have shown and Chapter 6 goes on to discuss, Auster believes the telling of stories to be a powerful social practice, through which we might begin to make sense of a complex world. Indeed, Auster thinks of himself primarily as a storyteller. However, he shows how, in this city, even storytelling is unable to impose any kind of order on the chaos. Consequently, in *Last Things*, the inhabitants are only able to use stories to create an intangible, insubstantial and unsustainable social practice, indicating that it is no longer possible to locate the self in relation to this city. Effectively storytelling is able to defer rather than mediate reality for the inhabitants of this dystopic metropolis. Varvogli notes how Anna is a figure much like Scheherazade from *1001 Arabian Nights*, a narrative Auster has frequently cited as an influence (Varvogli, 2001: 7). Scheherazade owes her life to the stories she tells as each night she defers the moment of her death. Anna too remains alive by setting down her story. However, Anna's story survives, as indeed Anna may, beyond the pages of her notebook. When the end of the notebook comes, we know her story carries on, but her fate remains uncertain. In other texts, particularly the much later films, stories are shown to be both a powerful social force in the metropolis and an essential aspect of Auster's own practice and commitment as an author.

Levitation has a similar significance for Walt. Through it he can escape his body, and at the same time it gives him an artificial identity as 'Walt the Wonder Boy'. Walt describes his technique for flight as a combination of loft and locomotion. First he must rise from the ground, and then proceed forward 'the way an aerialist advances along a high wire' (Auster, 1995a: 81), as if following 'the shape of an imaginary bridge' (Auster, 1995a: 130). Auster's inspiration for Walt and his levitation act is Philipe Petit, a French high-wire walker and street entertainer whose exploits and book Auster celebrates in the essay, 'On the High Wire' (reprinted in Auster, 1997). There are striking affinities between Walt's levitation act and Petit's guerrilla acts of urban spectacle. Auster writes of how he continues to see in his mind the newspaper picture of Petit walking between the towers of Notre-Dame cathedral in Paris. He describes 'an almost invisible wire stretched between the enormous towers of the cathedral, and there, right in the middle, as if suspended magically in space, the tiniest of human figures, a dot of life against the sky' (Auster, 1997: 251). This event and its magical quality have the power to alter Auster's perception of Paris forever. In a pamphlet that influenced Auster's thinking, *Two Towers I Walk*, Petit writes of his walk between the towers of the World Trade Center in New York. He describes how the city stops to look up and gasp, and he feels 'the breath of the city that has changed its rhythm' (Petit and Reddy, 1975: 17–18). Auster considers high-wire walking an art, comparable to other physical arts such as dance (Auster, 1997: 251–2), and Petit's writing emphasises this quality of his work. Auster observes that (like poetry): 'the high-wire is an art of solitude, a way of coming to grips with one's life in the darkest, most secret corner of the self' (Auster, 1997: 257). During his initiation, Walt too is forced to explore his most intimate inner spaces. In a showdown with himself, Walt learns to separate his mind from his earthly body (Auster, 1995a: 49), so that he is able to achieve 'the ascension into actual flight, the dream of dreams' (Auster, 1995a: 89).

Equally, Mr Bones in *Timbuktu* uses dreams as a way to escape the reality of life without Willy, and to re-establish the equilibrium he had known with his old master. Once suburbia has proved to be nothing more than a fantasy, Mr Bones longs to be at Willie's side again. Willie comes to the dog in dreams, offering advice and encouragement on finding a new family. He also offers him the hope of a reunion in the mythical 'Timbuktu'. For Mr Bones, Willy's ethereal presence is a comfort. 'Mr Bones was ill-equipped to parse the subtleties of dreams, visions, and other mental phenomena,' Auster tells us:

> but he did know for certain that Willie was in Timbuktu, and if he himself had just been with Willy, perhaps that meant the dream had taken him to Timbuktu as well. . . . And if he had been to Timbuktu once, was it too much to think that he might not be able to go there again – simply by closing his eyes and chancing upon the right dream? It was impossible

to say. But there was comfort in that thought, just as there had been comfort in spending that time with his old friend. (Auster, 1999: 123–4)

Mr Bones wills himself to a place which is at once a 'no-place' and 'the good place', where he can again be Willy's disciple.

A dream or reverie also constitutes the dominant and central part of Auster's film, *Lulu on the Bridge* (1998).[14] The central dream sequence in the film is framed by the shooting of jazz saxophonist, Izzy Maurer (Harvey Keitel), and his trip to hospital in an ambulance. This short spell of 'real' time encompasses a number of days of dream time in both New York and Dublin (one of Auster's favourite cities). The story includes a glowing stone with magical properties, and the now ever-present emotional relationship upon which the artist (here a musician) is able to reconstruct some sense of self after a catastrophic loss – in this case Izzy's ability to play. Izzy endures kidnapping and danger to be with the woman in his dream, Celia (Mira Sorvino). She helps him to come to terms with life without music, and to investigate the mystery of the stone. Once again, dream represents an escape from corporeal reality, a shift in the experience of time and space, and the re-establishment of a stable focus and personal social references. The film ends, however, on a nihilistic note, making it clear that the things Izzy sought in his dream are intangible and ephemeral. He dies in the ambulance as it passes Celia on the street in New York.

The projection of the image and the audiences' desires onto the screen makes film an ideal form with which to explore the nature of illusion. In *The Book of Illusions*, both Zimmer and Hector use film to suspend the reality of loss. The slapstick of Hector's early silents draws laughter from Zimmer for the first time in months, and triggers a release from his misery (Auster, 2002a: 9–10). In the 1920s film making created a 'delirium' and was 'exhilarating' for Hector (Auster, 2002a: 147). Thus, by forcing himself to abandon the happiness of making films Hector punishes himself for his part in Bridget's death and its concealment (see Chapter 4). By returning to film making at the Blue Stone Ranch – itself a reference to an illusion – after the death of his son, Hector rescues his marriage and saves himself from a nervous breakdown (Auster, 2002a: 207). *The Inner Life of Martin Frost* demonstrates that film can present the inside of a man's head – the space of dream and illusion. In his imagination, Martin Frost conjures the image and person of Claire to appear in Tierra del Sueño (which is, of course, the land of dreams). Like Celia in *Lulu*, she is able to break his solitude and provide focus for his work as 'a spirit, a figure born of the man's imagination, an ephemeral being sent to become his muse' (Auster, 2002a: 243). But to keep Claire alive, Martin Frost must destroy his work. The role that the insubstantial person of Claire plays in Frost's survival exemplifies the powerful forces at work in dream, imagination and illusion.

Storytelling, dreams of flying, dreams of a better place, the creation of flickering images; for Auster's characters these are all ways of creating a space in which a balance – an equilibrium with another person – can be sought, and the construction of a stable sense of self embarked upon. In dreams and under the conditions of illusion, the points of reference upon which self can be built remain stable and constant in a world that is typified by change and uncertainty. The logical extension, then, is the creation in material space and social process of the same practices that are available through dream, imagination and illusion. By grounding them in real space and real practice, there is the hope of generating a robust sense of a relational and situated self – with others as a focus and a secure way to locate oneself in the world. These are to be found in community, and community is to be found, predominantly in Auster's work, in the culture of baseball. The next chapter explores the different functions served by baseball in Auster's work, and considers its central role in constructing a communal consciousness in the global capital, New York City.

Notes

1 Leo Marx describes how pastoral thinking of this kind would view 'America as nature's garden, a new paradise of abundance' (Marx, 1967: 75). Marx also examines a pamphlet called 'The Golden Age', which has similar celestial ambitions as Stillman's (Marx, 1967: 105–7). On the tension between America's Edenic innocence and its potential as a new Babel in 'City of Glass', see also Brault, 1998: 228–38.
2 This collision and combination of seemingly incompatible philosophies is explored in detail in Oberman, 2004: 191–206.
3 Rykwert, 2000, traces urban planning and utopian thinking from the Greeks, through the Enlightenment thinking of More, to the industrial metropolis, the new towns of the early twentieth century, and the global cities of the twenty-first century.
4 Citadel-LA is the former working-class Bunker Hill neighbourhood of central Los Angeles, which has been redeveloped as a civic centre. It contains institutions of state surveillance and control (police and court buildings, and a jail), various municipal buildings (including City Hall)

and a complex of cultural venues (including the Frank Gehry-designed Disney Concert Hall). See Soja, 1989: 222–48 and Soja, 1996: 204–37.

5 Ilana Shilo investigates the relationship between money, power and enslavement in *Chance* (Shilo, 2002b: 504–6). Eyan Dotal sees the meadow as a site for the playing out of 'a hostile encounter' 'between Baudrillard's account of late capitalism and contemporary Marxist thought' (Dotal, 2000: 162).

6 Gender does not figure significantly in Auster's work as a theme. He does, though, seem to suggest that female characters, particularly when they are artists, are more able to consistently bring appropriate strategies to their urban lives, and it is often through these women that his male protagonists achieve some sort of equilibrium between their inner and outer terrains. However, it is an individual character's relationship with language that will ultimately determine her or his capacity to establish a stable sense of identity.

7 Woods too contemplates the correspondences in Auster's earlier works between Anna's wandering and de Certeau's 'walkers' (Woods, 1995b: 111). He describes the city as 'a place and non-place, in which people are completely indifferent to reality, knowing no logic or negotiation or causality or contradiction, wholly given over, as they are to the instinctual play of the desires and the search for survival' (Woods, 1995b: 112).

8 The article, 'Cairo Garbage Gives Migrants a Good Living', is included with early drafts and other materials relating to *In the Country of Last Things* in the Berg Collection, New York Public Library.

9 Peter Kirkegaard also comments on the relationship between Auster's characters and Benjamin's description of urban types (Kirkegaard, 1993: 165–6).

10 Walker notes that Anna 'seeks out traditional institutions of stability and meaning to provide herself with sanctuary and identity' in the roles of 'daughter', 'wife' and 'nurse/employee' (Walker, 2002: 408).

11 Isabel's deterioration reflects that of the city, even down to the erosion of language. For Auster, a person's presence in the world is clearly composed, at least in part, by their language and speech. This episode parallels the end of Kafka's life, which Auster describes in the essay 'Kafka's Letters'. As Kafka was dying of tuberculosis of the larynx he, like Isabel, was unable to speak, eat or drink. To communicate he wrote 'conversation slips', and these were published along with his collected letters (Auster, 1997: 138–9).

12 Auster has discussed with the author his interest in the figure of Rose Hawthorne (pers. comm., 13 December 2001).

13 Anna, Sam Victoria and Boris Stepanovich escape the city in Woburn House's ancient Pierce Arrow and tour the countryside beyond, performing their magic tricks.

14 The only critical comment in Anglophone scholarship that I am aware of is Brooker, 2002: 131.

6

The global metropolis

The magic isn't just simply a dream. It's real, and it carries all the emotions of reality. (Auster, *Lulu on the Bridge*, 1998b: 145)

The notion that illusion can provide stable points of reference for identity, as secure coordinates on which to anchor self-formation, emerges as a central theme in Auster's film work. In the companion films *Smoke* and *Blue in the Face*, he embraces practices with poetic or mythical dimensions through which his characters are able to locate themselves in the world. In this final chapter, I will show how Auster presents storytelling and baseball as ways of promoting friendship and community in an urban setting, and how they each provide ways for characters to reconnect to their metropolitan environment. These practices overlay the material reality of the metropolis and offer the inhabitants the chance to 're-enchant' their relationship with their environment. Storytelling functions in these texts as a way for characters to forge connections with supportive networks of friends, their immediate neighbourhood and wider society. Throughout this study, I have argued that Auster believes that stories help us to make sense of the world we live in, and that metropolitan stories help us to make sense of the metropolis. In *Smoke* and *Blue in the Face*, storytelling initiates and perpetuates a sense of community which is more than an introverted mode of metropolitan living. Instead, by acknowledging and negotiating the larger social processes that surround individual experience, Auster's characters are better able to comprehend their place in the world, and so locate themselves more securely than characters in his earlier fictions.

An incomprehensible New York, typified by the experience of characters such as Fogg in *Moon Palace* and Sachs in *Leviathan*, is to a large extent a result of the incomprehensibility and determinism of Manhattan, which stands in contrast to the human warmth of Brooklyn. A broad view of Auster's work shows that 'the monstrous sum / of particulars' (Auster, 1991: 61) is too vast to contemplate, while, at the same time, the solitude of the singular is too lonely to bear. This suggests that, for Auster, individuals need to be able both to relate themselves to the social and physical landmarks of their own metropolitan experience and to meaningfully situate themselves in relation to the processes at work beyond those boundaries. In his films – in their representation of the metropolis and as a consequence of the mode of their production – Auster proposes friendship and community as a way to connect to the wider social world, and to locate oneself in the complexities of the global metropolis. In what follows, I will briefly examine how recent urban theory has related the global processes of spatial formation in the city with the immediate and personal experiences of urban living, before exploring how the characters in Auster's films combine knowledge of the global and the local, and how he fashions from this knowledge a qualified celebration of the contemporary metropolis.

The central space of the films is the Brooklyn Cigar Company store, where baseball is the usual subject of discussion. Baseball in Brooklyn will always mean the Brooklyn Dodgers, who were moved to Los Angeles by the club's owners in 1957 in search of higher revenues. Auster demonstrates how the history and memory of the Brooklyn Dodgers provides his characters with a resource for communal identification, and a powerful focus for action. As a consequence, the films present the Dodgers and the store as the foci of a community able to extend from the store to the neighbourhood, and beyond. Auster's fiction demonstrates how social relationships help characters to form a coherent relationship with their physical environment. In his film work, community also enables characters to engage with a matrix of social contacts at once stable enough to provide secure coordinates, while at the same time sufficiently connected to encompass a range of social relationships on a number of geographical scales. Individual characters are thereby able to achieve a degree of stability by situating themselves in their Brooklyn neighbourhood while also establishing a relational sense with a wider social world. Consequently, in some ways, the focus of Auster's work contracts to the scale of a small community of people in and around the store and the neighbourhood. But, in other ways, the focus also expands to embrace the larger

metropolitan and global processes beyond the boundaries of neighbourhood, which impact on the daily lives of those individuals.

There has been a dichotomy in urban theory between exploration of
the quotidian experience of the metropolis, and discursive study
of urban process. As this study has shown, Fredric Jameson has
attempted to 'disalienate' the metropolis (itself another way of
describing 're-enchantment') by extending the discoveries of local
positioning to allow us to comprehend 'our insertion as individual
subjects into a multidimensional set of radically discontinuous
realities, whose frames range from the . . . spaces of bourgeois private
life all the way to the unimaginable decentering of global capital itself'
(Jameson, 1991: 413). Jameson attempts to locate the individual and
her or his geographically limited experience in the broader networks
of social relations that extend beyond the local into 'multinational
space' (Jameson, 1991: 49). However, Jameson's project is hampered
by its reliance on the abstractions of mapping, constantly requiring
the translation of experience into the codes and conventions of
cartography. In short, the ambitions of 'cognitive mapping' to translate
comprehension of local experience into global understanding are
problematised by over-abstraction on all geographical scales (Jameson,
1991: 416). As Mike Davis points out, Jameson's project is also
overdetermined by his class position, which extends his findings in
the Bonaventure Hotel (a 'large vivarium . . . for the upper middle
classes') to the totality of global economic activity (Davis, 1988: 86).

David Harvey rearticulates the relationships within Jameson's
economic equation, investigating the place of the body ('the geography
closest in'[1]) in the processes of globalisation. He is concerned to
integrate 'body talk' with 'globalisation talk'; to comprehend how the
metropolitan, national and regional forces at work today are shaping
the metropolitan environments and experiences of individuals, and
how those personal experiences are, in turn, related to the larger
(global) processes (Harvey, 2000: 15). In short, Harvey seeks to
comprehend the relationship between micro and macro discourses –
the 'local' level of metropolitan experience, and the larger forces of the
'beyond local' (Harvey, 2000: 199).

Doreen Massey also adopts the term 'local' to emphasise the
everyday experience of metropolitan subjects, and uses the term
'global' to designate the context in which that takes place. She
reimagines how we might understand the relationship of the personal
and immediate with larger temporal and geographical forces in a

discussion of the global in the local, and identifies their interpenetrating 'composite nature' (Massey, 1999a: 102). In the context of metropolitan cultures, this translates as a 'geographical imagination which can look both within and beyond the city and hold the two . . . in tension' (Massey, 1999b: 161).

In Auster's films community emerges as a way to comprehend the relationship of the personal, the particular and the local with the metropolitan, the general and the universal. At the same time, friendship, storytelling and baseball are aspects of the characters' lives from which communal feeling emerges. Raymond Williams elucidates a number of useful concepts that illustrate my understanding of community; amongst these are the ideas of 'militant particularisms' (Williams, 1989a: 249) and 'structures of feeling' (Williams, 1973: 158; 1977: 132). He proposes that local obligations and solidarities can be experienced at a larger geographical and social scale, and can subsequently be incorporated into 'the establishment of higher relations' for 'the total relations of a society' (Williams, 1989b: 115). 'Militant particularisms' are fugitive and clandestine social actions which secrete themselves in the interstitial spaces beyond the vision and command of the dominant order.[2] For Williams, small acts of 'militant particularism' accumulate and coalesce into 'structures of feeling' that are themselves informal and barely tangible senses of community and neighbourly relations. Auster adopts the Brooklyn Cigar Company store as just such an interstitial space in *Smoke* and *Blue in the Face*, where the non-conformist practices of storytelling and discussion stand in direct contrast to the dominant order of Manhattan's money relations. However, the translation of 'militant particularisms' beyond the place-bound action of their origin is often frustrated by 'systematic obstacles' (Williams, 1989b: 115). We need then to carefully consider the nature and function of community in these films, and to place it in the context of the contemporary metropolis, and in particular, New York City.

Community

The meaning of community is an important theme in Auster's work, though it only takes on the conventional sense of place-bound neighbourhood in the films. Previously Auster had acknowledged his debt to a 'community' of writers and a literary heritage that begins with Poe, Hawthorne and Melville. Nathaniel West, the New York Language poets and European modernists such as Mallarmé and Kafka have all been influential figures.[3] However, Auster's strongest influence is the historical connection he feels to other writers. With regard to 'The Book of Memory', but in comments that hold true for many of his works, Auster said:

> I felt as though I were looking down to the bottom of myself, and what I found there was more than just myself – I found the world. That's why the book is filled with so many references and quotations, in order to pay homage to all the others inside me. On the one hand, it's a book about being alone; on the other hand, it's about community. That book has dozens of authors, and I wanted them all to speak through me. In the final analysis, 'The Book of Memory' is a collective work. (Auster, 1997: 316–17)

In the stories of *The New York Trilogy*, the voices of Poe, Melville and Hawthorne are constantly present, as well as a cacophony of detective writers implied in the form. In *Moon Palace* Fogg's predicament is haunted by echoes of Knut Hamsun's *Hunger* and Kafka's 'The Hunger Artist'. In *The Book of Illusions* the writings of Chateaubriand frame the text as an influence shaping the narrative.

This 'community of collaboration', as we might term it, can take many forms. Auster has 'collaborated', for example, with the artist Sophie Calle on two projects.[4] In *Leviathan* he takes Calle as the inspiration for Maria Turner, appropriating a number of Calle's pieces for his character. These include the stranger's diary that is central to the story, but also a chromatic diet, and an 'archaeology of the present', recording spells as a chambermaid and a stripper (Auster, 1993: 63–7). In *Double Game* Calle inverts this process, and lives out her life according to the rules imposed on Maria by Auster – the 'life of Maria, and how it influenced the life of Sophie', as Calle puts it (Calle, 1999: 10–11). Part II of *Double Game* records those pieces that influenced Auster. But Part III, 'Gotham Handbook', is the photographic and written record of a true collaboration between artists who, despite working in different media, cooperate to produce a communal project. In a 'whimsical'[5] four-part manifesto for improved metropolitan living entitled 'Personal Instructions to SC on How to Improve Life in New York City (Because she asked . . .)', Auster reveals what is wrong with the contemporary New York environment and what can be done to put it right (Calle, 1999: 234–5). If Auster's failed urban characters (from Quinn to Mr Bones) had been armed with this model for urban engagement they may have faired considerably better. Under the instruction 'Smiling', Auster encourages Calle to '[s]mile at strangers in the street' to 'see if it makes any difference' (Calle, 1999: 239). He instructs her to talk to strangers. 'It doesn't matter what you talk about', he tells her:

> The important thing is to give of yourself and see to it that some form of genuine contact is made . . . it is good to remember the things that bring us together. The more we insist on them in our dealings with strangers, the better morale in the city will be. (Calle, 1999: 240)

Under the category of 'Beggars and Homeless People', the marginal and dispossessed of New York once again inhabit Auster's thinking, and he directs Calle to give away sandwiches, cigarettes and Mac-Donald's meal coupons to 'the miserable ones' (Calle, 1999: 241–2). Finally, he encourages her to impose some sense of her own identity on the anonymous city by 'cultivating a spot' (Calle, 1999: 242–3). In an echo of Stillman Sr, Auster proposes she does this because 'nearly everything is falling apart' (Calle, 1999: 242). However, unlike Stillman, Auster suggests that this space can help to nurture some sense of self. 'Pick one spot in the city and begin to think of it as yours', he instructs:

> Take on this place as your responsibility. Keep it clean. Beautify it. Think of it as an extension of who you are, as part of your identity. . . . Make a record of . . . daily observations and see if you learn anything about the people or the place or yourself. (Calle, 1999: 240)

The place Calle chooses is a phone booth on the corner of Greenwich and Harrison in Tribeca. She cleans it and equips it with a pen and paper, flowers, chairs, magazines and a sheet for comments. In a gesture that encapsulates the idea of 're-enchanting' the city by overlaying the rational and taken-for-granted with the poetic and reimagined, she covers the phone company's logos with her own messages. By adding signs exhorting New York to 'HAVE A NICE DAY' and 'ENJOY' (Calle, 1999: 246), Calle adds a personal, lyrical and positive communal dimension to the experience of the city. She also uses the comments callers leave to adapt her booth, deploying a flexibility in her task which allows her project to correspond with the needs and desires of the city's inhabitants. The experiment is bought to an end after seven days when AT&T's engineers tear down the decorations (Calle, 1999: 288–9).

This last act goes some way to justifying Auster's insistence on a degree of metropolitan nihilism. He warns that the sort of social contact he proposes for Calle can be dangerous in New York, and she should be wary at all times (Calle, 1999: 239). Although Calle is never personally threatened, her exploration of New York's human scale, experienced at street level, is cut short by the distant, dehumanised and inflexible forces of the city, here represented by the phone company. Her reward for her improvised and clandestine acts of kindness is destruction, and a return to the uniform, controlled and rational city space.

Communal practices have also emerged in Auster's work in the form of film making, which promoted a strong sense of collaborative production. Prior to *Smoke* and *Blue in the Face*, Auster collaborated on a number of other projects: with his friend Art Spiegelman on an illustrated version of 'City of Glass'; on a filmscript of 'City of Glass'; with Sophie Calle on *Double Game* (1999); with his associate editor Nelly Reifler and the contributors on *True Tales of American Life* for National Public Radio; on an introduction to Terry Leach's baseball autobiography *Things Happen for a Reason* (2000); on a story in Art Spiegelman's illustrated children's book, *Strange Stories for Strange Kids* (2001); and on the accompanying text for a series of paintings by Sam Messer, *The Story of My Typewriter* (2002). All of these projects are about connecting with others in the production of literature and art.

The 'community' of film making has had an enormous impact upon Auster. His first significant experience came when Wayne Wang asked to direct a film based on Auster's short story, 'Auggie Wren's Christmas Story', first published in the *New York Times* on Christmas Day in 1990. The story became the film *Smoke*, and the core team of scriptwriter, director and editor proved so creative that they went on to produce *Blue in the Face*. This film was made immediately afterwards as an improvised companion piece with Auster as co-director. Later, Auster would script and direct *Lulu on the Bridge*. Despite the film receiving bad reviews (leading to abandonment by its distributors), Auster gained a good deal of support and encouragement from the collaborative process of its production, and formed a particularly close working relationship with the director of photography, Alik Sakharov. In an indication of how these artistic understandings can develop, Auster told Rebecca Prime:

> We worked for weeks, just the two of us. . . . That was the foundation of the film. . . . Not only did we develop a plan that we both believed in, but

we learned to trust each other, to depend on each other's insights and judgements. By the time filming began, we were comrades, partners in a single enterprise. We worked together in a state of tremendous harmony. . . . He was my closest collaborator on the film, the one person who was with me all the way. (Auster, 1998b: 162)

In a wider sense of collaboration, and in a remarkable reinterpretation of his connection to a literary heritage, Auster found, 'standing there on the set every day with the crew, I somehow felt that they were creating the story with me – with me and for me. It was as if they were all inside my head with me' (Auster, 1998b: 165). Poe and other writers provide Auster with some of the voices and materials that inhabit his books, most notably in the *Trilogy*. Similarly, the working community constituted by the actors and crew of the film inhabit *Lulu* as an essential aspect of the creative process as well as the technical one.

Of the production of *Smoke*, Auster has said, 'I was the writer, Wayne was the director, . . . it was *our* film, and all along we had considered ourselves equal partners in the project' (Auster, 1995b: 8, original emphasis). In a statement that reflects the ethos of the films, Wang has added, 'I thank Paul Auster for the inspiration, for being my friend, my brother, and my partner' (Auster, 1995b: viii). To this core team of writer and director were added the actors, none of whom made a lot of money, but 'all seemed enthusiastic about being in the film. That made for a good working atmosphere all round' (Auster, 1995b: 9). Although Auster did not get particularly involved on set with the shooting, he contributed significantly to the editing. He, Wang and the editor Maysie Hoy formed 'an excellent three way relationship' where opinions were shared in an atmosphere of 'respect and equality' (Auster, 1995b: 11).

Place operates in *Smoke* on a number of important levels. New York, Brooklyn, Park Slope, the store – all these places form the basis of some kind of identification for the characters. Auster has said that he focused on his own neighbourhood because it 'has to be one of the most democratic and tolerant places on the planet' (Auster, 1995b: 14). *Smoke*, he says, is also a way of challenging some of the stereotypes that present New York as a hellhole, by showing how people from all races and classes can get along. Harvey Wang (no relation to Wayne), who shot video footage for *Blue in the Face*, fully understood Auster's sense of Brooklyn. He has written of 'this one-of-a-kind place' as a cacophony of voices and accents (Auster, 1995b: 200). This cacophony contributes a distinctive aspect to Brooklyn's very particular character in Auster's films, as the individual voices join in 'militant particularisms', which in turn accumulate into 'structures of feeling', and ultimately into a unique sense of place and community. Writing about the specific community represented in *Blue in the Face*, Auster has said: '[t]he characters are embattled, highly opinionated, relentless in their anger. And yet . . . the film is genuinely amusing, and one walks away from it with a feeling of great human warmth' (Auster, 1995b: 161).

The multitude of voices that inhabit Brooklyn operates in two ways in these films. First, it emphasises the fact that New York is at the intersection of large and distant geopolitical processes, highlighted by the borough's diversity. Secondly, it gives Brooklyn some of the peculiar characteristics that construct it as a knowable and warm place for Auster. The way that a multitude of voices combines in these texts is further indicated by Auster's use of a story about Bakhtin, first deployed in 'The Locked Room' and repeated in *Smoke* (Auster, 1995b: 101–2). During the siege of Leningrad, Paul Benjamin tells his young friend Rashid, Bakhtin was forced to use the pages of a manuscript he had been working on for ten years as cigarette papers. In an interview Auster states that Bakhtin's dialogic theory of the novel and the concept of heteroglossia come 'closest to understanding the complexity and the magic' of the form (Auster, 1997: 304). Where the focus is tight and limited, the novel is able to express some of the competing and contrasting voices within its fictional communities. But film is able to broaden that focus to incorporate the voices of contestation, contradiction and conflict which characterise communities. It is through the contestation of urban voices in the films, particularly *Blue in the Face*, that Auster expresses his most optimistic vision of community in the contemporary metropolis. Heteroglossia, and Foucault's idea of heterotopia (of which the store is an example), express a construction of place emerging from a multitude of potential identifications.[6] As this chapter will argue, it is through the construction of such flexible communities that Auster demonstrates how his characters might achieve a temporary, but nonetheless stable and coherent identity. The implication is that only in communities which are simultaneously supportive and outward looking can the array of personal and social coordinates one find to establish that identity.

Baseball

Baseball has performed a number of significant roles in the lives of Auster's characters, and has functioned on a number of symbolic levels. From *The New York Trilogy* to *Blue in the Face* it has been a pastime, part of a social strategy, a form of community and a trope for both metropolitan living and the metropolis itself. Like social relations in general, baseball can also be thought about on a number of different geographical scales. In terms of the rules, leagues and championships the game operates at a national and international level. It has a history and a culture that can be shared between fans anywhere, but like language itself, there are conventions and codes that make the sharing of baseball possible. At the same time, it also operates at a very local level, expressing team loyalties, local rivalries and the experience of 'being there'. On this scale the game becomes personal, immediate and emotional.

Because of these multiple levels it is also possible to think of baseball in similar terms to those Doreen Massey applies to the city. Baseball, after all, is a predominantly metropolitan activity, and impacts on the culture of American cities, and even the mythologised global view of them, through a universal lexicon of club symbols and popular idiom (talk of 'left-field', 'curve-ball', 'back-stop', 'three strikes and you're out', and so on), while continuing to provide a point of identification at a local, neighbourhood level. Thus, where Massey argues that the contemporary metropolis promotes a feeling of 'the outside as part of the inside' (Massey, 1994b: 5), we can also see the global scale of baseball, including both its regulatory structures and its extranational culture, influencing attitudes at the local level. Simultaneously, the global content of baseball culture is formed from an accumulation of games and results that emerge locally. That is, the global is formed by the local, while the local is constantly informed and constrained by the global.

The operation of rule and chance in Auster's urban environments generally, and in baseball specifically, emphasises the metaphorical relationship between the game and metropolitan living in his work. Auster consistently uses chance as a causal device in his metropolitan fiction. Fogg in *Moon Palace*, Maria Turner in *Leviathan* and Nashe in *The Music of Chance*, for example, all paradoxically rely on chance as an organising principle in life and art, and deploy it in metropolitan or allegorically metropolitan settings. There is also a historical association between games, chance and the metropolis, noted by the architectural historian Joseph Rykwert. He observes that the Greeks applied the word 'polis' both to the city and to a 'dice-and-board game that . . . depends on the interplay of chance and rule' (Rykwert, 2000: 5). The association Rykwert draws out between the game and the city also applies to baseball and the way Auster represents New York. Thus, in Auster's work the analogy between baseball and the metropolis is dependent upon the unfolding of a series of chance events operating within a tightly regulated set of structures or rules. In games, it is this interplay of chance (the roll of dice, the pitch of the ball, the strike or out) within the limits of rule (the constraints of the board, the diamond, and complex rules) that shapes outcomes and lives. In cities, it is the endless choice of destination and possible routes, with the infinite possible encounters along the way, which constitute chance, while the pattern (in New York, the grid) of streets constrains and orders. Rykwert recognises that a balance between rule and chance in the city is desirable. He sees that urban living is not entirely imposed from above by rule, nor quite determined from below by chance (Rykwert, 2000: 5). As in games, the contingent event is as vital as the rule that simultaneously contains and allows it, and a satisfactory outcome is dependent on an equilibrium between the two. Auster demonstrates this in the cases of Maria Turner and Lillian Stern in *Leviathan*. Because Maria is attuned to her metropolitan environment, she is able to take account of the boundaries and rules in which her aleatorical art is formed. Lillian, however, is 'out of control' and unstable, over-determined by the unbounded actions of contingency. Equally, when rule and chance inhabit the fragmented and disorientated lives of Auster's alienated (male) characters, baseball often offers them some sort of structure and focus. In complex and isolating metropolitan environments, therefore, baseball is able to offer isolated characters some small degree of order as well as connections to a world beyond their solitude.

Auster's adherence to the concept of chance having infinite interplay within a set of regulated boundaries – as expressed in baseball – is recreated in a card game he devised before he became a renowned novelist. Before *The Invention of Solitude* and *The New York Trilogy* had propelled Auster to literary success, he attempted to make some money with a card-based baseball game of his own design. 'Action Baseball', as he called it, clearly demonstrates how rule and chance, structure and contingency, operate in baseball for Auster (Auster, 1998a: 209–30). The turn of the cards as pitches within the structure of plays and innings creates a game which, Auster insists, 'unfolds with all the excitement of a flesh-and-blood game' (Auster, 1998a: 212).

Baseball, then, permeates Auster's life on many levels. On a personal level, he maintains a keen interest in all matters to do with the game. In the Berg Collection there is a postcard from Don DeLillo to Auster dated 6 April 1987. The handwritten message on the card amounts to just this:

Paul: Pay attention. This is <u>serious</u>.
NL East   NL West
Cardinals   Reds

AL East   AL West
Indians   Who cares?

(DeLillo)[7]

Baseball, though, has also had an originating role in Auster's literary career. In the brief autobiographical fragments, 'Why Write?' (first published in *Granta* in 1995, and reprinted in *Hunger*), Auster traces his career as a writer to a formative moment at the Polo Grounds, to express how writing and baseball are intrinsically linked. As an eight-year-old boy at his first major-league game, Auster asked Willie Mays for his autograph ('none was greater, none more perfect nor more deserving of worship than Willie Mays, the incandescent Say-Hey kid' (Auster, 1997: 393)). However, nobody in the party had a pencil and the young Auster was bitterly disappointed as the great Willie Mays 'walked out of the ballpark and into the night' (Auster, 1997: 394). As a direct consequence of this incident Auster started carrying a pencil with him at all times. 'If nothing else', he records, 'the years have taught me this: if there's a pencil in your pocket, there's a good chance that one day you'll feel tempted to start using it. . . . [T]hat's how I became a writer' (Auster, 1997: 395).

This association between writing and baseball is echoed in an unpublished article entitled 'Spring Fever'. Here Auster insists that '[m]ore easily than any other sport, baseball lends itself to the written word' (Auster, 1980: 8). Much of this article was incorporated into *The Invention of Solitude* in a section recollecting Auster's grandfather. Here Auster develops both the intensely personal aspects of baseball and its wider appeal, particularly as these things apply to his own life. As his grandfather lies dying in hospital, Auster records how baseball provided a connection between them. It was his grandfather 'who had taken him to his first game, had talked to him about all the old players, had shown him that baseball was as much about talk as it was about watching' (Auster, 1982: 117). It is this oral constituent of baseball culture that functions in *Smoke* and *Blue in the Face* to emphasise the importance of face-to-face relations in a community. But there is more to baseball and collective identity in the modern metropolis. As well as the here-and-now contact and dialogue between individuals, there is also the discursive component of baseball's histories, both personal and 'official', and its place in a wider culture. Through these baseball is shown as an 'introverted' constituent of community, reaching out to a wider social and organisational network. In 'Spring Fever' Auster identifies how baseball and its culture inhabits an American collective consciousness, making it simultaneously a national concern and 'part of our inner landscape' (Auster, 1980: 3).

On a personal level, Auster insists that old baseball photographs have the same evocative power as Proust's madeleines (Auster, 1980: 1). At the same time, on an institutional level, the archival aspect of the game has given it 'a vast and compelling tradition' created from a record of every play in every game since the late nineteenth century (Auster, 1980: 2). It is from this statistical legacy – along with the rules, the league frameworks, and the conventions of reports and figures – that the structural nature of baseball emerges. The contingent and chance events on the field become formalised and rationalised within these highly regulated structures.[8] In a sentiment that prefigures his use of baseball in the films, Auster also claims baseball as a national language which is able to cut across class, colour and ethnic origins because of its universal appeal as a 'male inheritance' (Auster, 1980: 3). At this point in his career (prior to the *Trilogy*), Auster sees himself connecting to a wider world through the masculine discourses of sport. As discussed, the fiction increasingly locates the possibility of urban redemption in the figure of female artists. It is possible to interpret this development as a reflection of the domestic stability he finds with Siri Hustvedt. However, as will be discussed, *Smoke* and *Blue in the Face* re-establish the possibility of a community of men, perhaps indicating that the cinematic form offers Auster the opportunity to incorporate both male and female urban strategies into the same narrative.

It is through the structural elements of baseball that Auster connects the game to wider social and historical discourses in his work. In 'The Book of Memory', for example, he explores the ways baseball has affected both his inner and outer lives. For A., when he was a child, baseball 'had been the thing that drew him out from the solitary enclosures of his early childhood. It had initiated him into the world of the other, but at the same time it was something he could also keep within himself' (Auster, 1982: 115). Baseball continues to connect A. to his grandfather in adulthood. To maintain his grandfather's presence in the material world, A. reads him the baseball reports from the newspaper. 'It was his last contact with the outside world', Auster writes, 'and it was painless, a series of coded messages he could understand with his eyes closed' (Auster, 1982: 118). A. comes to realise that baseball has become a comfort to him at a distressing and incomprehensible time – a point of stillness in a changing world. Staying in his grandfather's apartment, he is able to watch baseball on cable TV at almost any time of the day. Like Fogg, who finds, sitting in a bar watching baseball A. discovers that to watch baseball is 'to feel his mind striving to enter a place of pure form'. He goes on:

> Despite the agitation on the field, baseball offered itself to him as an image of that which does not move, and therefore a place where his mind could be at rest, secure in its refuge against the mutabilities of the world.
> (Auster, 1982: 115)

Beyond the personal experience of individual games, baseball can function to order the past along its own trajectory of landmark events. As with Proust's madeleines, baseball can trigger recollections across time. Auster describes how for A., 'the power of baseball was for him the power of memory . . . as a catalyst for remembering his own life and as an artificial structure for ordering the historical past' (Auster, 1982: 116). For example, 1960 is memorable as the year Bill Mazeroski won the World Series for the Yankees rather than the year Kennedy was elected or the year of A.'s Bar Mitzvah (Auster, 1982: 116).

The continuity of baseball in American national consciousness is, according to Auster, the result of the stability of its symbolism. As well as the style of the uniforms – which look much the same at the turn of the twentieth century as they did at the turn of the nineteenth – Auster identifies the diamond (unchanged since 1893) as an 'icon as familiar as the stars and stripes' (Auster, 1982: 116). In 'Spring Fever' Auster comes close to comparing baseball to a religion, describing the diamond as 'democracy's answer to the spritual icon' (Auster, 1980: 1). The diamond, of course, also represents a set of uniform and universal structures and boundaries within which the contingent events of each game are contained.

From personal experience to the national consciousness, then, Auster demonstrates that baseball is a means of connection with both the historical and the social. For A. in *Solitude* it provides a connection to others in childhood, a connection to his own development into the adult world (symbolised in Jewish culture by Bar Mitzvah), and a connection to the discursive world of politics and history, as well as here-and-now contact with his grandfather.

Baseball first appeared in Auster's literature in the pseudonymous detective novel, *Squeeze Play* (first published in 1982, and reprinted as an addendum to *Hand to Mouth*). The title derives from a play in baseball, and the novel follows the investigation into the death of former baseball star George Chapman. The solution of the case reveals that, in a reversal of the traditional detective story, Chapman's death is a suicide staged to look like a murder. As well as the 'crime' of the 'murder', Chapman has also transgressed the principles of baseball by betting on his own performance. He has attempted to impose an organising principle on the game that is contradictory to both its spirit and Auster's adherence to the rule of chance, and he is punished by his gangster bookmakers and his author (Auster) for doing so. The novel is more conventional in its form than the later novels, but does contain the germs of many of the themes that emerge and are problematised by later texts, particularly in the *Trilogy*.[9]

Auster's subsequent fiction has demonstrated how even the most alienated metropolitan individual can be reconnected to the social realm by baseball, if only temporarily. In *The New York Trilogy* both Quinn and Blue are baseball fans. Quinn's lonely life is punctuated by anonymous chats with the counterman at the Heights Luncheonette. Blue escapes the solitude of his observation of Black for the crowds of Ebbetts Field. For the first time in months he experiences the multitudes of a crowd as he rubs shoulders with the other fans on the subway. Once at the ballpark Blue is fascinated by Jackie Robinson, the first African American to play in the major-leagues. Blue is quickly caught up in the atmosphere and the spectacle of the game, 'cheering whatever Robinson does, and when the black man steals a base in the third inning he rises to his feet, and later, in the seventh . . . he actually pounds the back of the man sitting next to him' (Auster, 1988: 159). Baseball has the power to temporarily liberate Blue from the binary relationship with Black that the case has imposed on him, and to remind him of the potential pluralities of urban life.

Similarly, in *Moon Palace* baseball plays a large part in the lives of M. S. Fogg and his Uncle Victor. Victor believes that our lives have a potentially infinite number of coincidences and intersections calculated from the nine innings of a baseball game (Auster, 1992a: 14). Auster also relates the unpredictable nature of modern metropolitan living and of baseball in the parallels between Fogg's condition and two baseball teams. As Fogg descends into the abyss, his team, the Chicago Cubs, begins a 'spectacular fall', while, simultaneously, the New York Mets start an 'improbable surge from the depths' (Auster, 1992a: 62). All of this prompts Fogg to speculate that '[c]ausality was no longer the hidden demiurge of the universe: down was up, the last was the first, the end was the beginning'. For the disorientated and confused Fogg, the descent of the Cubs and his own misfortune appear to be connected.

Elsewhere, in *The Music of Chance*, Auster presents baseball as analogous to Nashe's organising principle, while Pozzi's worldview does not admit the intersection of a multitude of potential outcomes, each delicately balanced. Instead, he persists in seeing their misfortune as the result of Nashe stealing the figures from the model and violating a universal law. In *Leviathan* Aaron returns from Paris because he misses baseball. This novel also displays the power of baseball to inhabit tangential narratives. Sachs uses Dwight's softball bat to kill his victim Dimaggio, who carries the name of one of the most famous baseball players ever. In *Mr. Vertigo*, Walt follows the St Louis Cardinals through his many lives, with pennants, World Series and inaugural live radio broadcasts having a greater impact on Walt's narrative than world events such as the Wall Street Crash, the Depression and the Second World War. The gangster section involving Dizzy Dean is a reworking of the plot of *Squeeze Play* (Auster, 1995a: 255). Mr Bones encounters baseball in *Timbuktu*, but the game and its culture present an impenetrable lexicon (or code) to the uninitiated dog (Auster, 1999: 110). Finally, Auster contributed an introduction to the autobiography of Mets pitcher Terry Leach (Leach and Clark, 2000: xix–xx).

One of the common themes that runs through all of the above, in Auster's representations of baseball in his own life and the lives of his characters, is the capacity of the game to overlay everyday metropolitan life with magical and mythical qualities. Best of all, it seems, this lyrical sporting discourse can be shared through the common vocabularies of histories and experiences that promote and nurture a feeling of belonging. Friendship provides the entry to one such community of belonging.

Friendship

Smoke and *Blue in the Face* explore the development of friendship and community in New York through the practices of storytelling and baseball. Auster's earliest literary creations, A. and Quinn, struggle against overwhelming isolation only to fail and be erased from the urban text (in Quinn's case). But in the films we find similarly alienated characters establishing connections back into the society of people, and back to the 'language of men' (Auster, 1997: 33), through friendship and community.

The friendship at the centre of *Smoke* is between Paul Benjamin (the pseudonym Auster used for *Squeeze Play*), a novelist; Auggie Wren, the manager of the Brooklyn Cigar Company store; and Rashid Cole, a black kid from the Boreum Heights projects. Their friendship develops from the kind of metropolitan contingencies and chance events we have seen emerging across Auster's literary works. Paul buys his cigars from Auggie, and uses the store to escape the loneliness and isolation caused by the murder of his pregnant wife during a bank robbery. Rashid meets Paul when he saves him from being run down by a truck. The bond between them develops from Paul's insistence that he must 'put the scales in balance' (Auster, 1995b: 30), an image that is invoked a number of times in the film. As the film progresses, the friendships between these three men develop into a series of solidarities and mutual obligations.

One of the ways Auster chooses to express this solidarity is through money. On the face of it this seems like a restatement of the values and ethos of the system of international finance capital, as encoded in the Manhattan skyline across the East River. However, Auster treats the circulation of money as an act that contradicts the 'money relations' of New York's global finance centre, by suspending the accrual of profit. Rashid is hiding out in bourgeois Park Slope because he has come into the possession of the proceeds of an armed robbery carried out by a notorious Boreum criminal known as the Creeper.[10] While staying with Paul he hides the money on a bookshelf, but it is discovered when Paul goes to retrieve a copy of Bakhtin to illustrate a story. With Paul's encouragement Rashid passes the money to Auggie to compensate for ruining a consignment of illegal Cuban cigars. Subsequently, despite being severely beaten by the Creeper and his accomplice, Paul's attachment to Rashid remains true and he protects Rashid by keeping his whereabouts secret. Finally, the money passes out of the group to

Ruby, Auggie's one-eyed former lover, for the rehabilitation of her drug-addict daughter. Thus, the money traces the development of obligations within the group of friends, but it does not generate a profit for any of them, suggesting that within the small community the dominant capitalist organisation of social relations can be evaded for a time.

The different narrative strategies and visual codes adopted by Auster and Wang subtly reinforce the social and spatial emphases of the films. The representations of community in *Smoke* are tightly focused, with the camera work foregrounding the core friendship between Paul, Auggie and Rashid. Auster describes how the 'visual language' of the film reflects the narrative, adopting more close shots of the three men as the friendship grows closer (Auster, 1995b: 12–13). The structure of the film also suggests a conventional and linear mode of artistic creation with the participants working from a script and to a storyline. The friendships in the film develop within structured sections, echoing the organised and stable core relationship between key artists at the centre of the film-making process.

The establishment of a community, and the identification of connections to it in the form of solidarities and obligations, then, is a primary concern of these films. Auster demonstrates how the familiarity of neighbourhood provides comfort and stability for his Park Slope characters in *Smoke*. *Blue in the Face*, meanwhile, broadens the scope of Auster's vision by encompassing the concerns of a wider Brooklyn community, and engaging a cross-section of its population in the film-making process. He thus simultaneously affirms his belief in the community of place and the community of artistic practice. This vision of community is able to incorporate the local and personal experience of family and friendship, like that illustrated by 'Paul Auster' and the Narrator in *The New York Trilogy*, Fogg in *Moon Palace* and Aaron in *Leviathan*. At the same time, though, the characters in *Smoke* and *Blue in the Face* are able to turn outwards and experience the networks that extend beyond their own place-bound experience.

The support and comfort Auster has drawn from the communal process of film making is recorded above, and the collaborative aesthetic practices of a community of artists are illustrated by the combined activity of Auster and Calle to produce *Leviathan* and *Double Game*. More specifically, in *Smoke*, Auster presents this same artistic community coexisting alongside and within the community of place.

The bond between Rashid and Paul is strengthened by Rashid's status as a painter. Similarly, the solidarities between Paul and Auggie are reinforced when Auggie shows Paul his photo-project. The relationship between the writer and the photographer parallels that of Auster and Calle, and that between Maria and Aaron in *Leviathan*. In *Smoke*, Auster once again demonstrates the power of art to add a mythical dimension to the metropolitan experience, and in a small way to make the city a better place on a personal level. The project consists of photographs of the cigar store taken from the same place at the same time every day for thirteen years. The images are arranged chronologically in albums, one for each year from 1977 to 1990. In its aleatorical openness to the admission of unplanned content within a highly regulated structure of routine, Auggie's project mirrors the work of Maria Turner in *Leviathan*, and that of Sophie Calle. The project also illustrates Auster's understanding of the interplay of rule and chance in the metropolis. The balance described by Rykwert, between the determination of rule and the undetermined nature of urban chaos, emerges in the project to create a significant contemporary urban record (Rykwert, 2000: 5). Consequently we can also trace parallels between the project, the metropolis and baseball as Auster represents urban lives constituted from random events constrained by structures and limits. The overall project seeks to be a totalising vision, while individual pictures and groups of pictures exemplify almost undetectable shifts in the rhythms of the metropolis. Together, the photographs represent, as Brooker suggests, 'a modernist sensibility keen to order the randomness of the everyday' (Brooker, 2002: 112).

In an exchange between Paul and Auggie, Auster's dialogue illustrates how the project and the metropolis display constraining practices, while simultaneously allowing an almost limitless array of variations and interplays. Paul is flicking through the second album of photographs when Auggie tells him to slow down:

> AUGGIE: You'll never get it if you don't slow down, my friend. . . . you're going too fast. You're hardly even looking at the pictures.
> PAUL: But they're all the same.
> AUGGIE: They're all the same, but each one is different from every other one. You've got your bright mornings and your dark mornings. You've got your summer light and your autumn light. You've got your weekdays and your weekends. You've got your people in overcoats and galoshes, and you've got your people in shorts and T-shirts. Sometimes the same people, sometimes different ones. And sometimes the different ones

become the same, and the same ones disappear. The earth revolves around the sun, and every day the light from the sun hits the earth at a different angle.

PAUL: . . . Slow down, huh?

(Auster, 1995b: 44–5)

The image of the sun hitting the earth at a different angle every day captures the essence of metropolitan life in Auster's work: each day, week or season is the same, but also contains subtle changes that are the personal and particular elements of metropolitan life. Here is the analogy for the concept of community which admits, indeed rejoices in, difference. Within each photograph personal and immediate narratives are captured, while across the years processes of change are detectable. However, these urban nuances are only apparent to the urban observer who takes his time.

In *Blue in the Face* Auster widens his focus to include the community of place. This extends from the shop, to the neighbourhood of Park Slope, and beyond that to the community of Brooklyn. This Austerian vision of community thus builds on the certainties of place to extend into wider geographical and social networks. In a scene that encapsulates the 'precartographic' (to borrow Jameson's term, 1991: 51) nature of local spatial knowledge, Lily Tomlin, playing the part of a street vagrant, searches for number 209 and a half. One of the store boys, Tommy, tells her: 'this is Brooklyn. We don't go by numbers' (Auster, 1995b: 230–3). His statement illustrates the way in which people navigate their own personal city, negotiating spaces that are too familiar to require the rational cartographic practice of numbering. Tommy's local sense of his place in the world is relatively secure – secure enough, at least, not to need the empiricism and rational classification of mapping. This immediate and sensual experience is what de Certeau refers to as the 'disquieting familiarity' of the personal city, identifiable as the genesis of a contingent stable experience of place for Auster's characters (de Certeau, 1984: 96).

The store remains the focus of the community spirit for those who use it, and it becomes the location for sharing historical and present-day mythologies for Park Slope residents. Auggie is conscious of this and invokes the importance of community in an attempt to dissuade the owner, Vinnie, from selling the store to a corporation with no connections to the area. 'Sure, it's a dinky little nothing neighborhood store', he tells Vinnie:

But everyone comes in here. I mean, not just the smokers. The kids come in . . . for their candy . . . old Mrs. McKenna comes in for the soap opera magazines . . . fat Mr. Chen for his crossword puzzles. I mean the whole neighborhood comes in here. It's a hangout, and it helps to keep the neighborhood together. Go twenty blocks from here, twelve-year-old kids are shooting each other for their sneakers. I mean, you close this store, and it's one more nail in the coffin. You'll be helping to kill off this neighborhood. (Auster, 1995b: 254–5)

The battle for ownership makes the store itself a contested site, fulfilling Lefebvre's prediction that space would become 'the principal stake' of 'goal-directed struggle' in the battle to establish a new politics of place (Lefebvre, 1991: 410). The contest here is clearly between the communal and particular practices of Auggie's store and the placeless and monotonous practices of multinational capital. It is apparent that Auster sees the outcome of such battles as shaping community politics in New York.

The value of the store to the neighbourhood cannot necessarily be measured in financial terms, but the social benefits are obvious, at least to Auggie. Its role at the heart of the community is reinforced by its openness and diversity – a multiculturalism that reflects the wider Brooklyn population. Edward Soja would include the store among his 'spaces of radical openness' (Soja, 1996: 33). Drawing on contemporary writings on feminism, race and postcolonialism, Soja describes places able to hold out the possibility of becoming spaces of difference and inclusivity – tolerant and accepting of 'race, class, gender, erotic preference, age, nation, religion, and colonial status' (Soja, 1996: 107). Soja understands that the social differences arising through class, race or other factors, are made concrete in (social) space (Soja, 1996: 86). However, micro-sites – such as the store – are detectable within this social space, in which 'utopias' can be enacted in real spaces that are open and susceptible to mental and imaginative impulses (Soja, 1996: 157, 159–63). These 'heterotopias' (to use Foucault's term) offer the potential to both challenge the dominant capitalist order and offer sanctuary from the intensities of the contemporary metropolis. By acknowledging the racial reality of contemporary Brooklyn life and adapting to its material social conditions, the community around the store is able to avoid the introversion and nostalgia that Doreen Massey also identifies as characteristic of a reactionary sense of place (Massey, 1993: 236). Instead it exhibits an outward vision and cosmopolitanism that is both progressive and inclusive.

Echoing Massey, the intervention of the global in the local – in a way that enhances and renews local experience – is illustrated by a video montage of neighbourhood stores near the end of the film. The sequence includes Molloy's bar and restaurant, the Hong Kong supermarket, adjacent Polish and Chinese restaurants, a Kosher dairy, a Vietnamese restaurant and an Indian grocery. Together the video sequences of the film and the other non-narrative interventions, along with the improvised scenes, constitute a visual code. Like the shooting regime adopted for *Smoke*, the 'visual language' of *Blue in the Face* expresses something of the production practices and the ethos of the film. The impression that the viewer gets, which is supported by Auster's comments, is of a loose, informal and personal approach by all involved. The film was made in six days without a script, and achieves its particular visual impression because Auster and Wang decided that all the scenes were to be shot in masters, without the singles and close-ups that fill in the gaps in editing (Auster, 1995b: 183). The transition between each scene is made instead using the non-narrative material. As a consequence, the narrative path through the film seems chaotic, especially when compared with *Smoke*. Auster describes *Blue in the Face* as a 'puzzle' in which the different formats fit together to form a relatively coherent whole (Auster, 1995b: 199). By 'layering' their presentation of Brooklyn in this way, Auster and Wang also suggest that, like the urban environment itself, communal artistic production is a palimpsest of layered groups contributing to the community of neighbourhood and artistic production.

However, a mode of metropolitan living that acknowledges only local processes in these times of geographical, social and political extension is subject to erosion by the rapid pace of urban spatial change and reproduction. As Raymond Williams notes, relationships in the metropolis become 'distant and dehumanised', 'the apparent opposites of community' (Williams, 1989b: 116). The Auster characters who insist upon an introverted and confined urban existence often find their sense of identity undermined by their unstable environment and the anonymous or overwhelming forces that drive new social and spatial formations. Consequently, for the characters in *Smoke* and *Blue in the Face* to establish a coherent but open sense of self they need to turn their attention to the outside world as well as their own inner terrain and the personal space of the geographically bounded neighbourhood. Each film has an event to symbolise how a character has acquired the vision to look inwards to community while simultaneously looking outwards to understand the world. In *Smoke*, Paul recovers his capacity to write, while in *Blue* Auggie is able to save the store. Auster demonstrates how larger forces, such as multinational business and the discursive nature of New York race relations, shape personal and everyday metropolitan experiences, but also extend well beyond the geographical experiences of the individual. The essential point here is that individual experience is embedded in vast and unknowable processes, and Auster is seeking to represent a mode of urban living able to account for both. In *Smoke* he demonstrates the way that his characters' particular Brooklyn lives are embedded in the networks of international finance markets, such as those driving the privatisation of space for profit or involving a baseball club in a secretive conspiracy. The opening of *Smoke* illustrates how the skyline of Manhattan, symbolic of New York's place at the centre of global capital, is a presence in the lives unfolding on the streets and in the stores of Park Slope. In his filmscript Auster describes the scene:

> *Against the backdrop of the Manhattan skyline, we see an elevated subway train heading toward Brooklyn.*

> *After a moment, we begin to hear voices. An animated discussion is taking place in the Brooklyn Cigar Company.*
>
> (Auster, 1995b: 19)

Here Auster is clearly setting up the homeliness of Brooklyn in contrast to the worldliness of Manhattan. The lives of the men in the cigar store in Brooklyn are, in some part, shaped by the forces flowing through the institutions on the other side of the East River. The story of Paul, Auggie and Rashid is concerned with how these men challenge or evade the social relationships formed through the intersection identified by Harvey of 'money, time and space' (Harvey, 1990: 226). If they succeed in doing so, they may be in a position to challenge capital's 'superior command over time and space', and generate a series of social relations particular to their own place and time (Harvey, 1990: 238).

Blue in the Face also emphasises how local and personal experience is embedded in the larger geographical scales of the metropolis and beyond. The opening sequence of the film expresses Auster's desire to locate his characters in the world. In this scene, a series of shots shifts the perspective from the global to the particular, via a map of the United States, then a map of the north-east region, then a map of Brooklyn. Finally the legend 'YOU ARE HERE' reinforces the exact the location at 16th Street and Prospect Park West, but also gives a context to the local on a national scale (Auster, 1995b: 204).

Writing in *Dissent* magazine at the end of the 1980s, Jan Rosenberg sketches out the racial geography around Brooklyn's Prospect Park. 'The southern and eastern sides of the park, bordered by predominantly black neighbourhoods, seem a distant land', she observes, uncannily anticipating Rashid's presence in *Smoke*. She continues:

> The park serves as more of a barrier than a meeting ground between white upper-middle-class and black and Hispanic Brooklyn. . . . [F]or even the most apolitcal of Slopers, there is a nagging doubt that their good fortune can endure in a Brooklyn increasingly overwhelmed by an underclass as cut off from prosperity as they are connected. (Rosenberg, 1989: 160)

Auster is acutely aware of the racial complexion of his own neighbourhood and addresses it in *Smoke* through the figure of Rashid. In the film, Paul attempts to engage with the discourses of race and is surprised to find it a source of considerable disharmony between himself and Rashid. In one scene they discuss the geography of racial inequality in Brooklyn. Their neighbourhoods are only separated by a mile, but Rashid is prompted to observe, 'It might not be far, but it's another galaxy. Black is black and white is white, and never the twain shall meet' (Auster, 1995b: 82). Attempting to emphasise the connection he and Rashid have made, Paul optimistically suggests that black and white have met in his apartment, to which Rashid responds: 'Let's not get too idealistic' (Auster, 1995b: 83). Here Auster acknowledges the complexity of the issue of race in New York. He also demonstrates how Paul as a writer is drawn to a liberal interpretation of his own role as a member of the white middle class, while at the same time his position and isolation make him blind to the urban realities of life in the projects. Auster does not suggest any special social or political insight on the part of his writer-character, and does not propose that artists can advance much beyond an idealistic optimism. This is graphically illustrated when Paul and Auggie inadvertently intervene to reveal Rashid's identity to his estranged father, Cyrus. There is a violent confrontation between father and son, followed by an uneasy reconciliation and the acceptance of Rashid into his father's new family (with a young wife and a child). However, Auster does not present this episode as a conflict resolved by Paul. Instead there is an uncomfortable silence as the black family shares a picnic with the two white men. The only communication is between Paul and Cyrus as they exchange cigars. Consequently, the conflicts of race (and paternity, which is also a significant form of troubled connection in Auster's work) are not resolved in *Smoke*, but they do find an uneasy accommodation.

Here Auster indicates that the 'resolution' of social tensions and contestations cannot be deferred endlessly, but that an adequate and provisional halt must be called to allow the participants to move on. The racial and paternal tensions that inhabit the relationships in this scene could be deferred, left unresolved or resolved along unrealistic lines of liberal paternalism. Instead, Auster chooses to adopt a moral relativism which results in an attainable and 'good enough' outcome. These films display a moral relativism in a number of other ways too. The utility of the Creeper's hold-up money, the purchase of illegal Cuban cigars, Auggie's stolen camera and the bag-snatch scene at the beginning of *Blue* all combine to demonstrate that the metaphysical bases for the measure of right and wrong are elusive, and the distribution of personal responsibility in the metropolis is a delicate balance. The constant deferral of judgement by or of these characters also reflects and reinforces the way in which Auster understands and constantly represents the deferral of language and the postponement of a permanent and stable identity in his work, which has been the subject of much of the discussion in the preceding chapters.

Storytelling

As the opening scene of *Smoke* suggests, the cigar store stands in contrast to the dominant order of New York's money ethos. Here Manhattan represents the 'perceived' space that Lefebvre identified in his 'representations of space' which encode the rational and institutional nature of urban living, including the grand symbolic gestures of, for example, the skyline (Lefebvre, 1991: 37–8). The store, however, displays the characteristics of 'representational', or lived, spaces (Lefebvre, 1991: 39). These spaces are inhabited by the dreamlike qualities of art and literature, and once again operate below the threshold of visibility. They are associated too with the practices that de Certeau names as 'the ruses and combinations of powers that have no readable identity' (de Certeau, 1984: 95), and David Harvey sees as embodying liberatory and emancipatory possibilities in the interstitial spaces between capitalism's panoptic powers (Harvey, 1996:

420). Storytelling inhabits these films both as a constituent of 'representational' space and as a militant particularism from which community can be formed. An early scene in *Smoke* sets the tone for both films. Before he has been accepted into the society of the shop Paul contributes to a discussion on women and cigars. He tells Auggie and the store boys the story of a bet between Walter Ralegh and Queen Elizabeth I. Ralegh bet that he could weigh smoke, which Paul compares to weighing someone's soul. Raleigh weighed the smoke, Paul tells them, by tapping the ash from a cigar into the pan of a balance, adding the butt and subtracting the combined weight from the weight of the unsmoked cigar, the difference being the weight of the smoke (Auster, 1995b: 24–6). From this point on, smoke becomes an important image in the film. Visitors to the store, for example, take time to share a cigarette with Auggie – creating a community of smokers. But this scene, in particular, reinforces the idea of an amorphous, transient and insubstantial quality at the centre of the store community, to which storytelling significantly contributes. However, like smoke itself, the elusive constituents of community are also present, detectable and effective. Auster clearly associates weighing a soul with the soul of his fictional community.

The penultimate scene of the film takes place in a diner decorated with baseball memorabilia, where Auggie gifts Paul the story of how he came to acquire the camera now used in his project. The closing shots of this scene are the closest and tightest of the film; Wang fills the screen with the characters' smiles of friendship wreathed in smoke. At the end of the scene the screen is filled with a close-up of Auggie's mouth that highlights the orality of storytelling in this relationship. This is the story that becomes 'Auggie Wren's Christmas Story' and breaks Paul's writer's block. By the end of this film, the city has become a place made tolerable, even exciting, by the myriad opportunities to discover, tell and share stories. Thus, storytelling itself becomes an urban strategy – a way of placing oneself in the world and 're-enchanting' the metropolitan environment.

Baseball, as we have seen, has been a consistent presence in Auster's fiction. In *Smoke* and *Blue in the Face* it is a central theme and the topic of much of the discussion in the store. The store guys debate the relative merits of current players and their teams' chances. They also reflect upon past glories and the history of the Dodgers. This practice exemplifies Auster's assertion that baseball is 'as much about talk as . . . about watching' (Auster, 1982: 117).

While *Smoke* is concerned mostly with storytelling and friendship, *Blue in the Face* focuses more on baseball and community. The contemporary plight of the store at the hands of anonymous financial institutions echoes that of the Dodgers in 1957. These resonances are felt by the characters, and the history of the Dodgers becomes a focus for the community involved in trying to save the store. Auster adds another layer of communal pride in the anti-racist stance that the Dodgers took in 1947 when Jackie Robinson became the first African-American to play major-league baseball.[11] The film adopts Robinson as a point of identification around which to rally. A resident summarises the importance of the Dodgers to Brooklyn life when he tells an interviewer: 'when they moved the Dodgers out of Brooklyn, I don't believe there ever was a worse day. Maybe when the war was declared' (Auster, 1995b: 253). However, despite their absence, the memory of the Dodgers remains so palpable to the residents of Brooklyn that when the ghost of Jackie Robinson appears to Vinnie, Robinson is able to connect the sale of the store to that of the ball club. 'I was the man that changed America', he tells Vinnie:

> And I did it all right here: in Brooklyn. Oh, they spat at me, cursed me, made my life a never-ending hell . . . and I wasn't allowed to fight back. . . . Things changed after me. And not just for black people. For white people, too. After me . . . well, white people and black people never looked at each other in the same way anymore. And it happened right here: in Brooklyn. . . . Dollars and cents, Vinnie. Ebbets Field may be gone now, but what happens there lives on in the mind. That's where it counts, Vinnie. Mind over matter. (Auster, 1995b: 256)

Vinnie is won over by the arguments of Auggie and Robinson. He sends a singing telegram, played by Madonna, and the neighbourhood celebrates with an impromptu street party led by the transsexual performer Ru Paul. Auster thus demonstrates how the community's simultaneous historical awareness and outward-looking embrace of diversity have been instrumental in generating a communal conscious-ness able to save and keep the store. As Peter Brooker notes, '[t]he best of old Brooklyn, its stand against prejudice and profit speaks in the present, not as nostalgic whimsy but as a living and active influence' (Brooker, 2000: 106).

However, ultimately the Dodgers did leave Brooklyn, and Auster includes a warning in *Blue in the Face* that is also a call to vigi-lance. The final shot of one of the video sequences shows a plaque commemorating the demolition of the stadium and the building of the Ebbets Field Apartments, and a sign on the building that says 'NO BALL GAMES' (Auster, 1995b: 60). Clearly the panoptic and governing powers of the metropolis are able to intervene to suppress non-conformist and improvised activity wherever it emerges.

These films, then, present a particular understanding of metropolitan living and community in the contemporary environment. As the above shows, Raymond Williams's terms for the emergence of a sense of community and of place are appropriate in elucidating how Auster understands the same process. 'Militant particularisms' and 'structures of feeling' are most easily identified in Auggie's photo-project. 'Militant particularisms' are present in the individual photographs. 'Structures of feeling', meanwhile, are identifiable in the wider movement recorded by the photographs, the people who pass by every day, the routines and habits of Auggie's personal metropolitan place and space, and the idea of the sun hitting the earth at a different angle every day. Elsewhere in the films, individual acts of friendship and sharing, such as gifts of money and stories, illustrate the capacity of 'militant particularisms' to arise out of and affect individual lives. These then accumulate into the indistinct and elusive qualities of community that make the city a better place, such as the culture of storytelling centred on the store, and the wider sense of belonging that inhabits Brooklyn. All of these things become detectable when you are able to slow down and look for them.

There still remains a suspicion that Auster's view of Park Slope is somewhat nostalgic and reactionary, where the ethnic poor are only admitted to engender a frisson of urban authenticity.[12] However, Auster demonstrates that Paul Benjamin's extension of social relations beyond his place-bound experience is genuine, if not entirely successful. Although *Smoke* is a film that exclusively explores friendships between men, it portrays openness to racial and class others as a positive social impulse.[13] *Blue in the Face*, meanwhile, redresses the gender balance, by including women as full participants in all the communal contestations that characterise the neighbourhood.

The metropolitan vision Auster presents coincides with Jan Rosenberg's view of Park Slope as a 'middle-class "utopia"'. Rosenberg describes the neighbourhood's development into its contemporary social and spatial formations in this way:

> To the middle class among a generation wary of suburbia's soured promise, places like Park Slope came to be seen as a contemporary

alternative, the chance to build a family centred urban life that is distinctly not suburban. The mix of people in public institutions, the subway rides to and from "the City", the architecture, the shared public grandeur of a partially restored Prospect Park – these eddies against the tide of privatization are reminders that one has embraced a post-suburban dream of a vital, complex, dynamic urban life. (Rosenberg, 1989: 161)

To Rosenberg's complex of public social spaces one might add the semi-privatised but wholly open dialogic and social space of the cigar store.

Ultimately, Auster's representation of the Brooklyn community succeeds as an alternative to the reactionary vision of neighbourhood because it is able to simultaneously embrace both the myths of the past and the material social conditions of the present. This allows his characters the flexibility to accommodate shifts in material social conditions and the subsequent changes in the spatial formations of the metropolis. The capacity of the characters to engage with diverse histories of Brooklyn, and their location at a particular intersection of contemporary networks and flows, also mark out their associations as the construction of an affirmative community. However, Auster's literary works suggest that social connections are fragile, and it is the multitudinous nature of social intersections that makes the contemporary metropolis such an intense and fluid experience. Thus, in Auster's New York, the individual must remain flexible and adaptable to maintain a stable understanding of her or his place in the city, and a coherent but open sense of identity.

Doreen Massey describes a similarly progressive sense of place that breaks free of the stasis of nostalgia but is flexible enough to acknowledge that people like to have the comfort of things such as 'place', which most 'progressive' models would decry as reactionary (Massey, 1993: 236). She calls for a new 'sense of place', which should be 'progressive; not self-enclosing and defensive, but outward looking' (Massey, 1993: 233). Auster strikes just such a balance. Park Slope, the Brooklyn Cigar Co. store, Brooklyn and the Dodgers all provide Auster's fictional community with those familiar things that are associated with place, while characters are aware of and engaged with social forces that extend beyond their local geographical experience. Their metropolitan lives provide them with a situated and relational sense of self, constructed from the certainties of local history and shared experience, and at the same time are engaged with the realities of the material social conditions of the here-and-now.

What Auster demonstrates across his work is that the experience of the metropolis wholly in the terms of a global or panoptic, or through a local or street-level perspective, is unable to secure for the individual a stable or coherent relationship with her or his metropolitan environment. Instability and incoherence occur for reasons: on the one hand, the panoptic view privileges the large, anonymous forces of the metropolitan process. On the other, the street-level experience overemphasises the underdetermined aspects of metropolitan life, and is unable to take account of the constantly shifting social and material formations of the metropolitan condition. Ultimately, Auster shows that some combination of perspectives is necessary in contemporary New York. As we have seen, only Massey's conception of 'the local in the global' is able offer a realistic model for Auster's fictional scenarios of metropolitan experiences – especially as he displays them in the films – placing in tension the specificity of place and personal experience with the processes in which it is embedded. As she points out, places 'can be imagined as articulated moments in networks of social relations and understandings' that extend beyond how we think of place-bound community, '[a]nd this in turn allows a sense of place which is extroverted, which includes a consciousness of its links with the wider world, which integrates in a positive way the global with the local' (Massey, 1993: 239). Auster presents Brooklyn as a locus of intersecting multinational forces, and its inhabitants as representatives of a complementary cosmopolitan worldview, where because of their awareness of the forces shaping their lives, the characters are able to occupy capitalism's interstices and resist some of its corrosive practices.

Consequently, we can see how Auster demonstrates the necessity of maintaining a social perspective on the metropolis able to incorporate both the near and the far, the particular and the general, the personal and the political, the 'phantasmagorical' and the physical, the imaginary and the social, and rule and chance, in order to locate oneself in the world. But he does much more than just this confirming what theorists have shown us (and common sense suggests): that personal experience is embedded in large and complex social processes.

This study opened with a discussion of how an urban poetics can overlay the physical metropolis with a mythical dimension to 're-enchant' urban living. James Donald in particular identified a 'traffic' across the boundary between the 'symbolic constructs' of urban imagination and the 'consequences' they manifest 'in an enduring reality' (Donald, 1999: 27). Auster's work too explores the boundaries between the material and the imaginary, going beyond the empirical accounts of urban life and showing how art, literature and storytelling can invest space with illusory and imaginary elements. These practices can, under the right conditions, add to the metropolis a dreamlike and mythical quality which 're-enchants' the contemporary experience of New York City, and combine in a 'poetics of place'.

Notes

1 The phrase is Adrienne Rich's, and is quoted in Soja, 1996: 36.
2 For a fuller discussion of Williams's theoretical and fictional works that emphasise place and community, and a fuller exploration of the relationship of 'militant particularisms' and 'structures of feeling' to community, see Harvey, 1996: 23–45. See also Donald, 1999: 147–52.
3 Auster in interview with the author, 13 December 2001.
4 Sophie Calle's art is difficult to classify. *Double Game* exhibits the full range of her expression. Most often her pieces consist of a photographic record of a series of events. For example, her work includes 'The Birthday Game', a collection of all her birthday presents, and 'The Detective', the record of a private eye Calle hired to tail her. Her work is often about decoding fragments of a life in an attempt to reconstruct a picture of the individual, and could be broadly categorised as 'conceptual'.
5 This is the term Auster used to describe his instructions for Calle in a recent interview (*South Bank Show*, 2005).
6 For Harvey the concept of heterotopia 'encourages the idea of a simultaneity of spatial plays that highlights choice, diversity, and difference. It enables us to look upon the multiple forms of deviant and transgressive behaviours and politics that occur in urban spaces ... as valid and potentially meaningful reassertions to some kind of right to shape parts of the city in a different image. ... It is within these spaces that alternatives can take shape and from these spaces that a critique of existing norms and processes can most effectively be mounted' (Harvey, 2000: 184). See also Soja, 1996: 157–63.
7 DeLillo's powers of prediction proved to be rather poor. Only the St Louis Cardinals for the National League East was correct. The American League West ('who cares?') was won by the Minnesota Twins, who went on to beat the Cardinals in the World Series.
8 Joseph S. Walker notes that for Auster 'baseball is seen as symbolic of human existence ... a continual confrontation between order and chaos' (Walker, 2002: 399–400).
9 Walker provides the only critical treatment of the novel to date (Walker, 2002: 395–6).

10 In interview with Lewis Jones, Auster described how he and his wife Siri live like a 'bourgeois king and queen' in Park Slope, a contrast to the penury he describes in *Hand to Mouth* (Jones, 2001: n.p.).

11 Jackie Robinson was recruited from the 'Negro leagues' to the Dodgers' farm team, the Montreal Royals, in 1947. After one successful season, he was promoted to the senior team, where he agreed not to react to racism for the first few years of his professional career. After that he was constantly embroiled in controversy, and was an influential figure in the Civil Rights movement in the 1950s and 1960s. Robinson acts in the film as a symbol of potential community action for the members of the neighbourhood. It can be argued that the Dodgers' president (Branch Rickey), in initiating the desegregation of baseball, acted not in the name of racial justice, but in the interests of sporting and financial expediency. It should also be remembered that there was significant resistance to Robinson from within the Dodgers' ranks and from just about every other club. In his first season Robinson led the league in being struck on the body by the pitcher (Tygel, 1998: 1–8).

12 Jan Rosenberg notes that the gentrification of Park Slope has been underway since the 1950s. The openness that typifies its neighbourhood spirit can be seen as the result of an influx of artists and radicals who have been instrumental in the neighbourhood's community politics (Rosenberg, 1989: 160–1).

13 For more on the limitations of the female characters in *Smoke* see Nichols, 1998.

Afterword

The events of 11 September 2001 have had a profound effect on the city of New York and its inhabitants. The impact on Auster's work has, so far, been tangential, though in the weeks after the terrible events he was a vocal spokesman for his city in the media around the world. In newspaper articles and essays he has tried to come to terms with the implications for his fellow New Yorkers of a morning which has changed the city for ever. If, as the preceding pages have argued, Auster's work is intrinsically bound up with the culture of New York City, then what bearing will these events have on his work in the future? *The Brooklyn Follies* ended with these lines:

> It was eight o'clock when I stepped out onto the street, eight o'clock on the morning of September 11, 2001 – just forty-six minutes before the first plane crashed into the North Tower of the World Trade Center. Just two hours after that, the smoke of three thousand incinerated bodies would drift toward Brooklyn and come pouring down on us in a white cloud of ashes and death.
>
> But for now it was still eight o'clock, and as I walked along the avenues under the brilliant sky, I was happy, my friends, as happy as any man who had ever lived. (Auster, 2005a: 303–4)

Time will tell how these events will change the way New York writers such as Auster, his wife Siri Hustvedt and their friend Don DeLillo (also a strong voice in the media in the weeks afterward) will come to represent their city in the future. In Ulrich Baer's collection of writers' responses, *101 Stories* (a title which reflects both the power of writing and the height of the buildings which were destroyed), Hustvedt notes both the power and potential inadequacy of language in the face of incomprehensible events. 'We have to talk', she writes, 'but we should be careful with our words' (Hustvedt, 2002: 159).

In the same collection, Auster describes how the citizens of his city carry on with their everyday lives. When a subway train stops in the tunnel, he pays tribute to his 'fellow New Yorkers [who] sit in the dark, waiting with the patience of angels' (Auster, 2002b: 36). More recently, Auster has narrated a walking tour and history of the neighbourhood around what is now Ground Zero. In this 'sonic memorial soundwalk', he describes himself as 'Paul Auster; writer, New Yorker', and guides the listener on a tour of 'the streets of lower Manhattan' (Auster, 2005b) that has the same geographical exactness as Quinn's plotting of Stillman's footsteps (and his own) around the Upper West Side.

Auster's belief in the angelic patience of his fellow New Yorkers, and the power of the soundwalk project to join people – victims and witnesses – together, suggest that Auster has travelled a good way from the belief that language can only struggle to memorialise that which has been lost, and that walking the streets of New York creates only emptiness. It seems fitting that Auster should return to the theme of walking. Here, two decades after *The Invention of Solitude* and *The New York Trilogy*, instead of emphasising the isolation and confusion of the streets, his pedestrian exploration of the World Trade Center site creates a 'walking memorial' (not unlike de Certeau's 'long poem of walking') able to memorialise both those who died, and what Auster sees as the indomitable spirit of the people whose lives are shaped by the poetry of New York City.

Bibliography and filmography

Works by Paul Auster

Published works

(1982) *The Invention of Solitude*. London: Faber and Faber.
(1987) 'Moonlight in the Brooklyn Museum'. *Art News*. 86.7 (September). 104–5.
(1988) *The New York Trilogy*. London: Faber and Faber.
(1989) *In the Country of Last Things*. London: Faber and Faber.
(1991) *Ground Work*. London: Faber and Faber.
(1992a) *Moon Palace*. London: Faber and Faber.
(1992b) *The Music of Chance*. London: Faber and Faber.
(1993) *Leviathan*. London: Faber and Faber.
(1995a) *Mr. Vertigo*. London: Faber and Faber.
(1995b) *Smoke and Blue in the Face: Two Films by Paul Auster*. London: Faber and Faber.
(1997) *The Art of Hunger*. London: Penguin.
(1998a) *Hand to Mouth*. London: Faber and Faber.
(1998b) *Lulu on the Bridge*. London: Faber and Faber.
(1999) *Timbuktu*. London: Faber and Faber.
(2001) (ed.) *True Tales of American Life*. London: Faber and Faber.
(2002a) *The Book of Illusions*. London: Faber and Faber.
(2002b) 'Random Notes – September 11, 2001, 4:00P.M.; Underground'. In Ulrich Baer (ed.) *101 Stories: New York Writes After September 11*. New York: New York University Press. 34–6.
(2004) *Oracle Night*. London: Faber and Faber.
(2005a) *The Brooklyn Follies*. London: Faber and Faber.
(2005b) *Manhattan, Ground Zero: A Sonic Memorial Soundwalk*. New York: Soundwalk.

Films

(1995) *Blue in the Face*. Dir. Wayne Wang and Paul Auster. Miramax.

(1995) *Smoke.* Dir. Wayne Wang. Miramax.

(1998) *Lulu on the Bridge.* Dir. Paul Auster. DVD release 2006.

(2001) *The Center of the World.* Dir. Wayne Wang. Story by Paul Auster and Siri Hustvedt. Artisan Entertainment.

Unpublished works in the Berg Collection, New York Public Library

(undated a) 'The Poem as Object'. Typescript.

(undated b) 'Invasions'. Holograph.

(undated c) 'New York Spleen'. Typescript.

(undated d) 'A Little Book of Colors'. Typescript.

(undated e) 'New York Confidential: experiments with color'. Typescript.

(undated f) 'Ghosts'. Holograph.

(undated g) 'Columbus's Egg'. Typescript.

(undated h) 'The Mysterious Barricades'. Holograph.

(undated i) 'City of Words'. Holograph.

(undated j) 'Eclipse'. Holograph.

(1967) 'The Dis-jointed Skeleton of Something Less than an Argument'. Typescript.

(1978–9) 'Happiness or a Journey through Space'. Typescript.

(28 March 1980) 'Spring Fever'. Typescript.

Collaborative texts

Auster, Paul and Sam Messer (2002). *The Story of My Typewriter.* New York : Distributed Arts Publishers.

Calle, Sophie (with the participation of Paul Auster) (1999). *Double Game.* London: Violet Editions.

Leach, Terry with Tom Clark (2000). *Things Happen for a Reason.* Introd. Paul Auster. Berkeley, CA: Frog Ltd.

Spiegelman, Art and Françoise Mouly (with a contribution by Paul Auster) (2001). *Strange Stories for Strange Kids.* New York: Harper Collins, 2001.

Interviews

Auster, Paul and Michel Contat (1996). 'The Manuscript in the Book: A Conversation'. *Yale French Studies.* 89. 160–87.

Gregory, Sinda and Larry McCaffery (undated). Draft interview, Berg Collection.

Reich, Allan. *Interview with Paul Auster: Keepsake Number 9.* New York: The Menard Press, 1988.

South Bank Show (1997). Granada Television.

South Bank Show (2005). Granada Television.

Vida, Vendela (ed.) (2005). 'Jonathan Lethem talks to Paul Auster'. In *The Believer Book of Writers Talking to Writers.* San Francisco: Believer Books.

Secondary works on Paul Auster

Alford, Steven E. (1995a) 'Mirrors of Madness: Paul Auster' s *The New York Trilogy*'. *Critique*. 37.1 (Fall). 17–33.

—— (1995b). 'Spaced Out: Signification and Space in Paul Auster' s *The New York Trilogy*'. *Contemporary Literature*. 36.4 (Winter). 613–32.

Barone, Denis (1995). 'Introduction: Auster and the Postmodern Novel'. In Dennis Barone (ed.) *Beyond the Red Notebook*. Philadelphia: University of Pennsylvania Press. 1–26.

Brault, Pascalle-Anne (1998). 'Translating the Impossible Debt: Paul Auster's *City of Glass*'. *Critique*. 39.3 (Spring). 228–38.

Brooker, Peter (1996). *New York Fictions*. Harlow: Longman.

—— (2000). 'The Brooklyn Cigar Co. as Dialogic Public Sphere: Community and Postmodernism in Paul Auster and Wayne Wang' s *Smoke* and *Blue in the Face*'. In Maria Balshaw and Liam Kennedy (eds) *Urban Space and Representation*. London: Pluto. 98–115.

—— (2002). *Modernity and the Metropolis*. Basingstoke: Palgrave.

Dotal, Eyan (2000). 'The Game of Late Capitalism: Gambling and Ideology in *The Music of Chance*'. *Mosaic*. 33.1. 161–76.

Dow, William (1996). 'Never Being "This Far From Home": Paul Auster and Picturing *Moonlight Space*'. *QWERTY*. 6. 193–8.

—— (1998). 'Paul Auster's *The Invention of Solitude*: Glimmers in a Reach to Authenticity'. *Critique*. 39.3 (Spring 1998). 272–81.

Drenttel, William (ed. and compiler) (1994). *Paul Auster: A Comprehensive Bibliographic Checklist of Published Works, 1968–1994*. New York: William Drenttel with Delos Press.

Finkelstein, Norman (1995). 'In the Realm of the Naked Eye'. In Dennis Barone (ed.) *Beyond the Red Notebook*. Philadelphia: University of Pennsylvania Press. 44–59.

Fleck, Linda L. (1998) 'From Metonomy to Metaphor: Paul Auster' s *Leviathan*'. *Critique*. 39.3 (Spring). 258–70.

Front Row (2003). BBC Radio 4 (17 January).

Herzogenrath, Bernd (1999). *An Art of Desire: Reading Paul Auster*. Amsterdam: Rodopi.

Holzapfel, Anne M. (1996) *The New York Trilogy: Whodunit?* Frankfurt: Peter Lang.

Irwin, Mark (1994). 'Inventing the Music of Chance'. *Review of Contemporary Literature*. 14.1 (Spring). 81–91.

Jones, Lewis (2001). 'The Accidental Novelist'. *Sunday Telegraph Magazine*. 10 November. No pages.

Kirkegaard, Peter (1993). 'Cities, Signs, and Meaning in Walter Benjamin and Paul Auster, or: never sure of any of it'. *Orbis Litterarum*. 48. 161–79.

Lavender, William (1993). 'The Novel of Critical Engagement: Paul Auster's *City of Glass*'. *Contemporary Literature*. 3.2 (Summer). 219–40.

Lewis, Barry (1994). 'The Strange Case of Paul Auster'. *Review of Contemporary Literature*. 14.1 (Spring). 53–61.

Little, William G. (1997) 'Nothing to Go On: Paul Auster's *City of Glass*'. *Contemporary Literature*. 38.1 (Spring). 133–63.

Malgrem, Carl D. (2001). *Anatomy of Murder: Mystery, Detective and Crime Fiction*. Madison, WI: Bowling Green State University Popular Press.

Max, D. T. (2002).'The Professor of Despair'. *New York Times* (1 September). 6.

Nichols, Hayden Bixby (1998). 'Review: *Smoke*'. *Film Quarterly* (Spring). http://findarticles.com/cf_0/m1010/n3_v51/20563905.jhtml (accessed 24 January 2001).

O'Hagan, Sean (2004). 'Abstract Expressionist'. *Observer* (8 February). http://observer.guardian.co.uk/magazine/story/0,,1141719,00.html (accessed 16 April 2006).

Oberman, Warren (2004). 'Existentialism Meets Postmodernism in Paul Auster's *The Music of Chance*'. *Critique*. 45.2 (Winter). 191–206.

Osteen, Mark (1994). 'Phantoms of Liberty: The Secret Lives of *Leviathan*'. *Review of Contemporary Literature*. 14.1 (Spring). 87–91.

Rowen, Norma (1991). 'The Detective in Search of the Lost Tongue of Adam: Paul Auster's *City of Glass*'. *Critique*. 32.4 (Summer). 224–34.

Rudman, Mark (1994). 'Paul Auster: Some "Elective Affinities"'. *Review of Contemporary Literature*. 14.1 (Spring): 44–5.

Russell, Alison (1990). 'Deconstructing *The New York Trilogy*: Paul Auster's Anti-Detective Fiction'. *Critique*. 3.2 (Winter). 71–84.

Saltzman, Arthur (1995). '*Leviathan*: Post Hoc Harmonies'. In Dennis Barone (ed.) *Beyond the Red Notebook*. Philadelphia: University of Pennsylvania Press. 162–70.

Shilo, Ilana (2002a). *Paul Auster and Postmodern Quest: On the Road to Nowhere*. New York: Peter Lang.

—— (2002b). 'A Place Both Imaginary and Realistic: Paul Auster's *The Music of Chance*'. *Contemporary Literature*. 43.3 (Fall). 488–517.

Swope, Richard (1998). 'Approaching the Threshold(s) in Postmodern Detective Fiction: Hawthorne's "Wakefield" and Other Missing Persons'. *Critique*. 39.3 (Spring): 207–27.

—— (2002). 'Supposing a Space: The Detecting Subject in Paul Auster's City of Glass'. *Reconstruction*. 2.3. http://reconstruction.eserver.org/023/swope.htm (accessed 15 March 2005).

Varvogli, Aliki (2001). *The World that is the Book: Paul Auster's Fiction*. Liverpool: Liverpool University Press.

Walker, Joseph S. (2002). 'Criminality and (Self)Discipline: The Case of Paul Auster'. *Modern Fiction Studies*. 48.2 (Summer). 389–422.

—— (2004). 'A Kink in the System: Terrorism and the Comic Mystery Novel'. *Studies in the Novel.* 36.3 (Fall). 336–51.

Weisenburger, Steven (1995). 'Inside *Moon Palace*'. In Dennis Barone (ed.) *Beyond the Red Notebook.* Philadelphia: University of Pennsylvania Press. 129–42.

Woods, Tim (1995). '"Looking for Signs in the Air": Urban Space and the Postmodern in *In the Country of Last Things*'. In Dennis Barone (ed.) *Beyond the Red Notebook.* Philadelphia: University of Pennsylvania Press. 107–28.

—— (1995). '*The Music of Chance*: Aleatorical (Dis)harmonies Within the "City of the World"'. In Dennis Barone (ed.) *Beyond the Red Notebook.* Philadelphia: University of Pennsylvania Press. 143–61.

Zilcosky, John (1998). 'The Revenge of the Author: Paul Auster's Challenge to Theory'. *Critique.* 39.3 (Spring). 195–205.

General

Barthes, Roland (1993). 'Authors and Writers'. In Susan Sontag (ed.) *A Barthes Reader.* London: Vintage. 185–93.

Baudrillard, Jean (1988). *America.* London: Verso.

Benjamin, Walter (1997). *Charles Baudelaire, Lyric Poet in the Era of High Capitalism.* Trans. Harry Zohn. London: Verso.

—— (1999). *The Arcades Project.* Trans. Howard Eiland and Kevin McLaughlin. Cambridge, MA and London: The Belknap Press of Harvard University.

Blair, Sara (1998). 'Cultural Geography and the Place of the Literary'. *American Literary History.* 10.3 (Fall). 544–67.

de Certeau, Michel (1984). *The Practice of Everyday Life.* Trans. Steven Rendall. Berkeley: University of California Press.

Davis, Mike (1988). 'Urban Renaissance and the Spirit of Postmodernism'. In E. Ann Kaplan (ed.) *Postmodernism and Its Discontents.* London: Verso. 79–87.

—— (1998). *City of Quartz.* London: Pimlico.

DeLillo, Don (1992). *Mao II.* London: Vintage.

Doctorow, E. L. (1985) *Ragtime.* London: Picador.

Donald, James (1999). *Imagining the Modern Metropolis.* London: Athlone Press.

Freud, Sigmund (1953). *On Aphasia.* London: Imago Publishing.

Foucault, Michel (1991). 'What is an Author'. In Paul Rabinow (ed.) *The Foucault Reader.* London: Penguin. 101–20.

Harvey, David (1990). *The Condition of Postmodernity.* Oxford: Blackwell.

—— (1996). *Justice, Nature and the Geography of Difference.* Oxford: Blackwell.

—— (2000). *Spaces of Hope.* Edinburgh: Edinburgh University Press.

Hawthorne, Nathaniel (1987). 'Wakefield'. In Brian Harding (ed.) *Young Goodman Brown and Other Tales.* Oxford: Oxford University Press. 124–33.

Haycraft, Howard (ed. and commentary) (1946). *The Art of the Mystery Story.* New York: Grosset and Dunlap.

Holquist, Michael (1971). 'Whodunit and Other Questions: Metaphysical Detective Stories in Postwar Fiction'. *New Literary History.* 3.1. 135–56.

Hustvedt, Siri (1994). *Blindfold.* London: Sceptre.

—— (2002). 'The World Trade Center'. In Ulrich Baer (ed.) *101 Stories: New York Writes After September 11.* New York: New York University Press. 158–9.

—— (2003). *What I Loved.* London: Hodder and Stoughton.

Hutcheon, Linda (1998). *A Poetics of Postmodernism.* New York: Routledge.

Jameson, Fredric (1991). *Postmodernity, or, The Cultural Logic of Late Capitalism.* London: Verso.

Johnson, Allen (ed.) (1928). *Dictionary of American Biography.* 20 vols. London: Humphrey Milford, Oxford University Press.

Kafka, Franz (2000). 'The Hunger Artist'. In Malcolm Pasley (trans. and ed.) *Metamorphosis and Other Stories.* London: Penguin. 210–19.

Lefebvre, Henri (1991). *The Production of Space.* Trans. Donald Nicholson-Smith. Oxford: Blackwell.

Marx, Leo (1967). *The Machine in the Garden.* Oxford: Oxford University Press.

Massey, Doreen (1993). 'A Global Sense of Place'. In Ann Gray and Jim McGuigan (eds) *Studying Culture.* London: Edward Arnold. 232–40.

—— (1994a). 'A Place Called Home'. *Space, Place and Gender.* Cambridge: Polity Press. 157–74.

—— (1994b) 'Introduction'. *Space, Place and Gender.* Cambridge: Polity Press. 1–XX.

—— (1999a). 'Cities in the World'. In Doreen Massey, John Allen and Steven Pile (eds) *City Worlds.* London: Routledge. 99–156.

—— (1999b). 'On Space and the City'. In Doreen Massey, John Allen and Steven Pile (eds) *City Worlds.* London: Routledge. 157–71.

Mazzoleni, Donattella (1993). 'The City and the Imaginary'. Trans. John Koumantarakis. In Erica Carter, James Donald and Judith Squires (eds) *Space and Place: Theories of Identification and Location.* London: Lawrence and Wishart. 285–301.

McHale, Brian (1987). *Postmodernist Fiction.* London: Routledge.

Oldenburg, Ray (1989). *Great Good Places.* New York: Marlowe and Company.

Petit, Philipe and John Reddy (1975). *Two Towers I Walk.* Pamphlet reprinted from *Reader's Digest* (April).

Priestman, Martin (1998). *Crime Fiction: From Poe to the Present.* Plymouth: Northcote House in association with the British Council.

Robins, Kevin (1993). 'Prisoners of the City: Whatever Could a Postmodern City Be?' In Erica Carter, James Donald and Judith Squires (eds) *Space and Place: Theories of Identification and Location*. London: Lawrence and Wishart. 303–30.

Roger, Georges (ed.) (1926). *Chateaubriand: Selections*. Oxford: Oxford University Press.

Rosenberg, Jan (1989). 'Park Slope: Notes on a Middle-Class Utopia'. In Jim Sleeper (ed.) *In Search of New York*. New Brunswick, NJ: Transaction. 159–62.

Rykwert, Joseph (2000). *The Seduction of Place*. London: Weidenfield and Nicolson.

Soja, Edward (1980). 'The Socio-Spatial Dialectic'. *Annals of the Association of American Geographers*. 70.2 (June). 207–25.

—— (1989). *Postmodern Geographies*. London: Verso.

—— (1996). *Thirdspace*. Oxford: Blackwell.

Todorov, Tzvetan (1988). 'The Typeology of Detective Fiction'. In David Lodge (ed.) *Modern Criticism and Theory: A Reader*. London and New York: Longman. 158–65.

Tygel, Jules (1998). *The Jackie Robinson Reader*. New York: Prime.

Williams, Raymond (1973). *The Country and the City*. Oxford: Oxford University Press.

—— (1977). *Marxism and Literature*. Oxford: Oxford University Press.

—— (1989a). 'The Forward March of Labour Halted'. In *Resources of Hope*. London: Verso. 247–55.

—— (1989b). 'The Importance of Community'. In *Resources of Hope*. London: Verso. 111–19.

Index

Note: 'n.' after a page reference indicates the number of a note on that page.